ACTIVE MEDITATION

The Western Tradition

OTHER BOOKS

by Robert R. Leichtman, M.D. & Carl Japikse:

The Art of Living (5 volumes)

The Life of Spirit (5 volumes)

Forces of the Zodiac

by Robert R. Leichtman, M.D.:

From Heaven to Earth (24 books)

by Carl Japikse:

The Hour Glass

The Light Within Us

ACTIVE MEDITATION

The Western Tradition

by Robert R. Leichtman, M.D.
& Carl Japikse

ARIEL PRESS
The Publishing House of Light

First paperback edition
Fourth printing

This book is made possible
by a gift to the Publications Fund of Light
by Richard & Marilyn McCraney

ISBN 0-08904-041-8
Library of Congress Card Catalog Number: 82-072785

Contents

TO

The Real Herman

ACTIVE MEDITATION

The Western Tradition

We Meet Herman

For years, our students have been asking us to write a comprehensive book on meditation—one that would examine the purposes and traditions of meditating, list basic techniques, and describe the common difficulties people might encounter. For years, our usual response has been: "But that would be encyclopedic!" Eventually, however, we began to entertain the possibility seriously. We got together and started to exchange our views.

"There are a lot of books out on meditation," Bob noted. "Who would really want to buy another one?"

"Do we know enough?" wondered Carl.

"It would be a lot of work," said Bob.

"Maybe we should just put it all on cassette tapes," suggested Carl.

The trend of the discussion had become evident. Finally, Bob remarked, "How did we ever get it into our heads that we should write a book on meditation in the first place?"

The room brightened visibly with that comment—but not through the doing of either of us. A voice which sounded as clear and pure as the primordial Word came to us from out of the light. "So, what makes you think it was your idea, anyway?" Slowly, a form emerged from the light to possess the voice. It looked like an angel.

"The idea was mine," the angel said.

"Yours?" we chorused in disbelief.

"Yes. I've eavesdropped from time to time when you've taught, and I've heard you grumble about how many people are misled by phony gurus and stupid techniques—and the books that have been written about them. I like your common sense style."

"You do?"

"Oh, yes. And I've waited long enough for you to get the hint: it's time to put up or shut up, as they say. You invoke a certain responsibility when you talk that way, you know. So, now it's your chance to spread the word about effective meditation. I will help you."

Carl looked at Bob, and Bob looked at Carl. "Do you suppose we've gone around the bend?" asked Carl.

"I don't know, but maybe we ought to find out what the bend has to offer," replied Bob.

So we decided to humor the angel. "If you want us to write the book, where are the gold tablets? Show us the gold tablets, and we'll do it."

"Have you seen what's happened to the price of gold lately?" the angel replied. "I'm asking you to write a book, not make a movie. You'll have to come up with your own gold."

"Our own gold?"

"Sure. The real gold is the substance of inspiration."

"Ah, so you're going to dictate the book to us?"

"No, you know what to say. This should be a book of common sense, not spiritual nonsense. If I dictated it, people would do it just because an angel told them to. That's a stupid reason. They should do things because they make sense. So use the ideas you already have. But you can mention me at the beginning."

"Is that such a good idea?" we asked. "There are some who would be too impressed by an angel, like you say, but there are a lot of others who don't accept things like angels. Mentioning you might strain our credibility."

"Nonsense! If they can't accept an angel, how are they going to accept their own higher self? How are they going to meditate? Talking with the higher self is just like talking to an angel, you know. It should be an intelligent communication and relationship with the angelic nature of the human spirit.

"Listen: don't be afraid to tell it like it is. Don't worry about the people who might be offended if you spell out what meditation is and what it isn't. Or if you spell out what the nature of the human spirit really is, and what it isn't. That's the whole purpose of this book. The people with the eyes to see won't be offended. Even by me."

We were becoming more impressed by what our visitor had to say. Even without the gold tablets, we began to believe that we ought to write the book. But we still had reservations. "Communicating with the spirit is more than just talking and getting ideas," said Bob. "It involves tapping all the light and love of the spirit, too. Are we going to be able to convey all that in a book?"

"I speak many languages other than English, and so can you. And I'm not referring to French or Russian, either. I'm talking about the languages of courage, peace, reassurance, enthusiasm, and hope—the very power of these qualities. You don't have to write *about* these qualities; just write *with* them. Your readers will get the message.

"Listen: I have to fly. Materializing like this isn't easy, you know."

"Hey!" Carl called after the angel, who had half vanished. "You haven't told us your name. What do we call you?"

"If I tried to pronounce my real name," the angel smiled, looking much like the Cheshire cat by now, "I would burn down your house. So just call me Herman."

"Herman?" we cried together.

"Yes, Herman. That will remind you that I am both a he and a she, and neither he nor she, too. I'm an angel. I'm a Herman. Your spirit is a Herman, too. Keep that in mind as you write."

And the last of Herman disappeared. But the angel that is both a he and she, and neither a he nor a she, did not go far. Herman graces every page of this book, just as spirit graces the life of every human being. As you read, look for Herman. The effort will be well rewarded.

1

The Western Approach

IT MAKES SENSE

The two most important elements of human consciousness are the personality, which we use in daily self-expression, and the higher self, which most of us largely ignore. These two aspects of our life are linked by a bond of intelligence and goodwill. In a primitive person, the bond is not highly developed, and the personality operates most of the time without the benefit of the love, guidance, and strength of the higher self. In a very advanced individual, the bond is strong, and the rapport between personality and higher self is both intimate and effective. For most of us, the development of this bond falls somewhere in between.

An intelligent person recognizes the need for strengthening this bond, and will endeavor to do so by any means or technique which proves helpful. There are a number of practices which can contribute to this strengthening.

Religious worship can help, for example, by magnetizing us to the divine nature of our higher self. But worship has the limitation of ascribing all divine attributes to a transpersonal force which is to be adored; it tends to downplay any realization that we can form a direct and active relationship with that divinity, and express it in our daily lives.

Good acts are an excellent way of strengthening the bond, too, for they draw forth the interest of the higher self in the responsible and creative behavior of the personality. The good acts, however, must be in harmony with the plans of the higher self; if they are not, our good intentions serve only to widen the gap, not close it. Sadly, much of what is labeled "good" in the world is not truly in harmony with the life and purposes of the higher self.

Prayer is beneficial, of course—provided the prayers are not just for the selfish wants of the personality. But too many people pray with the odd conviction that all they have to do is "believe" in their prayer and it will be fulfilled. They are not really interested in communicating with the higher self—just in getting what they want.

Each of these practices has merit, but there is another practice to consider as well: meditation. Properly approached, meditation is *the* technique for strengthening the bond between the personality and the higher self. It is the practice of contacting the life of our spirit, learning to focus it, and building the higher elements of life into our daily self-expression. To put it in simple terms, meditation is the practice of communicating with the highest aspects of our humanity and learning to work in cooperation with them. For the intelligent person, therefore, it makes sense to meditate.

Little has been written about meditation, however. Oh, there are scores of books which have been published recently and in times past which allegedly describe the nature and the techniques of meditation. Indeed, this glut of books purporting to explain meditation may prompt some people, upon first picking up this new one, to exclaim, "What, *another* book on meditation?"

But very few of these books have actually dealt with the communication of the higher self with its personality. They have taken a subject which is eminently sensible and intelligent and stripped it of its most basic virtues, presenting it instead to the public as something mystical, magical, and difficult to comprehend. In the process, the practice of meditation has been debased to the point where many thoughtful and cautious people simply stay away.

They have good reason to stay away, when the practice of meditation is advocated by the likes of:

• Greedy opportunists who will stoop to anything to make a buck. These are the con artists who, sensing the mood of the "me generation" and its craving for self-improvement, are all too willing to pluck the feathers of waiting turkeys.

• Ignorant followers of fads who will fall for anything, especially the glowing promises of greedy opportunists. These, of course, are the turkeys who are being plucked.

• Seekers of laboratory phenomena who tirelessly trivialize the subject of consciousness by discussing it in terms of brain waves and changes in skin resistance, rather than in terms of *thought, quality,* and *inspiration.*

• Reporters who have a talent for library research and writing, but who cannot distinguish a mystical experience from a good fantasy.

• Religious fanatics of all hues (and cries) who promote their dogma and traditions with dedication and fervor but intensely fear the insights and growth that genuine meditation can bring.

• Certain psychologists who view human nature exclusively in terms of sickness and malfunction, and therefore have no meaningful understanding of the higher self. To them, meditation is just a chic way to overcome stress or "get in touch with their feelings."

• Dilettantes who embrace meditation as a new and more sophisticated way to escape reality.

• Very passive people who fall into a trance-like condition and never reemerge. Even though they continue about their daily business, not all of them is ever present and accounted for.

• Anti-intellectuals, who fear clear and lucid explanations of anything.

Frequently, these types of people tend to be the loudest voices promoting meditation, but the person who seeks to understand meditation and use it wisely and productively in his or her life must realize that loudness alone is not a guarantee of authority. The ability to pander to a wide range of people is likewise not a guarantee of helpfulness. There *is* value in meditation, even if most of the people who preach it and teach it do not yet understand what that value is. It is an important and effective tool for self-improvement and the exploration of the higher realms of life. It is an indispensable means of training the mind in various skills of abstract and concrete thinking—and for making sense of life. It should therefore be seized by intelligent people and given its proper place and value. Surely it makes little sense to leave something so worthwhile to the hordes who can only offer us platitudes, boredom, and bed-sores.

Properly practiced, meditation offers us access to a realm of intelligence, benevolence, guidance, and creativity. It is worthy of our investigation—and our use.

AN ACT OF COOPERATION

In the public mind, the practice of meditation has become equated with sitting still, quieting consciousness until it is blank, and then concentrating on a mantra or some other device, such as the flame of a candle. It is described as "entering into the silence"; we are frequently admonished to "become passive" and withdraw from the physical plane. These ideas are so ingrained in the public consciousness that it is difficult to shake them loose.

But shake we must, because these are false perspectives on meditation, engendered by multitudes of beginners who do not know any better. For them, blanking the mind *is* a step forward--but not for the intelligent individual who is seeking to strengthen the bond between the higher self and personality. For such an individual, emptying the mind is a tragic regression into numbness and dumbness.

Meditation is much more than the act of withdrawing from the physical plane and the concerns of the personality; the art of meditating requires much more than just a vague expectation that God will swoop down, lift us up to heaven, bless us and bliss us, and then gently set us back down on earth, healed and enlightened. Such notions inevitably appeal to those people who do not want to have to make any effort, other than surrendering, to become spiritual. But they do not make sense when scrutinized with intelligence. They are just empty acts—shadow play with spirit.

True meditation, by contrast, is a communion with the deepest, most powerful, most wise and loving part within us—our higher self, or soul. The God within us. Meditation is not a surrender to this inner self, but an act of cooperation. It does not just establish communication with the higher self; meditation *is* the communication. And it is therefore active!

A moment's reflection will confirm the reasonableness of this idea. We do not communicate with other people on the telephone by becoming passive and letting them suck our ideas out of us, or impose their ideas on ours. We talk, we listen, and we exchange thoughts. It is a very active process. So is the real communication with the higher self—our spirit. We must learn the proper techniques for dialing the inner being, but once we have made the contact, we can expect the exchange of ideas to be lively, active, and enriching. It will help us cleanse the personality and enhance our daily self-expression. It will assist us as we confront the challenges and problems of daily living. It will complement our attempts to interact with life in intelligent, constructive, and helpful ways.

The higher self never encourages anyone to enter into silence; it invites us to enter into the symphony of life. Nor does it encourage us to become passive; it seeks to activate our wisdom, compassion, and talents more fully. It does not require us to mumble a mantra or stare at a candle; it much prefers us to think and become intelligent.

It is important to keep this perspective in mind as we approach an understanding of meditation. The practice of meditation is designed to serve the intelligence of our higher self. Its techniques and goals should therefore all be reasonable, logical, and sensible.

WEST MEETS EAST

Much of what has been written about meditation in recent years has been imported from the East—from India, Japan, and Tibet. There is much richness in these traditions which can be of value to the Westerner who is seeking to learn to use meditation intelligently; in many ways, the East has preserved its traditions of communicating with the higher self better than the West has. The Western traditions of mysticism and meditation have generally been obscured by the ravings of smallminded Christian fundamentalists, much to our loss. But in turning to the East, we must be careful to choose what is valuable to us, and not adopt traditions which are unsuitable for the modern Western mind.

It is always dangerous to oversimplify, but it can be stated that the purpose of the spiritual path is quite different in the East than in the West. It is a mistake to naively assume that techniques which work for one set of people will work equally well for another set, especially when widely separated in geography and culture. Different peoples make different contributions to the progress of mankind; the intelligent person learns to recognize these differences and the purposes they serve.

One of the many contributions of the peoples of the East, spiritually, is to ponder the nature of God and perfect methods of attuning themselves to divine forces. As a result, the literature of the East and its spiritual practices describe the *way* to God. The spiritual contribution of the West, by contrast, has been to perfect the *expression* of divine virtues and qualities—in daily work, creativity, personal relationships, and behavior.

Consequently, our religious and cultural traditions have been designed to embody and demonstrate divine qualities on earth, in ourselves and in society.

This represents a significant difference, and one which must be reckoned with in translating Eastern practices of meditation into something useful for the West. In the East, for example, it is a common practice to use meditation to withdraw from the personality and the duties of mundane life; quietness is prized as a proper climate in which to adore God and contemplate His abstract nature. The goal is union with God "up there"—God in His transcendent nature. The Easterner is motivated not so much to know God as to identify with Him. His meditative techniques are therefore designed to achieve these ends.

In the West, the study and adoration of God is also important, but *as part of* the larger effort to express divine virtues and skills in all that we do. Before we can express these qualities and talents, however, we must become aware of them and understand them, at least to some degree. We cannot just express the light blindly; we must serve the unfoldment of the divine plan for humanity and civilization intelligently. We must connect heaven with earth and give expression to the immanent nature of God—the God "down here," in us. As a result, we are charged with enlightened living, actively involving ourself in work, relationships, and the duties of a citizen of earth.

Given this assignment, the passive approaches of the East simply will not work—not without major modification. We must do more than just contemplate esoteric schemes and ideas; we must comprehend and apply them. We must likewise do more than just love an abstract God; we must love the God we find indwelling in all life forms. Our expression of goodwill cannot be made in the silence; it must be made in daily life.

In no way should these comments be interpreted as suggesting that the destiny of the West is superior to the East; they are set down here only for the purpose of showing that differences do exist between East and West. Nor are these comments intended to suggest that no one in the East teaches or practices a life of compassionate service, or that everyone in the West is a saint in disguise. Common sense indicates otherwise. But common sense also tells us that a rose does not serve its spiritual heritage by imitating a petunia. It is dangerous for the people of the West to try to imitate, in every way, the lifestyle, culture, and spiritual path of the East—and vice versa.

Nonetheless, the West does have much to learn from the East in terms of techniques for contacting our higher nature and aligning with it. The Westerner, oriented to action as he is, often seeks to master his nature and self-expression before he has found the sources of virtue, wisdom, compassion, and talent which will enable him to succeed. He frequently becomes so absorbed in his active pursuits that he excludes the spiritual life. When that happens, he very much needs to be inspired by his Eastern brother, and turn to the higher self.

At the same time, the East has much to learn from the West regarding the value of demonstrating and expressing the divine powers and qualities which have been contacted. The Eastern individual usually knows very little about integrating the higher qualities and insights he has contacted into his personality and daily self-expression. In fact, throughout much of the East it is considered a virtue *not* to be very involved in the outer expression of self. This is a deception wherever it appears, either in the East or the West. The goal of meditation is *not* to become absorbed in an otherworldly rapture of divine bliss, to the exclusion of practical activity. It is to increase our effectiveness as an agent of the higher self.

Throughout this text, we will try to honor the best elements of the Eastern tradition, as they suit the needs and challenges of the modern Westerner. But we profess no allegiance to any one tradition. Our sole allegiance is to the higher self itself; our guiding light will be common sense. We are interested in setting forth what will work in the West in the twentieth century and beyond, not what helped Chinese or Hindu peasants two thousand years ago, or Sufi mendicants in the glory of Islam. We will therefore rely on what our own experience has taught us to be practical for the average, intellectually-oriented Westerner who seeks to know more about his or her spiritual potential, and what to do with it. Dedicated fanatics and sentimental lovers of faded spiritual traditions should inquire elsewhere.

The ideas presented in this book are meant not to be believed in, but experimented with—in the great laboratory of experience. They are to be taken into your mind and heart and tested. If they prove effective, as they have for us, then use them. If not, then try something better. *This* is the key of the Western tradition.

TAPPING INNER DEPTHS

The Western approach to meditation is not a program which has been handed down from on high; it is a natural outgrowth of the basic Western tradition for solving problems, enriching culture, governing ourselves, and discovering scientific truths. A thoughtful review of our civilization will reveal a definite pattern of characteristics which are typically Western in nature. These include:

1. The Western approach is intelligent, thoughtful, goal-oriented, and logical. It seeks to understand.

2. In exploring the phenomena of life, it gives more importance to the results of intelligent experiments than the formulations of dogma and tradition. It seeks to discover.

3. It is active, not passive. It seeks to make a contribution.

27

4. It assigns tranquillity and good feelings to a secondary importance, emphasizing results as a higher priority.

5. It constantly aspires to greater efficiency, by examining and reviewing the effectiveness of what has been done. It adapts to new conditions as needed.

6. It prizes intelligence. At times, this has caused the Western mind to overvalue doubt and skepticism, but that can be corrected by blending faith and hope with sound practices of the mind.

7. It is pragmatic in its purpose, always looking for practical results, not just theories, philosophies, and rituals.

8. It dares to challenge opinions and socially accepted values.

9. It cherishes individuality and places a high value on the responsibility of the individual to contribute to society.

Any good approach to meditation in the West should be compatible with these fundamental characteristics, and for a very sensible reason. Being born in the West, we possess subconscious and unconscious taproots which have been developed over many centuries; they are our inheritance from earlier generations. To the degree that we recognize these taproots and draw our nourishment and inspiration from them, we can grow rather quickly in our capacity to explore consciousness. But if we adopt techniques which are fundamentally opposed to our cultural origins, we will experience a certain amount of frustration which will be hard to trace and overcome. If we attempt to render ourself passive and immobile, for example, the active nature of our cultural heritage will be offended—and it will let us know. Or if we fail to use our intelligence in pursuing spiritual growth, the intelligence of the Western tradition within us will sound an alarm—which we had better heed.

A good way to conceptualize these somewhat abstract characteristics is to think of the way an intelligent person would embark upon the exploration of new territory, be it a jungle or desert or forest. He would take with him suitable tools of exploration: a map, a light to shine on the path, and a compass. He would use these tools often, to check his bearings and keep him progressing in the intended direction. Moreover, he would have a definite purpose in mind for making this trip; he would be seeking to discover something he could bring back with him—something which would be useful in his career or personal progress. He would therefore keep a record of what he encountered and experienced, and where he found it, so he could return to the same spot time after time, for further exploration. The more frequently he returned, of course, the more efficient he would become in traversing these new regions. Eventually, he might even settle there.

Much the same can be said about the intelligent Westerner's approach to the exploration of the inner depths of consciousness. He would not enter these regions unprepared, leaving behind him his capacity to think or his common sense. He would see these as necessary tools for exploration, and scoff at anyone who suggested that he should not think or reason while making the trip. Indeed, before he left, he would consider the purpose of his journey and develop a thorough plan for proceeding. This plan would then help him stay focused in his intent; he would not be vulnerable to the advice of idlers and mountebanks who might lounge around the border of the territory, nor the grandiose stories of "tour guides" who might offer to lead him to places they had heard about but not explored themselves.

The intelligent explorer would be intent on staying alert throughout the whole journey—rather than going into a trance or becoming absorbed in what his body or feelings told him. He would laugh at the silliness of traditions that he must wear a certain color shoe, or regulate his heartbeat, or practice breathing exercises in order to make progress. He would be offended by the notion that he did not have to make any effort on this journey, or that there really was no object to the trip—that all he had to do was enter a bland state of passiveness and "just be." Common sense alone would guide him otherwise.

Indeed, he would work to establish techniques and clear paths in consciousness he could follow time after time. In doing this, he would not just follow paths which had been blazed by stone age travelers; he would pursue trails of exploration suited to his modern needs. He would seek to contact the treasures of intelligence and, having found them, bring them back into his own conscious awareness and use. After having worked in this way for a while, he would know beyond all doubt that those who would advise him to "be here now" and mouth monosyllabic mantras have no idea of their limitations and lack of comprehension.

PROPER MOTIVES

Meditation is an activity in consciousness, linking the higher self with the personality. Because it is an activity, it is an expression of force; as such, there must be certain motivations which we harness in order to practice the discipline of meditation. Understanding these motivations, and separating the false ones from the genuine ones, is part of establishing a proper perspective about meditation.

Far too often, the principal motivation for what is loosely called "meditation" is just the need to relax and escape the problems of daily living. Many people, especially active and thinking individuals, become stressed and tense during the course of their daily activities; they need a way to soothe their frayed nerves and distressed bodies. For these people, a simple relaxation technique can be a real tonic. But we must take care not to label these elementary techniques "meditative"; they are not. They are techniques of relaxation and recreation, not meditation—regardless of what is claimed by devotees of certain popular brands of "meditation."

Why is simple relaxation not justifiably labeled meditation? The explanation is simple. The purpose of meditation is to establish better communication between the personality and the higher self. A technique which directs its practitioners to empty their minds of all content may possibly be useful in reducing stress—but it certainly is contrary to the goal of enriching consciousness. One does not build a better fire by removing the embers which are already burning!

This is not to say, however, that the only proper motivation for meditation is the determination to improve communication with the higher self. Many people, properly offended by the absurdities of unimaginative religious fanatics, will not be interested in the "higher self" or the God within them. For them, the motivation to meditate will be to contact a greater resource of goodwill, insight, peace, and strength. Others will be motivated by a strong impulse to grow; they are constantly seeking to overcome the limitations of their consciousness and discover what is unknown, occult, and hidden. Some are inspired by a strong motive to serve, but they realize they cannot serve the higher self effectively and wisely until they have established a meaningful contact with it. Others are spurred on by the need for healing of mind and body or for creative inspiration they can focus in their work. All of these are proper motives in addition to the central spiritual motive of seeking a close relationship with our innate divinity.

ENRICHMENT, NOT ESCAPE

Whatever our motive, as we seek to transcend our human nature, we move toward the source of our life, wisdom, and goodwill. We enter into a realm of consciousness which is already enriched by a more intense and unadulterated quality of love, intelligence, and strength than we have experienced before. It is this *enrichment* of awareness which is the true goal of meditation. The technical term for it is *transcendence.*

Transcendence always involves the act of entering into an enriched and active state of mind; it is not just the escape from something unpleasant or mundane. There are many steps which must be climbed before transcendence is achieved; it is not the simplistic act of "getting yourself out of the way" that many people want it to be. Indeed, some of the popular meditative systems, in describing the nature of transcendence, actually trivialize and distort it. A concentrated effort to forget our body, emotions, and mind, for example, can actually result in *disconnecting* us from our capacity to be aware and mentally alert. It unplugs us from our daily activities—and also from our capacity to receive the greater wisdom, goodwill, and strength of the higher self. It may serve to relieve some stress, to be sure, but the price we pay for the benefit is outrageous. It makes no more sense than does amputating an arm in order to cure a rash.

The purpose of transcendence is enrichment, not escape. If our expectation in meditating is simply to escape a dull and disappointing existence in the physical plane, we will have no chance of entering a legitimate state of heavenly consciousness. Instead, we will go directly to the fantasy department of our own emotions, where we will play with papier-mâché dolls of God and saints and angels—and maybe a demon or two. We will pretend to be meditating, just as children who play with dolls pretend to be grownups—and we will believe in our pretense. But we will not in fact be communicating with the higher self—just our wish life.

Transcendence is something like visiting a bank, whose vaults are filled with the treasures of ability, wisdom, faith, courage, love, and benevolence, rather than money. But visiting the bank is not enough; we must also make withdrawals. And we cannot make these withdrawals unless we have cultivated, to some degeee, an active, intelligent expression of the treasures of the higher self.

In other words, meditation is a skill which, when sufficiently practiced, provides us with access to the inner, transcendent realms of life. And it is important to recognize that it *is* a skill—a skill which can be learned and mastered. It most certainly is not a passive state of quiet, blissful expectation— the expectation that God, Whoever that is, will do all the work of life for us. After all, the teller does not throw money at us as soon as we walk in the door of the bank. We have to learn to make out a withdrawal slip and present it properly. A similar amount of common sense and intelligent enterprise is expected in meditation—and transcendence.

Meditation is a means to an end—not an end in itself. It is rather amazing that anyone has ever thought otherwise, but many have. Thousands of people seeking to escape from a dull reality, lulled by fantasies that a few touches of catatonia now and then are good for us, have tried to promote this tiresome fiction. Sloth has always been attractive to certain elements of the human race, especially when dressed in the robes of saintliness. But illusion is still illusion, no matter how many people accept it and believe in it. The goal of meditation is enrichment of consciousness. The skills of meditation are designed to enhance the richness of self-expression. Its focus is to bring heaven to earth—not to escape to heaven and stay there.

A HOUSE CONDEMNED

What is unfortunate is that many good people will read these ideas and agree with them—and then proceed to practice meditation as though it were a passive observation of their thoughts, feelings, and associations. They will read the words but miss the message. A certain measure of self-observation, of course, is an important part of any program of self-understanding, but it is useful *only* if coupled with intelligent activity. All such passive forms should be avoided as directly contrary to the goals of meditation.

In this regard, we have conducted extensive experiments to determine the value of passive observation in life. We have done this by observing the dirt and dust in our kitchens and living rooms, without interfering with it. We have just let it be. These experiments have indicated to us that mere observation does not clean dirt and dust! Of course, these are only *preliminary* results; they will have to be checked in scientific laboratories. But there is a basis for concluding, tentatively at least, that observation alone is *not* sufficient activity—either in the home or in the mind and heart.

This evidence will probably not be enough for lovers of laziness, however. For them, it should also be reported that one of our friends did allow an experiment in observing household dirt to run for several years. He declares that the dirt ceased to bother him after the first year, and he has not noticed any increase in dirtfulness since the fourth year. Of course, no one is visiting him anymore, and the Board of Health has condemned his house. But he is quite happy.

For the rest of us, this little parable should remind us that responsible and intelligent action is an important aspect of meditation and the work of transcendence. Meditation requires the effort to cooperate with our inner life. Our higher self has much in store for us to receive, but we must be ready to do more than just sit on a rug on the floor with our mouth and hands open and our mind empty.

Our emotions must be used actively and skillfully to love the ideals of the higher self and to trust in the value of a close relationship with it.

Our mind must be used to comprehend the nature of our higher self and to act and think as the higher self would have us act and think in our daily life.

Keeping alert and awake and involved in what we are doing will be as vital in meditation as it is in driving a car—and for the same reasons!

2

The Role
Of Meditation

STRETCHING THE MIND

There are many practical ways the potential of meditation can be harnessed. We can be inspired by good ideas which will assist us in our work; we can establish a healthier rapport with others, helping us build better relationships. We can work to improve our self-image and accelerate our personal and spiritual growth. The list of practical applications of the skills of meditation is virtually endless. Yet no matter how we choose to focus the potential of meditation, our efforts will inevitably bring us back, time after time, to a fundamental realization. *The work of meditation is to bring the life of the higher self into expression in the activities of the personality.*

The problem is that most people know very little about the higher self—and what it means to integrate the resources of spirit into the activities of the personality. Their eyes tend to glaze as they encounter these terms; they gloss over them as quickly as possible, skimming on to something they understand. To master meditation, however, we must not skip over these ideas lightly. We must stretch our minds and strive to understand:

- The nature of the higher self.
- Its relationship with the personality.
- How the resources of spirit are integrated into the activities and needs of the personality.

All effective techniques of Active Meditation are based on this understanding. That is why they work.

THE HIGHER SELF

Volumes can be written about the nature of the higher self. For the purpose of this book on meditation, it is enough to state that the higher self is the essence of our humanity—the source of our inspiring wisdom, our healing love, and our basic will-to-life. It is abstract, but certainly not unknowable. The higher self can be known through our most noble acts, our highest aspirations, our tenderest moments, and our best insights. It is the impelling force behind all these expressions, and many more.

The higher self is also intangible—but this does not mean that it is the creation of the personality. It is not the invention of philosophers, religious leaders, or the superstitious. The higher self existed long before our body or our personality came into being; it does not owe its existence to our physical body or anything in the physical plane. Quite simply, it is the presence of God within us. To employ religious terms, the higher self lives in the realm of heavenly wisdom, love, talent, and strength; it possesses these heavenly treasures—and more. It stands ready to serve as a benevolent parent to the personality, if the personality will accept this relationship and learn to make the higher self its basic source of guidance and inspiration, love and forgiveness, courage and steadfastness, dignity and beauty.

Of course, there is no way these bold statements about the higher self can be proven in print. We have no figures and graphs which plot the statistics of spirit; we have heard of no laboratory which has yet dissected or weighed the soul. Brain waves can be tested, but they prove nothing about consciousness; neither would an opinion poll of one thousand random meditators. The factual reality of the higher self can be proven only in the experiences we each have and the experiments in meditation we each conduct. There are, naturally, many tales which could be told about the miraculous transformations that can occur, and have occurred, when the personality and body come in full contact with the higher self. But these are tales—meaningful to the people who have lived them, but just examples to others who have not. No matter how impressive they may be, no evidence is as impressive as our own evidence in proving the fact of the higher self.

To those who have not yet experienced the reality of the higher self, we can only suggest that there is good reason to pursue a meditative discipline designed to establish this contact, until some of the inspiration, healing, or strength of the higher self has been tapped. It makes sense to do this, just as it made sense for the Portuguese and Spanish explorers to sail in search of the New World, even though they had no proof it was there, or what it would be. And, as inspiration, healing, or strength is discovered, it should be taken as a sign—a sign that there is more whence this has come. Indeed, the source is inexhaustible. Therefore, the reward for discovering it and learning to use it is great.

In seeking to make contact with the higher self, we are venturing forth to do nothing less than make contact with God Himself—the God within us. Unfortunately, this is a hard concept for many people to grapple with because God, quite frankly, has been on the losing end of some rather poor publicity over the years. The very ministers and priests who have been charged with leading us to a closer union with God have often been eager to tell us how sinful our spiritual nature is, and how evil our origins and destiny are. The impact of these intensely ignorant, and sometimes, willfully malicious people has polluted our understanding of the nature of our higher self, and its relationship to our personality and body. These misguided individuals have reduced the subject of spirit to an issue of hysteria and superstition—often making it difficult to discuss the nature and purpose of meditation without being seriously misunderstood. The advanced practitioner of meditation, of course, will have already found the evidence which shatters these concepts of sinfulness and evil, but this is of little help to the beginner. More frequently than not, our cultural conditioning on these issues represents a serious problem in our endeavor to comprehend the purposes of meditation—and pursue an effective program.

The best way to handle these difficulties, of course, is to apply some common sense. If we are seeking to contact the source of our highest intelligence and greatest love, why should we expect to run into the devil? It does not make sense. If we are looking for the most transcendent elements of strength and purpose within us, why should we expect to discover something inherently marred? It does not make sense. If we are intent on pursuing our noblest ideals with faith and steadfastness, why should we be afraid that calamity will befall us? It does not make sense. What does make sense is this: that as we think and act on the wavelengths of love, wisdom, and joy, we will gradually become attuned to greater measures of love, wisdom, and joy, wherever they exist. The evil we might do becomes overshadowed by the good that we choose to do, until the evil disappears.

Clearly, the ministers of fear and the priests of original sin are trying to sell us something other than the best within us. They are trying to persuade us to accept the worst within us, rather than the wisdom, love, courage, and dignity of the human race. Their untiring effort to find a devil to hate in the heart of every man and woman—while professing to lead a spiritual life—is the height of silliness. The merest whiff of intelligence will blow them away as though they were the most insubstantial puff of dandelion fluff—which they are. It makes sense to ignore such distortions of the spiritual life.

Meditation establishes contact with our higher self, the God within us. It does not connect us with the devil or our sinful nature. Common sense, therefore, dictates that we should put the devil, whatever that is, behind us—and put the higher self before us. We should pursue knowledge and wisdom with intelligence, compassion and goodwill with loving devotion, and courage with all our strength.

And even though we are contacting ideas, qualities, and powers which are abstract, we should expect our contact with the higher self to be intelligible, clear, and helpful. A benevolent parent does not speak vaguely or in secret code to his or her child, and neither does the higher self hide behind the veils of mushiness or conundrums. It guides us in reasonable and meaningful ways—but we must learn its language. That is the purpose of meditation: to help us develop the eyes to see, the ears to hear, and the mind to know.

OUR HUMAN NATURE

In addition to our spiritual nature, the higher self, we also have a human nature, the personality. This personality is the offspring of the interaction between our higher self and our earthly experiences. It is the sum of our thoughts, emotions, habits, and behavior—but it is not designed to be static. It may *appear* to be static, because the physical body is relatively solid, emotional patterns tend to be repeated, and thoughts generally adhere to certain grooves. And in some people, the dynamic potential of the personality does become bottled up and stagnant. But this is not what is meant to be. Ideally, the personality learns to be responsive not just to its experiences in the physical plane, but to the guidance, love, and strength of the higher self.

There are many departments in our human nature. The personality as a whole is composed of the mind, the emotions, and the physical body. Each of these three aspects, or bodies, of the personality in turn has conscious, subconscious, and unconscious expressions.

The conscious element is that part of the personality which we happen to be expressing at any given moment.

The subconscious is a much larger portion of the personality—the sum of our memories, habits, skills, and potentials for action. It is a very busy part of the personality, but it operates behind the scenes of our conscious awareness.

The unconscious is even more remote. It contains the seeds of our character and our taproots in mass consciousness.

Each of these departments of the personality can be thought of as a matrix in consciousness, capable of responsiveness. It can be responsive to our environment and experiences—as it is in most people—and it can also be responsive to the guidance, healing, and love of the higher self. But it can only become responsive to the higher self *if taught.* Left to its own devices, the personality will simply remain trapped in what it experiences, what it feels, and what it needs. That may be satisfying to some people, but it is woefully incomplete, just as a fruit tree which bears no fruit is barren.

Moreover, it is important to realize that before a rapport with the higher self is possible, each of these departments of personality must be aligned and attuned with it. It is not just enough to link our conscious awareness with the higher self, through devotion and affirmations. It is a beginning, to be sure, but if we stop at this level, our contact may be sabotaged from the subconscious and the unconscious. Nor is it enough just to link the unconscious parts of the personality with the higher self, which is primarily what happens when people fall into trance. That leaves out the conscious and subconscious. The whole of the personality must be involved in our intercourse with the higher self, if our meditations are to be effective and productive.

Unfortunately, people of little wisdom frequently confuse their human nature and their spiritual nature. Some believe the subconscious to be the higher self, because as they explore its content, much of it is new and different to them. Others believe that if they have tapped into mass consciousness, they have contacted great power. These people fail to appreciate a

44

basic distinction between the personality and the higher self. Our human nature has its home in our daily activities and reactions; our spiritual nature has its home in heaven.

The confusion engendered by the failure to make this distinction can be great. Many people, intent upon finding the higher self, go exploring in the subconscious instead, where they discover pockets of ignorance, sickness, greed, laziness, anger, or jealousy. They then mistakenly conclude that this is the nature of the higher self and cannot be changed. This is a tragic error.

A person of goodwill and intelligence will push beyond these imperfections and seek to find that which is worthwhile—in himself and in others. He will connect himself with the abundance of nobility, grace, love, and wisdom to be found in his spiritual nature, and then focus this abundance into his personality to heal the imperfections. But not everyone does this.

There *are* imperfections in the personality and these must be dealt with and overcome. But why anyone would seek to enshrine and sanctify the imperfections of humanity is beyond reason. And to glorify these imperfections and turn them into a sort of pagan religion is even more puzzling—yet that is often what is done. Emphasizing the deformities and deficiencies of the personality in this way is a peculiar materialistic practice which has crept into much modern thought—especially in religion, meditative philosophies, and certain psychiatric therapies. It is there, but it does not make sense.

It could be said that ever since God created man, man has been returning the favor by creating God—by deifying and excusing our imperfect human nature through myths and theologies. Naturally, this phenomenon can also be found in the practice of meditation; many people, in meditating, simply deify their wishes and feelings and label them the "higher self," rather than make the distinction between higher self and personality, between spiritual nature and human nature. As a result, the entire process of meditation breaks down.

It is therefore important to pursue the legitimate qualities and strengths of the higher self, not just the intriguing sights and sounds of a slightly deeper level of the personality. We must pursue those qualities which bring to us more gracefulness, more intelligence, more peace, and more courage—nothing less. At first, we may be puzzled as to how to proceed, but we can overcome this hesitancy by embracing our higher self with faith and hope—the expectation that it will help us in our efforts. In no way is this a rejection of the personality, however; on the contrary, it is the intelligent and sensible recognition that our human nature is designed to cooperate with and express the best within us. As the personality seeks to embrace the higher self, it will in turn be embraced—and profit from it.

If we experiment with meditation skillfully and cautiously, therefore, we can reasonably expect to progress—from faith to knowledge, from experience to understanding, and from need to fulfillment. As we do, we build a base of common sense which will add knowledge to our faith and wisdom to our experiences. It will add light and love and power to our personality.

THE MISSING LINK

How to link the personality with the higher self in meditation is a subject which has generated many different and opposing perspectives. Some people are quick to tell us that the personality is virtually useless and must therefore be all but destroyed in order to make room for the unveiling of the higher self. Unfortunately, the devotees of this approach usually end up being more successful at damaging the personality than at delivering spiritual wisdom and power.

46

Others listen to their emotional fantasies and feelings, until they become drunk on sentiment and lost in artificial dreams. When they enter a "meditation," they head for a place in consciousness which feels good to them—not for the higher self. Their goal in meditating is more to be soothed and entertained than enlightened. As a result, they become victims of self-deception.

There are many other variations on this theme as well: students being encouraged to plug into their guru instead of their higher self or loving a god of their own creation. It should be understood that the subconscious is very willing to put on makeup and costumes and strut about in a meditation looking absolutely divine; such god games can be sustained for a long time through wishes and affirmative platitudes. But when serious problems arise, the gods we have subconsciously created turn out to lack the power to offer genuine assistance and guidance.

The sensible way to link the personality with the higher self, by contrast, is through the practice of *integration*. We seek out whatever treasures of the higher self we need—for example, greater compassion, goodwill, wisdom, or skill—and work to blend them into our daily self-expression. We replace our pettiness with nobility. We replace our anger with tolerance. We replace our jealousy with appreciation. We fill the holes of our ignorance with intelligence.

Integration implies something more than the acceptance of new perspectives on living; it implies active work to change our daily behavior and the attitudes and convictions which influence it, making them more constructive, more healing, and more inspired. Integration is the work of making our human nature more compatible with and expressive of the power, love, and wisdom of our spiritual nature. Obviously, as this occurs, the higher self will draw nearer to the personality and use it more completely and powerfully.

The practice of integration is not guaranteed to be free of illusion, self-deception, and silliness. But its great advantage, over other methods of linking with spirit, is that it keeps us focused on growth. Therefore, as we encounter self-deceptions and silliness, we are more prepared to see them for what they are and remove them. The work of integration constantly reminds us to strive for a better definition of the higher self—and to use its power to animate our daily living.

CENTER STAGE

A good analogy for the proper relationship between our higher self and personality, and the work of integration, can be found in the legitimate stage. When we go to the theater, we expect to be entertained by a polished performance of accomplished actors in a witty, well-plotted play. We do not want to see them stumbling through their lines, covering up for poor writing, or trying a scene five different ways, until they find the best variation.

And yet, we know that this polished performance we are seeing is not a fortuitous accident, or improvisation. The activity leading up to this performance began many months before, when a producer and a director chose a script to stage. They hired actors, engaged a theater, set stage and costume designers to work, scheduled rehearsals, and found funding. The actors, at one time, did stumble through their lines—and perhaps tried certain scenes many different ways, until the director was satisfied. Stage hands, costume designers, and dialogue coaches all made their contributions. We see only the actors and the polished performance, but the play would not be possible without proper preparation and rehearsal.

Much the same can be said about our daily performances at work and home. They are not meant to be improvisations.

Although many people do approach life spontaneously, there really is no virtue in "going with the flow." Our acts and attitudes should be carefully thought out and rehearsed before they are performed, and guided by our noblest convictions, ideals, and inspirations. The personality is the actor of the drama of our life—but it is the higher self who ought to write the script, direct the action, and produce the show.

This only makes sense. Our highest intelligence *ought* to be the part of ourself which writes our dialogue and sets the plot we are to act out. Our highest power *ought* to be the part of ourself which produces this script, arranging opportunities, relationships, and learning situations. And our highest ideals and convictions *ought* to be the part of ourself which directs the play, giving it meaning, scope, and drama, as indicated in the script. The personality, on the other hand, should focus its efforts to acting out the part it has been given. This is a sufficient challenge: one requiring great talent, integrity, and self-mastery.

If we could see the invisible influence of the higher self in our life, we would understand how apt this analogy is. Behind the outer expression of our overt behavior and our spoken words lies the true "center stage"—the convictions, ideals, strengths, intuitions, and patterns which are our counterparts of director, dialogue coach, costume designer, and producer. Indeed, there is a progression of "directors" and "producers" which await our discovery. But they will remain unknown to us until we learn that the personality and the higher self *need each other,* just as actors and producers and directors need one another to stage a proper performance of a play. We need to rehearse, we need to perform. Both go together, and must be properly integrated.

Those who do not accept the need for this integration of personality with higher self condemn themselves to a very incomplete existence. One such person is the ardent materialist who disclaims the reality of anything greater than the personality and body, either in word or deed. Through this attitude, he becomes an actor who scorns the script, director, and the rest of the company. Another is the otherworldly dreamer who holds the personality and all activity in the world in contempt. Through this belief, he becomes a director without actors—or a stage to perform upon.

The higher self is the source of healing and enrichment for the personality. The personality and physical body are the vehicles the higher self must use to express its wisdom, talent, love, and potential on earth. Without a certain measure of contact and interaction between the two, the personality becomes just another ignorant, arrogant egotist—and the higher self becomes just another disembodied spook, unable to act on the physical plane.

Meditation is center stage for inspired activity. It gives the higher self the opportunity to reveal to us our lines and role—and it gives the personality the opportunity to rehearse its performance and be guided by the higher self. Meditation is not the performance itself, but without it, our performances in life fall far short of what they otherwise could be.

THE PROPER RELATIONSHIP

Much insight about the proper relationship between the personality and the higher self can be obtained by extending this analogy of the personality being an actor and the higher self being the director. Several factors are worthy of consideration.

1. It would be silly for an actor to show up for rehearsal and then fall into a deep sleep. He must be alert, awake, and ready to interact with the others in the cast and the director. Nonetheless, many people seem to believe that the best medita-

tive state is a deep trance. Suffice it to say that meditation is no time to fall asleep! We must participate in meaningful ways.

2. No good director is impressed by groveling or sycophantic adoration from his actors. A director needs allegiance and attentiveness, not mindless worship; cooperation, not abject surrender and slavery. It is important to approach the higher self in much the same spirit.

3. The good actor pursues his craft. He seeks from the director clear guidance, support and encouragement, discipline when he is wrong or ineffective, and constructive criticism when necessary—not just vague affection and approval. Many people who meditate do not approach their higher self in this way, however. They prefer to be comforted rather than guided, indulged rather than supported, exempted from consequences rather than disciplined, and "stroked" rather than criticized. We must understand that help is often more than a kind word.

4. Communication must be clear and established in both directions. The actor should articulate his needs; the director has the responsibility to give clear instructions. If the actor does not understand the director's intent, he should ask for further clarification. Naturally, it is presumed that the actor has already acquired certain skills of his craft and will be able to figure out some of what he needs to know for himself. But where he is confused or mistaken, the director will help him. The same is true in the communication between the higher self and personality. Divine guidance is never so strange or incomprehensible that it defies understanding. If it is muddled, it is usually our own confusion which has done the muddling.

As with actors, our personalities are at different levels of competence and brilliance. But the needs of each are met. It therefore makes sense to expect that communication *is* possible and that it will be reasonably clear. Either there is light in the higher self and in God—or there is not. Either there is wisdom in our higher intelligence and in God—or there is not. Either there is clarity of thought in our higher self and in God—or there is not. The assumption that there is not is untenable. So is the nonsense of gurus and others who claim that the inner life cannot be described clearly and precisely. The person who hides behind platitudes and generalities is usually just trying to camouflage his own lack of understanding.

5. A proper line of authority must be established. The director has reasonable authority over the final performance of the play. To this authority the actor must yield, but not in fear or intimidation. The director will not use his authority tyrannically, smiting actors who misbehave or are slow to learn. He would not have selected them for the play *unless* he thought them capable of acting the part! So he will work with them, train them, and support them in their efforts. He handles the actors gently, skillfully—not by issuing ultimatums or taking an adversary position.

The actor could, of course, defy the director and play the part any way he chose, but the good actor has no motive for doing so. He is not threatened by or covetous of the authority of the director; rather, he sees its advantage and seeks to cooperate with it.

These approaches to authority are also ideal in meditation. The higher self does *not* expect the personality to become mindless, simple, or passive; it does *not* desire the personality to surrender to it, either in fear or in awe. Passiveness and surrender reduce our capacity to respond meaningfully to the assistance of the higher self. The proper attitude, by contrast, is a healthy appreciation of the bond between the higher self and the personality. This is a bond of *sharing*, not fear; a bond of *cooperation*, not surrender. Just as the actor submits to the authority of the director in order to share in the staging of the play, so we ought to submit to the authority of the higher self in order to share in its greater wisdom, love, and power.

6. A commitment is required. An actor is not signed on to do a play only at his convenience; he makes a binding commitment for a certain period of time. As we approach the higher self, we are expected to make certain commitments as well—commitments of responsibility, ethics, and dedication. In return, we receive the opportunity to work with the greater life of the higher self. This is an agreement which is taken quite seriously by both parties.

7. There must also be a proper definition of the standards of performance. An actor does not have sole responsibility to decide how he will play a character; the character must be compatible with the rest of the play and the other parts. It is the duty of the director to make sure that the actor performs adequately. Sometimes, this requires pushing the actor beyond his talents and capacities, into new realizations of character. The actor may resent this for awhile, but after the new skills have been perfected, he will recognize the value of what the director demanded.

The same is true in the proper relationship between the higher self and personality—in meditation and in life. It is not the wishes of the personality which are to be stirred up and enforced in meditation, but rather the projects and standards of the higher self. At times, the higher self may actually push us beyond our limitations—but this must be accepted as the only real way growth can occur. And so, we must keep in mind that smug feelings about what we have accomplished are not really a very good guide to our performance. Meditation is not designed to be an exercise in self-flattery!

8. Together, the director and actor bring life to center stage. As the proper relationship is established, a true integration occurs. This does not mean that they literally become one and the same. But the inspiration, authority, and guidance of the director draw from the actor a response of talent, charm, and brilliance, as he performs the role on stage. The talent and

genius of each feed the talent and genius of the other. As a result, a transformation occurs. The play is no longer just a play; it becomes an act of magic which enchants, instructs, and lifts up the spirit of the audience.

The integration of higher self and personality is very similar. The wisdom, love, and power of the higher self draw from the personality a response of intelligence, genius, and goodwill which vivifies all it does, thinks, and says. The higher self still remains the greater, but a figurative union does occur. And there is a genuine transformation. The personality becomes infused with ever more of the life of spirit.

Once again, it must be understood that this process of integration is anything but mindless and passive. The director does not insert a tape recorder in the throat of the actor, or manipulate him like a marionette. The role of the actor is of great importance, requiring extensive training and talent. He contributes much and receives much.

The same is true for the personality.

TRANSFORMATION

The goal of meditation is to transfer some of the life of the higher self into the personality, where it transforms daily behavior and self-expression. As such, meditation is anything but a quiet, passive state; it is a dynamic process involving three distinct stages:

1. Contacting the higher self.
2. Transferring some quality, energy, or idea.
3. Using it to transform the life of the personality.

The first stage is similar to the activity of the actor trying out for a part. The director advertises the parts available; the actor responds and appears for an audition. To many, it might seem that winning the role is the hardest part of acting—but it is really just the initial stage. The same is true in meditating. Many people believe that contacting the higher self is the *entire* work of meditation. In reality, it is just the beginning.

For the actor, the next step is to learn his lines, walk through the paces of the role, and rehearse the part. It is much the same for the one who meditates. Having contacted the higher self, he seeks out the guidance or inspiration he will need to act. He rehearses ways to express this in his life.

Once the lines are memorized, then the actor faces his hardest task: mastering the state of mind, feeling, conviction, and movement of the part he plays—and how his character must react to and interact with the others in the cast. He becomes the character and brings to life a believable portrayal of a human being. The third stage is also the hardest one for the meditator: having glimpsed the insight or love or plan of the higher self, he must now assimilate that greater life into his own expression. He must remove old patterns of thought or behavior which will conflict with the new, and move beyond them, establishing new habits, new patterns of thought and feeling, new definitions of self-image, new ethics, new skills, new values, or whatever is required to properly honor the inspiration and intention of the higher self. He must permanently improve his self-expression in some significant way, while remaining flexible so that he can grow some more in the future.

Meditation transforms. The meditator needs to pattern himself after the mythical alchemist, who sought to transmute lead into gold. Meditation is the alchemy of human consciousness, seeking to transmute the dross of our habits and feelings and thoughts into something more refined and noble—the wisdom, compassion, and skill which characterize the enlightened individual.

What is tragic is that many a beginning meditator learns a few tricks and then assumes that he knows all there is to know.

He cleans up a few bad habits and then stops, content with the modest improvement made. The alchemy of transformation, however, is meant to be a continual process, with each succeeding meditation adding a new layer of richness to our character and creativity. We are meant to take peak experiences of love and become so acquainted with them that they soon become our customary self-expression. When we have, then we stand ready for even greater peak experiences than before. Just so, we are meant to convert awe-inspiring revelations into simple, common sense attitudes and perspectives toward life. When we do, we stand ready to be inspired by even greater elements of the higher self.

The sure sign of the novice is the meditator who gushes about the wonders of his or her meditations. "Oh, wow—you should have seen all the white light." The experienced meditator *has* seen all the white light he wants to see; he continues to be moved by truly profound experiences, but they become progressively more subtle. His meditations move him not to talk and exclaim, *but to act!* They move him to improve his character, learn new skills, make new commitments, contribute to life, and integrate the treasures of heaven into the rich opportunities of earth.

CONSCIOUSNESS

We would never believe that the efforts of a poor playwright were the equivalent of the masterpieces of a Shakespeare, just because they happen to be performed on the same stage and by the same company. But many people do treat meditation in this way, believing very different techniques to be the same just because they are performed by "meditators."

A meditation which does not bring in the life of spirit is no meditation.

A meditation which does not lead to growth of character or creativity is no meditation.

A meditation which does not lead to new revelations is no meditation.

To understand this distinction, it is helpful to realize the difference between sensation and consciousness. Briefly stated, sensation is any perception made directly by the personality, either through its physical, emotional, or mental senses. Consciousness, by contrast, is the knowingness of the higher self. The capacity to sense is a projection of consciousness, but consciousness itself is much greater.

Many people who profess to meditate simply deal with a somewhat higher level of sensation than usual; they close their eyes to physical phenomena but keep them focused on emotional and mental phenomena. Except as a very introductory stage, this does not serve the work of meditation. We must make the effort to climb out of sensation and enter into the realm of consciousness.

The goal of meditation is not just to get more ideas—it is to obtain the *power to think!*

The goal of meditation is not just to get more good feelings—it is to tap the *power to love!*

The goal of meditation is not just to slow down our heartbeat or breathe more deeply—it is to contact the *power to act!*

Consciousness *is* the staging ground of meditation. Meditation does not *alter* consciousness, as so many people glibly insist; nor does it *raise* consciousness. It turns our attention away from sensation and focuses it in consciousness. What may or may not happen to the physical body of the meditator is therefore inconsequential. It is what occurs in consciousness that is all important—and how successfully the meditator assimilates the power of consciousness into his daily self-expression.

In this regard, it is helpful to keep in mind that not all

actors are successful in projecting the essence of their character to the audience. Some fill the stage only with emptiness. But the truly inspired actor magnetically charges the auditorium from the very moment he appears.

The work of meditation is to magnetically charge our awareness and activities with the dynamic presence of the higher self—the presence of consciousness. If we are using meditation effectively, then eventually everything we think and do and say will reveal the wisdom, love, and power of our spirit.

MEASURE FOR MEASURE

Anyone can daydream, but daydreaming holds us in the world of sensation. How do we know when we have actually been meditating, and not just entertaining ourself with a series of daydreams?

The only sensible answer to this question is to look at the results. The effectiveness of meditation should always be evaluated in terms of the enrichment of our self-expression and growth in our understanding—not in terms of how many lights we see, how "deep" we go, or what sort of visions appear. Amid all the clamor about breathing, chanting, postures, and obeisance to a guru, one fact stands clear: the true activity of meditation occurs in consciousness, not sensation. The best measure of meditation, therefore, is our success in managing our thoughts, feelings, and intentions, so they become more enlightened. Our capacity to breathe deeply, visualize clear symbols or images, adore a guru, or sound certain words is no guarantee whatsoever of achievement in meditation. Even the most casual follower of fads can learn to imitate these phenomena.

It is always more appealing to focus our attention on

lovely images and superficial changes instead of disciplining ourself to make a substantial contact with the higher self.

It is more "fun" to pretend that a magical force such as kundalini is flowing up the spine than it is to struggle with the work of forgiveness.

It is easier to sound a mantra than it is to make our habits sound.

It is simpler to concentrate on a straight posture than it is to create straight thoughts about our self-deceptions.

It is more comforting to hold in mind a pleasant daydream than it is to generate benevolent thoughts regarding a tragedy we have experienced.

It is more restful just to relax and let go of tension than it is to remove the psychological reactions which caused the tension to build in the first place.

But none of these is a path to the higher self—just to superficial pacification. It is important to respect the tremendous richness which can be tapped in effective meditation, and not be fooled by insignificant phenomena. We have the responsibility to place our priorities for meditating in proper order. Only then will it be possible to evaluate accurately the progress we are making.

This is just common sense. If our goals and motivations do not amount to much, neither will our efforts. The person who meditates only to find tranquil respite from the harried activities of life will never tap the higher self or the riches of heaven. Instead of meditating, he ought to take a nap—or soak himself in a hot bath. But the person who wants to remove the elements of his own hostility, resentment, and intolerance which nip at him throughout the day will not only find a new measure of tranquillity once they are removed, but will also discover great resources of compassion, forgiveness, and peace within himself. Surely *that* would be an indication the work of meditation is proceeding well.

There are dangers in pursuing the practice of meditation without an intelligent definition of our goals and expectations, or a means for examining how well we are proceeding. One danger is that the whole effort will sink to a level of artificial catatonia; in the quest of peacefulness, we simply deaden our awareness. This, of course, is not peacefulness at all—just the avoidance of responsibility.

Another danger is the risk of being held hostage by the wish life of the personality. The subconscious of each of us is well-stocked with feelings, images, memories, and associations. It can be very exciting to pursue these—especially since the pursuit will quickly take us out of our subconscious (allowing us to conveniently forget our problems) into the subconscious of mass consciousness. The risk is that we may soon become trapped on the level of these images, and actually begin to believe that these images represent the higher self. In point of fact, however, they are several strata below.

This danger of being trapped by the wish life is far more common and enticing than might be suspected. The study of the images of the mind has always been popular, and for good reason—it is a science in itself, when properly approached. But when the study of images is promoted as a fad, or taught by people who have little knowledge of the limitations or scope of imagery, it can become a seductive diversion from the real work of meditation. In such cases, the images or symbols perceived are made almost wholly of emotional or astral energy— which is, of course, the primary energy of our wish life. The temptation to deal with them exclusively on this level, and not discover their counterparts in the mind and the higher self— where their true power lies—is enormous. *But it is always the highest level of consciousness which should be pursued in meditation—not the far more entertaining and pretty images of the subconscious.* The responsible meditator must learn this basic lesson.

The third danger of meditating without a sense of responsibility or true intelligence is the most obvious. It is just a waste of time. This also implies the most effective measure of the success of our efforts. If we are meditating well, it is time well spent. If not, it is just a waste.

INTO THE ABSTRACT

These principles of Active Meditation will undoubtedly be annoying and frustrating to some. The person who draws comfort from his wish life and the study of astral images will be irritated by the prospect of giving them up, and probably find some reason for not doing so. The individual who enjoys resting passively and doing as little as he can in meditation will be insulted by the invitation to be active, and will piously claim that activity is the wrong path to the higher self. The meditator who gets all wrapped up in chanting, deep breathing, postures, and a vegetarian diet will be upset by the idea that none of these constitutes meditation; none of them leads to the higher self. He will undoubtedly scurry off to find the nearest guru to reassure him. But this is like passing up a banquet in favor of a couple of lollipops.

The chief reason why Active Meditation is annoying to some is that it lacks the comfort of concreteness. The essence of our wisdom, love, and strength—the virtues of the higher self—is, to us, abstract. It is not formed into nice images we can contemplate; it is form*less*. Active Meditation does deal with forms and images, to be sure, but its principal focus is to connect us with the abstract levels of the higher self: the *power* of pure ideas, not the mantras which represent that power; the *power* of goodwill, affection, and forgiveness, not just passive adoration. Active Meditation seeks to harness the impelling intention to express ourselves—and that is abstract.

The average person is not accustomed to working with abstract thought, emotion, or power, but unless it is embraced and mastered to some degree, our efforts to meditate may just weight us down in the concrete elements of the personality. Yet we need not fear the abstract; we are all potentially capable of experiencing and interacting with abstract thought, feeling, and power, and focusing it usefully through the personality. Indeed, almost everyone has touched the abstract from time to time, often without realizing it. The peace and goodwill which can be perceived at Christmas worship services are abstract emotions. Flashes of insight are abstract thoughts. A sense of purpose is abstract power. The goal of meditation is to help us become more conscious of these abstract elements of life—and do something with them.

We should not turn away from the abstract, even though we are more accustomed to the concrete and the well-defined. It may be annoying or frustrating to deal with the abstract at times, until we become more familiar with it, but the process of bringing abstract life into concrete expression is the way we grow, develop, and become more useful. God seldom gives us concrete answers to our prayers, after all; instead, He gives us the wisdom to figure out our problems on our own. It is not always easy, but it does help us grow. And the support is real, even if abstract and indirect.

Still, the desire of some people to avoid activity is great. These people love the platitudes which enjoin us to turn all our problems over to God and let Him solve them. To the degree that we are truly seeking the help and support of God and intend to work *with* God to solve these problems, all is fine. But if we "give ourselves to God" as a clever way to avoid responsibility in facing our problems, we are seriously deluding ourselves.

The higher life is there for all to tap—but it is our responsibility to give it focus and expression.

IS THAT ALL THERE IS?

Because meditation is a technique used for self-improvement, exploring consciousness, and contacting the higher self, it is frequently confused with other systems and practices which are designed to do some of the same things. In order to properly understand meditation, it is useful to see how it *differs* from these other practices. The most common include:

Guided imagery. The heavenly states of consciousness are not populated with pictures or images; they are realms of force and abstract qualities. Symbols can be intelligently used to lead a meditator into contact with these forces and qualities, but most people who employ imagery never go beyond the images themselves. Their experiences are often no more valuable than looking out a car window as we drive downtown.

Guided imagery can be a useful way to learn the content of our subconscious—if we then use other techniques to clean up the problems we find there and better organize it. But because the images themselves originate in the personality—or in mass consciousness—the use of guided imagery or visualization is limited to the exploration of those levels. As commonly practiced, it is not a suitable vehicle for contacting the higher self or exploring the true realms of consciousness.

Hypnosis. This is a practice which is frequently mistaken for meditation, because many of the words used and methods of relaxing are very similar. Even most hypnotists tend to believe that meditation is a type of hypnotism—but then, hypnotists are the most hypnotized people in the world when it comes to the subject of hypnosis. It must be kept in mind that not all doorways lead to the same interior; the doorway of a church may resemble greatly the doorway of a courthouse, but the activities which occur inside each building are considerably different. In meditation and hypnosis, the methods of entering may be similar, but once inside, the activities are poles apart.

The object of meditation, as we have seen, is to contact the life of the higher self and transcend the limits of the personality. The object of hypnosis is to contact the subconscious of the person being hypnotized and make changes there which will influence daily behavior and attitudes. There is much of value in hypnosis; it can be most useful in strengthening or weakening certain trends of thought and feeling. But as it is commonly practiced,* hypnosis does not lead to transcendence. It does not bring in the life of the higher self or any of the richer dimensions of wisdom, love, courage, or skill. And so it differs fundamentally from meditation.

Hypnosis does sometimes stir up the wish life of the personality, engendering the illusion or fantasy that the personality is vastly more powerful and mature than it actually is, and this experience could be misconstrued for contact with the higher self. But this sense of strength usually fades in the face of subsequent experiences, as unresolved conflict, resurrected hostility, and ambivalence surface. Hypnosis can do nothing to put a person in touch with the resources of spirit needed to conquer these problems.

When used skillfully by people who are maturely aware of human nature and psychology, hypnosis can be a marvelous adjunct to the work of conditioning and healing the personality. But it is never more than one aspect of the personality (our own or someone else's) talking to another part of the personality. It does not contact the higher self.

Positive thinking. Like hypnosis, positive thinking is a practice in which one part of the personality speaks to another. In this case, it is the conscious mind speaking, attempt-

---

* There is one exception. When a person who is already psychic, mediumistic, or mystical is hypnotized, he will frequently rise above the subconscious and contact the life of his spirit. Edgar Cayce is a good example of this. But such exceptions should not be construed to be the general rule.

ing to control the reactions of the subconscious and unconscious by repeating affirmations. It is often quite effective, but it must also be realized that there are other sources of power available to us than our conscious thoughts. Positive thinking does not connect us with the higher self; after all, the higher self already knows that it is healthy, wise, loving, and well. Indeed, if positive thinking is pursued too fanatically, it can actually lead to self-deception, in which we believe we are doing all that is necessary to correct our behavior and grow. In fact, we are taking only the beginning steps.

The practitioners of positive thinking ought to reflect on the fact that there is a difference between uttering a statement which affirms truth on the one hand and comprehending and being able to express that truth on the other. This is the difference between positive thinking and meditation.

Self-observation. This is the practice of quietly observing our thoughts, feelings, and images as they arise to the surface of awareness. Self-observation is advocated in many circles as a true meditative technique—but it is not. There is, of course, much merit to self-examination, but to be effective, self-examination must include more activity than just self-observation. In reviewing an experience, thought, or attitude, we should forgive when necessary, rehearse the ideal, and build convictions for future action. All of these activities go beyond mere observation and, to some degree, call upon the power and intelligence of the higher self.

As usually practiced, self-observation is passive and undirected. It leads to an astralization of the personality—we become more and more immersed in our emotions and feelings, as our attention is progressively focused on our rich storehouse of memories and fantasies. We begin to "space out" and simply disconnect ourself from the mess in our subconscious—we do not transmute it. The short-term result is that we feel better, but the long-term consequences are more serious. The strength and quickness of our reactions to life are reduced; we accept an illusion of escape as the basis of our life. For hysterical and habitually over-reactive people, this may seem a blessing, but is something like cultivating deafness as a means of coping with noisy neighbors. It does not make sense.

At best, self-observation leads to a richer awareness of what has happened to us—and to the innate life of the personality. Employed selectively, this can have value—but what do we do once we have reviewed all there is to review? Is our past, our fantasies, our illusions, our memories, our feelings, and our fears all that we have? Is that all there is? Of course not—there is the full abundance of the higher self. But we cannot tap this merely by observing the life of the personality. We cannot even *change* the personality just by observing it! We must take action.

Laziness of thought and feeling, so attractive to so many people, has never had a more sophisticated cloak than the practice of self-observation. But like the emperor's new clothes, it is a bit thin. Meditation is much, much more than self-observation; intelligent activity *is* required for effective change.

Besides, the path to enlightenment should never be so boring!

Psychic awareness. As the activity of meditation is pursued, there often is an increase in psychic perceptions. We become aware of the phenomena of inner realms of creation which have heretofore been unknown to us. But these perceptions are incidental to the true activity of meditation, just as conversations we hear between acts at the theater are incidental to the action on stage. And it should be recognized that not all people who have psychic perceptions know how to meditate intelligently.

Some of the psychic phenomena which might come to us in association with meditation may be useful to us—if they lead to practical insights about life or the nature of the higher self.

But it must be understood that most psychic perceptions are the products of sensation, not consciousness. They are either emotional or mental (primarily emotional), but they are still sensations. And it is so easy to become charmed by the sheer fascination of these sights and sounds that we forget our more serious purpose for meditating: working with the higher self.

If we are more interested in chatting with someone who has died or in seeing auras than we are in discovering the abstract forces of the higher self, then we ought to watch television rather than meditate. We are obviously more devoted to being entertained than we are to enriching our consciousness. And yet, this is a common motive for "meditating"! Far too many people simply lust secretly to travel through the astral plane—and are quite content just to remain at that level. They conveniently label all of its psychic phenomena as "spiritual"—and even insist that the astral plane is the highest level of "consciousness" anyone can achieve. But these deceptions and dissemblings do not change the basic fact that they are not actually meditating. They are merely playing psychic games.

Some of the places and people we might meet psychically, on the astral plane, are quite real. But this level of life is no more the higher self than the physical plane is. So the meditator must not confuse his work with the pursuit of psychic impressions. Aside from this, the one who would travel astrally should beware the allurement of the many astral "Disneylands" which infest the astral worlds. They can be fun, but they are not real—and their entertainment can be had only at our peril.

Prayer. This is a valuable practice when performed correctly, but it should not be confused with meditation. The person who reads a little about meditation and then proclaims, "Oh, I do all that in my prayers," clearly knows very little about either prayer or meditation.

If we consider the realm of the higher self as a heavenly

state of consciousness filled with the rich treasures of wisdom, talent, compassion, courage, and beauty, then prayer would be akin to a phone call to heaven. Meditation, by contrast, would be more like an actual visit. Both practices can be used to bring new, enriching life from the spirit to the personality, but prayer does not require much preparation of consciousness—and is more limited in its results. Meditation involves a much more extensive change in our state of mind and emotion.

To oversimplify a bit, prayer is essentially a one-way communication with a higher power and intelligence; meditation is more truly a communion with that higher power. It is an interaction with wisdom, goodwill, and power. Prayer invokes aspects of our higher life for assistance in our daily activities. Meditation lifts aspects of the personality to the level of our higher self so they may be bathed with its wisdom, goodwill, and power. The practice of prayer is largely controlled by the personality. In meditation, we make far more of an effort to open our personality to the authority and guidance of the higher self. We can pray for a specific blessing, for example, and never expose or think about our prejudices, hypocrisy, or unresolved conflicts. In meditating, however, we do expose the weaknesses of the personality to the redemptive and penetrating life of the higher self, while also seeking its blessings. Thus, the opportunities for effective healing and transformation are far richer in the practice of meditation than in the common practice of prayer.

THE FUNDAMENTAL PRINCIPLE

The path we choose to follow to our higher self should be compatible with the nature of the higher self. If we are seeking to discover love and goodwill, the best technique is undoubtedly the expression of compassion and benevolence in all we do. If we are seeking to discover wisdom, the best technique is surely the use of intelligence and creativity. If we are seeking to discover strength, the best technique is unquestionably the expression of courage and determination in pursuing goals.

All techniques of Active Meditation grow out of this fundamental principle. There are many other systems of self-improvement which have great value, but it is important to comprehend that we reach the higher self *only* by learning to think and act and express ourself as the higher self would have us think and act and express ourself. Anything short of that will obviously not suffice.

This is also a good principle to keep in mind as we survey the vast array of meditative techniques available. We must strip away the nonsense and hysteria which attend a good many of these practices, and look for that which will truly help us. The meditative supermarket is overstocked with theories, gurus, and philosophies. Before we buy anything, we should ask: "How well will this help me become aware of the higher self and integrate more of its life and light into my own self-expression?"

And we should also ask ourself how willing we are to make these techniques work—for us.

Herman Returns

We turned off the typewriters and decided to take a break. "It's a shame that so many good people become trapped in nonsense about the higher life and meditation," remarked Bob. "Maybe now they won't."

As Bob said these words, the room began to glow again. Soon, Herman had reappeared. "It's a nice start, boys," the angel said, "but watch out that you don't become too negative."

"Well, we thought we'd better warn the reader about the obstructions and diversions he'll encounter on the road to the higher self," Bob responded.

"To say nothing of the potholes on the path," chuckled Herman. "Yes, that's quite important, but please keep in mind that some of those practices you would do away with were once very important and even considered esoteric. Why, I remember back 35,000 years ago when we..."

"You're not going to tell us to indulge or promote something just because it worked 35,000 years ago, are you?" interrupted Carl. "The chariot was quite the thing once, too, but I'd rather drive a car today. A lot of ideas and techniques which were suitable once upon a time just aren't good enough today. Humanity has grown beyond them."

"What's so outmoded about loving God?" asked Herman.

"Nothing," Carl said. "But loving God, in ourselves and others, can be an act of intelligence. It doesn't have to be an act of mindless idolatry."

"Then you had better tell your readers how to do it—intelligently," said Herman quietly. "And you'd better be convincing, or you might just get an unwelcomed visit from certain 'defenders of the faith.'"

"I'm not sure I like the sound of that," said Bob. "We know we can't please everyone—but I don't relish the thought of being tarred and feathered, either. We just want to put our ideas out in the marketplace, so they can reach the right people—the ones who can think and respect good ideas intelligently explained."

Herman sighed, as only an angel can sigh. "There's a certain momentum in mass consciousness and human traditions which opposes any change—even change for the better. You are going to run into that. In fact, I believe you've both already sensed a vague force of disapproval as you've written. That's not from me—it's from the masses. People are like that. Many of them just don't want to grow more than the next two steps. They are comfortable with the status quo—even when it's silly. But you are challenging that—and they will challenge you back."

"How will they challenge us back?" asked Carl. "Do you mean the Druids or someone will show up some dark and stormy night and hurl bricks at us?"

Herman laughed. "You know better than that. There won't be physical people. But mass consciousness and group minds do speak up when pricked by the kind of ideas you are setting down here. They speak through the forces of discontent, fear, and resentment. You hear it in your heart. But that doesn't mean it is imaginary. It can be quite distressful, as you both well know."

"Then what do you suggest we do?" asked Bob. "We're too far into the project to give it up. And neither one of us would set our hands to writing mush and sweet nothings. If we wanted to write about nothing, we'd write nothing at all, and be done with it!"

Herman appeared amused—as amused as an angel might be. He seemed pleased that he had finally struck the right chord. "No *living* person would want to refuse the opportunity to grow, to become more knowledgeable, or to learn new skills. People just misunderstand motives and ideas at times, especially when you insist a little too strongly that the old ways are outmoded. They want to be cajoled and comforted, not intimidated. Of course, some people believe that *all* criticism is destructive, even when it is offered constructively and compassionately. So just take care to devote more space to encouraging people to do what is effective and helpful than you do to pointing out what is dangerous or passé. Tell them why you think you are correct—and then let them decide for themselves. Invite them to put their own intelligence to work. If you have done a good job of explaining your ideas, their intelligence will see the light. It really is stronger than their resistance, you know."

"Absolutely."

"And anyway—you can't force people to be good or do good. Not even an angel can do that."

"You can't?" we cried in amazement.

Herman spoke very quietly. "Well, we do know how, and we have the power, but we choose not to. People have to learn to make the right decisions. Try to keep that in mind as you write. Don't try to force people to do anything, even if it's right. Instead, just carefully explain why your ideas and approaches are reasonable—as though you were loving parents entrusted with the duty of teaching your children what was helpful and what was not. Just make sure you don't betray that trust."

Herman paused to let that idea sink in, then announced: "I have to fly now. I'll be around now and then to nudge you as you need it."

And with that, the light faded and we were left in the lesser light of our own thoughts. Carl spoke first.

"I never intended to write a lurid exposé of 'Accidental Mindlessness.' People who practice things of that ilk expose themselves. But we can't pretend that passiveness is part of meditation."

"I don't think Herman would disagree," said Bob, "although I doubt that we could get an angel to say the things we say *in print*. I think Herman was just warning us to stick to the business of being helpful. He probably hears us joking about certain gurus as 'freaks in sheets' who wear sandals only because they are too dumb to tie shoelaces and worries that we'd stick a crack like that in the book. We'd better cool it on the sarcasm—even if the sandal fits. But we dare not pretend that there is anything spiritual about stupidity—or remaining silent in the face of stupidity. We must not be afraid to point out the practices we know to be a waste of time—or harmful."

Carl thought a moment. "I guess we should try to be helpful and kind, even as our higher selves have been helpful and kind to us. Over the years, we have found them to be trustworthy guides who respect our needs and abilities—but do not hesitate to nudge us toward our undeveloped potential. I suppose that writing in this manner—like our higher selves would speak to us—is what Herman wants us to do.

"You know, I think he's a bit more clever than we give him credit for."

A faint, disembodied chuckle echoed in the room.

3

The Importance
Of Being Active

THE ACTIVE MODE

There is an old axiom that if we want to learn how to play the piano, we had better play the piano. It will not help to stare out the window, gather daisies, manicure the dog, or take a nap. Only by practicing the piano can we learn to play it. It should be equally obvious that if we want to increase our wisdom, talent, courage, or goodwill, we had better practice expressing these qualities in our life. We cannot just *believe* in the goodness of these elements of life, or gather poems about them into a scrapbook, or surrender blissfully to God. It is not even enough to exercise our fantasies; we must activate and give life to wisdom, talent, courage, and goodwill in all we do.

The activity of meditation is the life of the higher self *moving* through us, awakening us, increasing our talents and understanding, enriching our life, and prodding us to transcend our pettiness. This activity is an inherent principle of life; it can be observed in nature, in groups, in civilization, in atoms, and in universes. The forms of life *can* come to rest, but growth occurs in the active mode. Accomplishment occurs in the active mode. Enlightenment occurs in the active mode.

We must appreciate that the wisdom, love, and power of the higher self are *active energies and forces.* They will not let us sit quietly and just observe them; if we are sitting quietly, then perforce we are observing something other than the higher self. These forces and qualities move through us and move us—to action. New ideas burst into our awareness, and with them comes the power to act. This is not to suggest that we are moved to act rashly or impatiently—not at all. We do, however, receive the dynamic motivation and support which enables us to act effectively.

But becoming active, either in meditation or in life, is not something which is as simple as drawing a straight line connecting two dots. There are strong forces within the subconscious and unconscious of each of us—and humanity as a whole—which resist enlightened activity. These are the forces of the status quo—primarily, laziness and fear.

DROPPING OUT

The lure of laziness is very seductive. People tend to be fascinated by the enchanting idea that they may be able to get more by doing less. And there always seem to be individuals who are all too willing to capitalize on this basic laziness—and feed and encourage it. Over the years, the "virtues" of inactivity and mental deadness have been carefully promoted and enshrined, to the point where many of our religions, philosophies, and traditions have been vandalized by apathy.

We must realize that laziness and apathy are dangerous to our health—especially our mental and spiritual health. But it is sometimes hard to keep this perspective in mind. It is commonly believed, for example, that hard work—particularly mental work—leads to strain and stress. The average person would say that no one ever died of relaxation, but many people succumb to excessive work. But this is just not true. Productive work actually leads to greater contentment, fulfillment, and comfort—not stress and strain. And the most common cause of declining health in older people is inactivity and boredom—not work. Still, the fictions persist.

One of the reasons why these fictions do persist is the fact that growth, either in consciousness or in form, always involves leaving something behind—or even destroying it. As a child grows, he must leave behind his old clothing, his less mature behavior, his favorite games, and many childish habits and attitudes. As an adult grows, he must leave behind comfortable conditions, outmoded habits, and sometimes even friendships.

80

A healthy approach to growth always emphasizes that genuine improvements in life should strike a balance between the old and the new. Rather than rejecting the old as undesirable, the primary endeavor is to update it and make it more ideal. Nonetheless, it is easy to become obsessed with and blinded by the presence of imperfection in ourself and in life— to the point where we start spending more time fighting off the old than we do in building the new and better. The results can be disastrous: we become consumed by our struggle to overcome our anger or depression or anxiety—until we become exhausted. At such a point, we are ripe to be plucked by a smooth-talking, charismatic peddler of simplistic solutions, who will tell us just to "let go" of our struggle—by blanking the mind or by "believing" in God's love. It sounds good—but we often forget that "letting go" is just a thinly-disguised version of laziness and apathy. Bums and drop-outs "let-go"—not responsible, intelligent adults.

It is possible to achieve a simulacrum of peace by letting go—or "blissing out"—but only because these practices produce a very effective suppression of our awareness of conflict, misery, and mistakes. We purchase peace by giving away some of our humanity—not through genuine growth in goodwill or strength. We actually have done nothing but trade our difficulties for indifference. But what is given to nothingness has a tendency to resurrect itself out of nothingness and be reborn. The only problem is that the individual who has let go or is blissed out now has nothing but nothing with which to act.

Some people would insist that altering our perceptions in these ways does represent a legitimate solution—but this claim does not hold up in the light of common sense. An illusion is an illusion, regardless of its origin. *Spiritual* apathy and passiveness are no less disastrous than more ordinary varieties.

Even if we do not go to these extremes, our efforts to grow, meditatively and otherwise, are frequently sabotaged by laziness and apathy. There are strong currents in mass consciousness which encourage us to hope that difficult conditions will just take care of themselves, without any activity on our part—and which discourage us from making too much of an effort to grow, lest the laziness of everyone else be exposed. We should understand, however, that any time we adopt a passive meditative or spiritual practice, we are in essence giving silent approval to the strong forces of resistance within us. We are slowing down our potential for growth. And that does not make sense—not to someone who wishes to grow in competence, wisdom, and goodwill.

It is important to realize that the apologists of apathy will not give up; *we* must give them up. They will be quick to point out, for example, that the active but unskilled mind is often rather destructive. This is true, but the solution does not lie in making such a mind passive; it lies in developing its skills and wisdom. They will warn that many people who are active are quite selfish and harmful. Once again, this is true, but the solution to the problem hardly lies in everyone becoming passive! That will merely let the selfish and harmful people manipulate us all the more easily.

The traditional meditative techniques designed to lull us into passiveness and laziness are all very simple. The more common varieties include:

1. The repetition of a mantra which has no real meaning. Concentrating on this mantra absorbs our attention while the rest of our thoughts and associations float away.

2. The passive observation of our subconscious thoughts, feelings, and images with studied indifference.

3. Staring at a symbol or object while ignoring everything else—especially the content of the subconscious and the activities of the mind.

4. The constant affirmation that we can do anything we want, anytime and anywhere, and it will be all right.

As simple as these practices are, they nonetheless pose a genuine threat to spiritual growth; they suppress awareness of ordinary thought and feeling by a) dissociating from them and b) damaging our associative mechanism so that we cannot connect with old problems and unresolved conflicts. If practiced long enough, these techniques can actually lead to a type of artificially-induced schizophrenia which is very difficult to remedy. The signs are:

• Forgetfulness and the inability to remember items readily.

• The inability to work creatively or deal with symbolic and abstract thought.

• A pleasant blandness of all feelings, without any strong sentiment—either negative or positive.

• Difficulty in concentrating.

• Irritability when out in public.

These conditions do not resemble enlightenment or genuine transcendence in any way whatsoever. They are just the fruits of militant and concentrated spiritual laziness.

ON OUR KNEES

The second major reason why many meditative and spiritual practices have plummeted into passiveness is the pervasive awe and fear of God in human consciousness. The ideal approach to God and the higher self is one of intelligent and loving cooperation, but this is something which many good people have not yet learned. For them, the thought of approaching an infinitely powerful and all-knowing, divine force is rather intimidating. They quiver, shake, and grovel.

Of course, there are many malicious opportunists who are all too eager to remind us of our "obligation" to crawl on our knees to God—and then stay on our knees while dealing with them. These people wrap themselves pompously in robes of wrath and arrogance and remind us that God knows all about our dirty little sins and is busily judging us. In return, most of us respond by feeling terribly guilty and hardly an inch high in comparison to God. We forget that we are of God and that God is within us—within our higher self. We proclaim how unworthy and wretched we are.

Mass consciousness is severely polluted by this notion, even if some of us have managed to escape it individually. As a result, many advocates of meditation and other spiritual practices insist that none of us should ever dare approach the presence of our higher self in any attitude other than abject surrender. Their philosophy of "we are nothing and God is everything" has done much harm to individuals and to civilization. Nowhere is this harm more obvious than in the common practices of meditation.

To be sure, the higher self *is* more wise, loving, powerful, and skillful than the personality—but this does not mean that the personality is wretched and unworthy. It does not mean that the personality must adopt a passive attitude of "I surrender" in order to please the higher self. Quite the contrary: we should approach the higher self as though we were a dutiful son or daughter of a wealthy businessman, seeking to be trained by our father so that we will be able to take over the family business. We would not learn much about our father's wisdom and management skills if we simply cowered in the corner, afraid to act. Nor would we learn much by limiting ourself to passive adoration of the mightiness of our father. Instead, we must work cooperatively with our father, performing the duties that he would have us do, until we had acquired his skills and competence. Active interaction with the father is required. Active experience in managing the affairs of the business is a necessity.

The same principle applies in Active Meditation. Even if

we are not the type to grovel, we should beware that fear of the higher self can often be very subtle, and adversely influence our thoughts and activity. It is of great importance to the success of meditation to cultivate a healthy, rational view of the higher self and the divine forces of life.

PROBLEMS IN RECEPTIVITY

The problem of passiveness in meditation is complicated by two other factors as well. The first is the need to be quiet in order to be receptive to the wisdom, will, and love of the higher self. It is easy to confuse this state of quiet alertness with passiveness; indeed, many teachers admonish us to become passive and still. Nonetheless, when correctly practiced, this state of quiet receptivity is far from passive: it is a highly refined state of intelligent alertness.

The truly passive person would not be able to hear or comprehend a thing. He would be like the individual who *appears* to be listening to what we are saying, but actually is not paying attention. Genuine listening of any kind, either to a friend or to the still, small voice of the higher self, requires poise and alertness—the ability to hear *and* digest what is being spoken. The higher self has no intention of filling us with wisdom and love in the sense of pouring soup into a bowl; we have the responsibility to interact actively with its ideas and forces and learn to do something useful with them. We have the responsibility to be alert, not passive.

The second factor stems from a misunderstanding of the nature of the qualities and treasures of the higher self. Many people assume that the love, wisdom, beauty, dignity, and courage of the higher self already exist in concrete form, ready to be tapped—almost like buying a loaf of bread at the grocery store. They believe the reason they do not have these qualities and forces themselves is that they are somehow *blocked;* if they could just remove the blocks and impediments, they would suddenly become fully loving, wise, gracious, and courageous. There is an element of truth to this notion; we often do let bad habits impede the good within us. But we must also understand that the good within us is abstract. It does not exist in prepackaged, ready-to-use form. In this sense, the treasures of the higher self are more like an abundant resource of wheat, ready to be made into bread—not the loaf of bread itself. We must learn to bake the bread—and that is an active process.

Just removing that which blocks us is not enough. Most people, after all, are hostile because they *lack* sufficient goodwill—not because their goodwill is blocked. They are afraid and anxious because they *lack* common sense and self-discipline—not because it is blocked. They are ignorant because they *lack* intelligence—not because it is blocked. They have not accepted the challenge of interacting with the treasures of the higher self and forming them into noble expressions and skills. They have remained passive.

THE CHALLENGE

Life continually summons us to grow in wisdom, talent, and love; it challenges us to be active. We are reminded, both in subtle and in obvious ways, of our frailties, our deficiencies, and our flaws. This is not done to embarrass us, but to inspire us to cooperate more fully with the life of the higher self.

This challenge cannot be met with laziness, for we are meant to be productive.

It cannot be met with surrender and fear, for we are meant to participate in the work of the higher self.

It cannot be met with silence, for we are meant to improve and increase our self-expression.

It cannot be met just by eliminating that which hinders us, for we are meant to build and create. Meditation is a means of building a superstructure in consciousness, so that we have better access to the life of spirit—and a means for bringing the riches we discover there into active expression in our needs and work.

It is only through intelligent and constructive activity that we can add to our stature and strength. The problems of living are to be met by actively overwhelming them with the enriching life of the higher self—not by blissfully hoping the problems will go away. Retreating from our problems is a regressive move which dulls us to the evocative challenge of life; it strips us of one of the fundamental virtues of our humanity.

We are designed to work as a partner with the higher self. It summons us to the activity of its labor and plan. In the process, we frequently find that we must summon it to assist us and heal or strengthen aspects of the personality which are inadequate for the tasks at hand. It is in this dynamic interaction between the higher self and the personality that the work of evolution is accomplished.

Not in "sitting."

4

Preparing To Meditate

CAREFULNESS

One of the great problems in spiritual growth is *careless-ness*—not paying sufficient attention to what we are doing, why we are doing it, or how well it is being done. Some people are casual almost to the point of being flippant. Meditation, however, is a very precise practice; it is important to hit the mark we aim for. After all, if we believe ourself to be in tune with our higher self but are actually only in touch with our warm and cozy wish life, we can grievously deceive ourself.

The antidote for carelessness is, quite obviously, careful-ness—the practice of taking the time and effort to do any endeavor properly. Carefulness includes making sure that our motives for meditating are proper; our understanding of what we are doing is thorough; and our goals are clear and well-defined. Haphazard efforts usually result in haphazard results. A modest amount of planning and preparation can go a long way in improving the quality of our personal development.

It is surprising how many people resent this idea, how-ever. They just want to be able to plop down and tune in. Usually, this is because they are still operating in the mode of wanting to see the sights—they want the higher self to act as a tour guide to something which will be entertaining and magical. That is not how the higher self works, however; the higher self responds to intelligence, not to requests for a dumb show. If that is what we want, it will turn the enterprise over to the subconscious, which is more than willing to entertain us.

It is therefore helpful to get in the habit of preparing our-self for the activity of meditation. This is not difficult or even time-consuming, but it is most beneficial. It keeps us focused on our goals and helps protect us from being sidetracked. It reminds us of the serious purpose of meditating and encourages us to proceed carefully. And it creates a matrix of expectation and need which helps invoke the presence of the higher self.

THOSE WHO CANNOT MEDITATE

One of the most effective ways to prepare for meditation is to face the fact that there are certain types of people who simply *cannot* meditate—not as long as they hold onto their cherished limitations and beliefs. To the degree that we may have traces of these attitudes in our own character, we can best prepare for meditation by removing them or at least putting them on the shelf for a while, so they will not disturb us. The people who cannot meditate include:

Those who maintain a poor self-image. As long as we feel inferior and unworthy of any help or friend, we will find it very difficult to contact the higher self and its treasures. We might discover the love of the higher self, but we would be unwilling to believe that we deserved it, or could do anything useful with it. This is not a healthy meditative state. And so, if we have in the past maintained a poor self-image, we should realize that part of preparing to meditate will include changing this fundamental attitude. We must begin to accept the fact that our higher self would not have selected us for the roles we play in life unless it knew we had the potential to do an adequate job. We may lack faith in ourself, but the higher self does not.

Those who sustain a martyr complex or depression. If we believe ourself to be a victim of life, or find life to be an unmitigated hell, it will not be possible to approach the higher self effectively. The forces and strengths of the higher self will be unable to penetrate the tent of gloom and pessimism we have chosen to camp in. It is our responsibility to strike this tent before we can expect the light and love of our inner life to enter.

Those who indulge a guilty conscience. Guilt can be a major hindrance, especially if we have allowed ourself to be excessively intimidated or have been the victim of the fundamentalist tenet that God is everything and we are nothing. If we believe that we are born in sin, living in sin, and doomed to die in sin, we will have to outgrow this nonsense and come to appreciate the higher self as a friend which can *help* us. We do have our problems, our limitations, and our peccadillos, but our spiritual nature is more important than any of these. It is certainly more important than our guilty feelings and our sense of nothingness. We are the child of our spiritual nature as well as our experiences, and so have the means of healing and enriching that which is imperfect or marred.

Paranoids. People who exaggerate hostile suspiciousness and fear of loss or criticism to irrational extremes become almost incapable of change. They project their fears and anxieties onto the world about them, to the point that they become obsessed with the expectation that they will be harmed, cheated, or criticized. Such attitudes foster a climate of defensiveness and hostility which prevents a proper relationship with everything—including the higher self. Paranoids need to realize that while some of their fears and suspicions undoubtedly do have a basis, there is no reason for projecting them onto the higher self. The higher self is a source of goodwill, peace, insight, and courage—not a malicious fiend. It is a powerful ally we all urgently need—but we need to be open to it and willing to cooperate with it.

Dilettantes. There can be no effective meditation without self-discipline and perseverance. The person who hops from one system to another, seeking but never using, is not really interested in growth—just the latest fads. The higher self could not care less about fads, however.

Sanctimonious know-it-alls. Like the dilettantes, these are people who will try any new fad that comes along—just to prove it does not work. They surround themselves in such a shell of Pecksniffian smugness that all they can hear is the echo of their own opinions. Their lack of vision and smallmindedness confines them to very limited possibilities; their smugness inhibits the acquisition of anything beyond what they already know. In order to meditate, these people first have to learn to accept the world as it is—larger than they are, richer in possibilities and opportunities than they suspect, and full of surprises, undiscovered joys, and marvelous new experiences.

The passive-dependent. These are people who are constantly on the prowl for assistance and approval. Their enormous craving for attention can quickly distort the activity of meditation into a search for the emotional goo of self-praise— or even the search for a guru who will flatter them for his own purposes. These people urgently need the strength and greater sense of individuality the higher self can give them, plus the dignity and knowledge which will let them stand independently. Effective meditation is *not* to be used for satisfying neurotic needs for affection and attention, but it can be used to cure the basic problem these people have—the lack of psychological self-sufficiency. First, however, they must shift from the perspective of giving all their attention to getting what they want, and adopt the responsibility for making their lives work more successfully.

Concrete thinkers who cannot accept anything unknown or formless. Some people believe that if they cannot knock it, taste it, see it, kick it, or at least take photographs of it, it does not exist. Before these people can meditate, they must learn that some of the most important things in life are rather nebulous or even intangible. The air we breathe, the production of our blood cells, the affection we receive from friends, the joy we experience at times, and the life force which animates us all are invisible to us. So is the life of the higher self and its influence on us. A little use of our imagination and common sense can open up new worlds to us, for our benefit.

Lovers of laziness. Some people are quite intelligent and curious, but expect nice ideas and techniques to work automatically. Unfortunately, thinking about an idea and making it work are two different phenomena. Meditation is not effortless. It is not hard work, but it *is* work. It involves change, not escape; self-appraisal, not self-indulgence. Before they can meditate effectively, lazy people must learn to be constructive and efficient in their use of these techniques. Sometimes, the help we need the most is the help that only we can give ourselves—self-help!

The skeptic. Doubt is not a hindrance to meditation, unless it is excessive. It leaves open the door to the possibility of surprise and discovery—and many doubting people are able to accept new ideas quite gracefully. But the person whose awareness and imagination have been dulled by an overdose of the mundane can find it difficult to conceive of a higher self and a level of consciousness filled with the riches of wisdom, compassion, talent, strength, and peace. Such a person runs the risk of missing important events and phenomena—even when they happen right under his nose. Skeptics often pride themselves on acute perceptiveness—but it has actually been blunted to pointlessness. They need to reflect on the possibility that they may be missing a great deal of life—fun, rich ideas, insights, new abilities and strengths, and opportunities for understanding themselves better.

The gullible. The person who believes *everything* will find it exceedingly difficult to meditate effectively. The ability to discern is one of the basic tools of the meditator. The person who accepts most any philosophy which claims to promote enlightenment is also prone to being deceived by a lot of silliness—from his own subconscious and from the mouths of others. The gullible person needs to add a healthy measure of common sense to his openness and trust.

The adjustments needed in these areas of attitude and concept should not amount to much of a strain for anyone seriously intent on self-discovery and self-improvement. It is rare to find anyone so imbued with these problems that they cannot begin to meditate and, in meditating, cure the problem. But it is important to realize that traces of these problems do tend to exist even in the best of us. And if we allow them to continue to fester, they will interfere with the work of meditation.

An important part of preparing to meditate, therefore, is the work of removing these problems, so that our access to the higher self will be clearer and more direct.

PACKING OUR BAGS

Preparing to meditate can be compared with the activity of preparing to drive from Chicago to Miami. We would not just jump in the car and drive off, hoping we were going in the right direction. We would plan the trip. This planning would consist of several elements:

• Considering the purpose of the trip and making sure it was worthwhile.

• Choosing the best route and making hotel reservations.

• Packing our clothes and loading the car.

• Making sure the car was ready for such a long trip.

• Visiting the bank to make sure we had enough money.

In preparing to meditate, we should plan in much the same fashion. A good place to begin is by considering the purpose of our meditative work and making sure it is worthwhile. If all we are interested in is conjuring up some pleasant fantasies about the higher self, or our psychic nature, or our karma, it probably is not worth the effort. That would just be the meditative equivalent of looking at a travel brochure about Miami and daydreaming about being on the beach.

In meditating, we are journeying toward the very essence of our life—the life behind the personality and body. We are pursuing our sources of wisdom, love, strength, and skill. We should have some definite purposes in mind for using them in our life—the more practical the better. If these purposes are then kept in mind constantly as we meditate, we will not be distracted by back roads, wrong turns, or detours.

We should then choose the best route. Having the intent to visit Miami will count for nothing if we head for San Francisco. Just so, having the intent to contact the higher self will count for nothing if we head for the wish life of the personality, or become passive, or simply chant a mantra. We must choose techniques which are compatible with the activity of the higher self—techniques which will help us make improvements in our self-expression. And we should set goals for making these improvements, just as we would make hotel reservations.

Next, we should decide what to take and what to leave behind, and pack for the journey. Instead of clothes and cameras and swimming gear, we will be more in need of mental provisions and equipment. And so, we should pack our common sense, a healthy measure of self-discipline, a satchel full of ideals, a supply of determination and dedication, reasonable expectations, and an alert mind. If we are tired, we should postpone the start of the journey and take a nap first.

In meditating, what we leave behind is sometimes even more important than what we drag along. Just as we would not take bulky furniture and bags of garbage along on a trip to Miami, there are numerous things we ought not take with us as we seek out the higher self:

- The bulky furniture of mundane habits and behavior.
- The garbage of worries, doubts, and fears.
- The poisons of anger, hostility, and malice.

As always, this is a matter of common sense. Fur coats are not needed in Miami for warmth, but they are often taken along for style and pleasure. But if we want to get a suntan, we have to take the fur coat off. In meditation, there are certain attitudes which keep out the light just as much as a fur coat impedes the sun. The light of our higher intelligence will generally be kept out by skepticism, vanity, prejudices, and stubbornness. The compassion, joy, and serenity of the higher self will usually be kept out by gloominess, self-pity, and criticism. The life of the higher self will be kept out by apathy, empty-mindedness, and depression. It is better to leave these items behind.

The equivalent of making sure the car is ready for the trip would be a quick check that the mind, emotions, and will are suitably prepared. Preparing the mind must include at least a brief reflection on the nature of the higher self as the benevolent source of our life—a power which ever seeks to help us as we provide opportunities for it to do so. We should recognize that we have a responsibility to contact and effectively respond to the higher self. And it can be very beneficial to contemplate the fact that the higher self already has plans, intentions, and a wealth of talent for helping us in our meditation. We therefore gear up the mind to work in partnership with this higher intelligence.

The emotions can be prepared by looking forward with anticipation and enthusiasm to the new discoveries and insights that will be made, and reflecting on the wonderful improvements we are working toward. We should especially cultivate the attitudes of hope, affection, reverence, and goodwill. As these qualities are responsive to the wavelength of benevolence of the higher self, they are quite useful in preparing us to interact with the greater love of our spirit.

The will is prepared by dedicating ourself to being the right person doing the right thing, supported by the power and direction of the higher self. If we are uncomfortable with the prospect of sharing our authority, we may have trouble interacting wisely with the higher self. We ought, therefore, to contemplate the many ways this greater power can enrich our life—if we cooperate with it.

Finally, the step of visiting the bank would correspond to the need to make sure that we have worthwhile activities planned for our meditations. Too many people sit down to meditate with hands, mouth, and mind empty—waiting for something to happen but not knowing how to make it happen. The key is to take a moment to outline specifically what we will do during this trip—and the best techniques for doing it. A morning meditation, for example, might include work on planning the day, transforming a specific emotional attitude, and seeking creative inspiration for a project at work. An evening meditation might include a review of the day, an examination of ideals and convictions, and an exercise in blessing and forgiveness. These schedules will change from day to day, but it can be useful to give our meditative work this kind of structure and format in advance—always leaving it flexible, of course, so we can be responsive to the guidance of the higher self.

It is unfortunate that many people assume that only a vague intent—such as identifying with God—is needed before sitting down to meditate. They often give more forethought to walking out to the mailbox than they do to their journeys into consciousness. We must keep in mind that because meditation is an activity of consciousness, skillful preparation and planning is of tremendous importance. Meditation is an opportunity to explore the hidden and richer dimensions of our humanity and spirit. The possibilities should quietly excite us, stimulate our curiosity, and appeal to our sense of adventure.

Meditating is not quite like a visit to a public library, with its brisk efficiency and clear access to information; it is more like a visit to a strange but intriguing mansion filled with rare and exotic furnishings and *objets d'art*. We are not quite familiar with it, so we must tread carefully, but there is much of value and interest to us if we proceed with intelligence, curiosity, optimism, a quiet enthusiasm, and the intention to make the most of this opportunity.

5

Entering
The Meditative State

SOMETHING DIFFERENT

Contacting the higher self in meditation is a bit more complex than plugging in a television set and turning it on. In just a matter of moments, the television image comes into focus; we may have to adjust the color and the fine tuning, but the set is designed to do most of the actual work for us. A good meditative contact, by contrast, is more of a process of discovery. It is almost as though we must first learn the principles of electromagnetic phenomena and then build our own television set! When it is finished, and we turn it on, we then discover that the higher self has been broadcasting to us all along—but only now can we receive the full signal.

The principles of electromagnetic phenomena, of course, would correspond to the basic tenets and principles of human nature and spiritual growth. Building our own television set corresponds with the work of preparing the mind, emotions, and physical body to be receptive to the higher self. This is a gradual process, requiring more than a moment's enthusiasm. From the very beginning, we get worthwhile results, but the activity of attuning to the higher self never ends—it simply becomes more sophisticated and expert.

In pursuing this contact, we must beware of techniques which are overly simplistic—or would have us build a television which can only tune in to one channel. There are many schools of philosophy ready to promote their special way to the higher self or God. Some offer more dogma than practical assistance; some have good techniques, but bury them under so much religious or philosophical baggage that the substance is all but obscured. Some would have us eliminate the channel of the mind and tune in only through the emotions. Others emphasize the exercising of the body and ignore the emotions and the mind entirely. Some even suggest that we do not actually need the television set—just the antenna! Given this plethora of technique and method, it is wise to remember the advice of H.L. Mencken—that for every complex problem, someone is sure to offer a simple solution, and it will be wrong!

We should not ignore these systems and schools, for much significant knowledge can be found among them. But we must comprehend that contact with the higher self is something we basically work out for ourself. No guru can do it for us, no holy faith can magically guarantee it. And because we are indeed individuals, the nature of the contact will vary from one to the next. It will be easy for some, a struggle for others. This is just common sense. The creative person will make a somewhat different contact than the religious devotee; the scientific mind will focus on certain elements of the higher self, while the artist will deal with others.

It should also be kept in mind that the personality and the higher self are in different dimensions or worlds. The higher self is *not* a part of the physical system. It may be a crushing disappointment for some to learn that the higher self does not really dwell in the spine or in the pineal gland of the brain, but it does not. It resides in a more subtle dimension of life. As such, it is unaffected by jogging, chanting, and physical exercise. Indeed, until contact is established meditatively, *there is no direct interaction between the personality and the higher self.* The personality, by nature, is accustomed to acting, feeling, and thinking in very concrete ways; the higher self, by nature, is abstract and free of mundane limitations. To make an effective contact with the higher self, therefore, we are somehow going to have to transcend the limits of our ordinary awareness and begin to operate at the level of the consciousness of the higher self itself. Given the proper practice, this is not especially difficult—but neither is it as simple as many people have assumed. We must avoid teachers who give us a formula or ritual and tell us that all we have to do is plug it in and we will go straight to the higher self.

Above all, we should remember that the goal of meditation is to integrate the life of the higher self with the personality. It is deceptively easy to form a pleasant alliance with the wish life of the subconscious and believe it to be an effective contact with the higher self. True meditation, however, transcends this level. It may be a step forward for some people to get in tune with this part of the personality, but it is at best only a beginning step; we must not stop there.

Therefore, we should expect contact with the higher self to be something different from what we have experienced before—something different from our feelings, our wishes, and even our aspirations and expectations. It will be the awareness of a new ability to think more clearly and with greater understanding. It will be the experience of being more forgiving and in better rapport with others. It will be the recognition that there is a powerful presence within us—a wonderful source of healing, courage, and new motivation.

IDENTIFYING WITH THE HIGHER SELF

The key to making contact with the life of the higher self is learning to *identify* with it—to identify with its power to be wise, compassionate, courageous, and noble. This identification goes beyond just an intellectual acceptance of the fact or the mightiness of the higher self, however. It is *not* enough to contemplate the virtues and wisdom of God; it is *not* enough to adore our divine origins. These practices have value, as they help us shift the focus of our attention, but effective identification with the higher self requires more. It requires us to *raise* the level of our awareness.

The average person identifies with his or her body, emotions, thoughts, habits, and experiences—not with the higher self. He may *think* about the higher self, but not really identify with it. To effectively contact the higher self, we must comprehend that we are more than these elements of our human nature, and begin to identify *primarily* with our spiritual nature—and only secondarily with the personality. We must realize that *we are, in fact, the higher self.* The personality and physical body are extensions of our consciousness that we use for creative and constructive work in the world. They are important to us—but do not define our identity.

This is not a concept which any one of us can master in only a matter of minutes; it is a dynamic idea which grows and matures through repeated interaction with it and reflection on its implications. It may be threatening to some, delightful to others, and nothing more than a nice philosophy to the rest. But whether we like this concept or believe in it is immaterial; to make effective contact with the higher self, we have to understand it and learn to live by it.

It is not an easy matter for the personality to make this shift in identification. Since birth, almost all of the information the personality has acquired has been about itself and the physical plane. It knows very little, if anything, about the higher self. Quite likely it has heard a goodly number of legends, stories, and myths concerning the higher self—both pro and con—but the fact remains that the personality has no direct, first-hand experience of the higher self and heaven. Everything it knows about these higher dimensions is hearsay—and probably unreliable.

Even when the personality begins to acquire trustworthy data about the higher self, it is not all that simple to make sense of it. The higher self lives in a world of universal themes and abstract forces; the personality lives in a world of finite events, concrete themes, and small concerns. The higher self dwells in a realm of ideals and perfection; the personality lives in an imperfect world, frequently hassled and frustrated by human error and pettiness. The higher self lives in the constant and full awareness that it is a divine and immortal being endowed with tremendous resources of power, wisdom, talent, strength, and dignity; the personality must live with constant reminders of its mortality, weakness, and limitations.

As much as we may wish to identify with such a lofty and noble higher self, the prospect almost staggers the imagination. True to its finite nature, the subconscious repeatedly will throw up objections and barriers of doubt and disbelief.

If the higher self exists, the subconscious will ask, why do so few people know about it?

If it is so benevolent, why do unfair circumstances arise?

If everyone has a higher self, why are some people so rotten—and why is there so much conflict?

Indeed, the personality often reacts as though it were an orphan who managed to grow up and successfully establish himself in early adulthood, only to discover he was actually the long lost son of an extremely wealthy parent—who now offers to help the "orphan." A certain degree of suspiciousness and wondering, "Where were you when I needed you," is reasonable.

What we have to work through is the fact that the idea of being lost and orphaned is only an illusion. The higher self never loses or abandons the personality; rather, we lose our awareness of the higher self and how to contact it. We lose it by identifying with the experiences of life and the innate sensations of the personality.

As we rediscover what we have lost, the conclusions we draw are sometimes almost comical. At first, for example, we may naively think of the higher self as some sort of year-round Santa Claus who passes out gifts. Or, the darker side of our human nature may paint the higher self as a god of wrath, who dotes on punishing us for our copious misdeeds. Neither of these concepts, of course, leads to a wholesome identification with the higher self. But eventually we outgrow them, by realizing that the higher self is a part of us, not apart from us; it is a higher octave of our own being. As such, it can provide us with the wisdom we need to make sense of the experiences of life, the compassion we need to heal our emotional wounds, and the strength we need to fulfill our responsibilities.

By identifying with the higher self in this way, we also develop a new perspective on the personality. Many people fear that as they identify more and more with the higher self, their regard for the personality will suffer, but this is not the case. Instead, we begin to see the personality as an *agent* of the higher self, representing it on earth and acting on its behalf. For the first time, it is connected with the treasures and noble life of the higher self, and this greatly enhances the stature and importance of the personality.

For the first time, the personality knows from direct experience that it has a divine heritage which cannot perish.

THE PROPER TRAINING

Making contact with the higher self is not a whimsical process, dependent on how much the higher self likes us, or thinks we are nice. It is a process we can learn and, through practice, master. And the higher self will help us learn!

In this sense, the process is something like attending a university in order to become an attorney or doctor. The university has tremendous resources which will help us learn: professors, classes, textbooks, a library, and much more. But we do not acquire an education merely by matriculating in the university and spending time there; we must study, go to classes, take exams, and work diligently and intelligently. Only then can these resources help us. The responsibility for getting the education the university offers lies entirely with us.

Making contact with the higher self demands exactly the

same sense of responsibility. The resources are there—they are inherent in every human being. They are accessible to every intelligent personality. But they remain latent until we begin to identify with them—and start to act as an agent of the life of the higher self. The person who reaches fifty and bemoans the fact that he is not as enlightened and as benevolent as he might like to be, therefore, really has no reason to be puzzled. He might as well be puzzled by the fact that he is not a heart surgeon! The simple fact is that he has not pursued the proper training.

Many intelligent people, poisoned by generations of ignorant teachers or just frustrated by their initial attempts to contact the higher self, have come to the conclusion that the higher self is so remote, so lofty, and so far beyond anything with which they are familiar that it is almost untouchable. This is a false conclusion. The higher self is *not* a blimp in heaven, soaring high above us, flashing obscure messages through the dark as it drifts gracefully off toward the horizon. The higher self is part of us. Wherever we may be, it is there, as well—within us.

The higher self understands us.

It loves us.

It seeks to help us.

Often, we are only able to respond to a fraction of its immense power, just as a tiny infant can only respond in the simplest ways to the much greater affection and intelligence of its mother. But we can train ourself to become more responsive; we can learn to be a better agent of the higher self. And just as the mother is probably more interested in the well-being and proper development of the infant than the infant itself, so also our higher self tends to be even more concerned with the effectiveness of our contact than we. It supports us and assists us as we seek to identify with it.

But we must initiate the effort.

THE GOOD HOST

Entertaining the higher self is not that much different from entertaining a good friend. Before receiving his friends, a proper host prepares the household and himself. He prepares the household by dusting the furniture, cleaning the floors, and fixing refreshments. He prepares himself by taking a shower and dressing for the occasion. He also primes his attitudes, looking forward to the arrival of his guests with enthusiasm. The good host takes care not to spoil the atmosphere, by having an argument with his spouse or becoming irritated over minor trivialities. He wants his guests to feel welcome, not uncomfortable. And this basic attitude continues to motivate the good host once his guests have arrived. He does not leave them to entertain themselves while he sneaks off to another room to watch television—or take a nap. Nor does he sit motionless and mute, expecting them to do all the talking. He treats them with friendship and respect, conversing with them, setting them at ease, and serving their needs.

In meditation, we are entertaining the saintly and angelic nature of our higher self, and we should treat this guest with the same respect and graciousness we extend to our friends. We should be ready to greet the higher self with charm, intelligence, good humor, affection, and dignity. We certainly would not want to leave him in the living room while we go play mind games and fantasies in the den. Nor would we want to fall into a trance or keep ourself focused on something else, ignoring our guest. Quite the contrary, we should embrace him, interact actively with him, make him feel at home in our awareness, and serve his needs as best we can. We should play the role of the good host, listening attentively and trying to understand what he has to say.

In other words, we have to be receptive to the higher self and its intelligence, benevolence, and power. In no way, however, should this state of receptivity be confused with passiveness or numbness—or even worse, parasitism. As impulses of the higher life emerge in our awareness, we are expected to relate them to the needs of our life, focus them in meaningful self-improvement, pursue a fuller comprehension of the fragments received, and ask questions where further clarification is required. This is not done just by sucking in as much of the power of the higher self as we can tolerate, or by feigning deadness so that the spirit can resurrect us. Rather, we must be alert enough to respond to the impulses which emerge, and sufficiently poised that we are able to restrain our reactiveness, fears, worries, or distractions which may arise. The mind and emotions should be subdued so that they do not rebel, but they must not be turned off. After all, these are the very vehicles needed to receive and contain what is coming to us from this transcendent source.

The state of receptivity is something more than just lying out in the sun and getting a tan. The practice of passively soaking up God's goodness is all right for rocks, melons, and rhubarb, but not for agents of the higher self. Receptivity is also something other than the capacity to tune into our emotions, prejudices, or what the body tells us. Ideally, it is like the responsiveness of a child who is patiently and intently listening to his parent tell him a story. The child's full attention is riveted on what his parent is saying; he is not looking out the window, or falling asleep, or wondering when dinner will be. He adores his parent and wants to hear the whole story. From time to time, he asks questions about the story, but mostly, he listens. And he listens to a good deal more than just the words; he is receptive and responsive to the full radiance of goodwill, concern, and affection with which the parent is reading.

For the meditator, the ideal state of receptivity is very much the same. It is the posture of the whole personality as it seeks to entertain the higher self.

The physical body is most receptive when reasonably relaxed and quiet—quiet enough that we can collect our thoughts and feelings without being unduly distracted.

The emotions are most receptive when focused in an attitude of tranquillity and quiet devotion to the life of the higher self.

The mind is most receptive when reflecting on the nature and wisdom of the higher self, and what this means in terms of daily activities.

The personal will is most receptive when focused on a sense of purpose, a willingness to change, and a commitment to the plan and direction of the higher self.

ENTERING A MEDITATION

When rain falls, it is quickly absorbed into the ground, or runs into drains and is carried away. If we want to collect it, we must set out barrels or pots. We cannot rely on the rain to gather itself. The same can be assumed for cloudbursts of wisdom, love, and inspiration from the higher self. If we are passive or inattentive in meditation, there may be a momentary cleansing and refreshing effect—but the true potential of the downpouring will simply wash away.

To be sure, the pots and barrels we put out must be cleansed of dirt and pollution; we do not want to contaminate the living water we are receiving. The mind must be purified of irrelevant thoughts and prejudices; the emotions must be cleansed of their crabbiness, fear, hostility, and resentment; the will should be cleansed of personal urges and desires. But cleaning a pot is vastly different than breaking it—or never setting it out in the first place.

The basic steps of contacting the higher self in meditation are each designed to build the vessels we need to receive new life from heaven. In all, there are four stages: relaxation, concentration, detachment, and attunement. Together, they form a very effective drill for beginning any meditation and invoking the outpouring of higher consciousness. As they are practiced, they vivify the hope, faith, belief, reverence, compassion, good intentions, commitment, and ideals we already possess, and focus them to be receptive to the higher self.

The needs of each person will naturally vary. A person who is already kind and devotional, for example, will experience very little difficulty in expressing reverence for the higher self—but he may have trouble preparing his mind to respond to its wisdom and intelligence. A passive, gentle person will have no problem accepting the benevolent authority of the higher self, but may have much more difficulty harnessing strength, hope, and conviction. The intellectual individual will be well prepared to receive insights and new understanding, but may be deficient in his capacity to mobilize the forces of devotion and faith.

One of the major problems encountered by beginning meditators is the tendency to emphasize one aspect of the process of contacting the higher self to the exclusion of all the others—usually the aspect they are most comfortable with, or feel they need the most. In other words, they put a lot of effort into learning to relax—but never go beyond that stage to the others. Or they work very diligently at mastering concentration but end up concentrating most of their attention on their problems and failures.

None of these stages alone constitutes meditative contact with the higher self. They are meant to be used in sequence, leading to a full and active state of alertness and readiness. Always, we must keep in mind the purpose of meditation: to lift our conscious attention to our higher self, so as to be nourished by its qualities and become a better agent for expressing its purpose.

RELAXATION

The first step in contacting the life of the higher self is *relaxation,* the process of releasing tension and establishing poise in the physical body, the emotions, and the mind. It is amazing how utterly simple relaxation actually is—and how little time it requires. The body already knows how to relax; it has rehearsed this procedure thousands of times. We do it every time we go to sleep. And what makes relaxation even easier is the fact that the body actually enjoys it—if we will just stop fussing over our little tensions and give it permission to relax.

It is not necessary to achieve any particular level of deepness in relaxing—in fact, too deep a state of relaxation can actually interfere with meditation. It will cause us to fall asleep or wander aimlessly. Nor should we pursue the practice of relaxation too fanatically. If our elbow itches in the middle of a meditation, scratching it is not a sign of poor relaxation or weak concentration. Common sense dictates that we should just go ahead and scratch it, and be done with it. That is what will let us most quickly return our attention to the higher self—not mounting some incredible mental effort to overcome the itch. The purpose of relaxation is to make the body comfortable—so we can forget it.

The position of the body is not terribly important—and again can be determined by common sense. Any position which is suitable for quiet, reflective thought will be ideal for meditation. If we have to shift in our chair every five minutes, we probably have chosen the wrong chair—or are not sitting properly in it. But these decisions are entirely incidental to the work and activity of meditating.

For those who find it especially difficult to release muscular or nervous tension, it can be helpful to check those areas of the body commonly associated with tension—the tiny muscles around the eyes, clenched jaws, hunched shoulders, and tensed hands. A simple thought of releasing this muscular tension is usually sufficient to relax that part of the body. If necessary, this check can be repeated as often as required until relaxation becomes automatic.

When properly poised, the body will very seldom distract us. As a result, we can focus the mind on the work to be done. But it should be understood that relaxation is not just limited to the physical body. Tension in the emotions and the mind must be released as well, not by making them passive, but by simply discharging the tension. Indeed, if we are troubled by excessive physical tension, it is probably the result of undue fussing in the emotions and mind. This level of tension can often be handled by recalling the memory of a tranquil state or scene, dwelling on the comfort and poise of peacefulness, or contemplating a firm intention to be calm and alert in the coming meditation.

If serious problems are encountered in achieving a reasonable level of relaxation, then a long-range program of healing major conflicts, fears, and irritations must be pursued.

CONCENTRATION

Even while we are still attending to the relaxation of tension, we can begin the second step in making contact with the higher self: *concentration*. The purpose of concentration is to keep our attention focused on the ideas we are considering or the work we are pursuing. Like relaxation, it is so simple to learn and master that it is amazing that so many people have made so much out of so little. Even the most witless person is able to concentrate on anything which interests him or fascinates him; even people who are very anxious and restless find no great difficulty in sitting through an exciting program on television or a good movie. They only find it difficult to concentrate on tasks which do not sufficiently interest them or have appeal.

To concentrate effectively in meditation, it is only necessary to cultivate a level of interest which will easily hold our attention. If we are more interested in the work and goals of the higher self than we are in our worries and irritations, we will have no difficulty concentrating. If we are more interested in discovering the treasures of heaven and what we can do with them than we are in what we ate for breakfast, then we should have no problem sustaining our concentration. Indeed, this level of interest should come naturally to anyone seriously involved in effective meditation.

This is a much different approach than is usually taught regarding concentration, but one which makes sense. We must take care not to become an addict of concentration—the kind of person who labors and labors and labors to achieve a single-pointed, uninterrupted concentration on a symbol, an object, his breath, or a mantra he repeats over and over. While feats of this nature can be performed, they belong more in the *Guinness Book of World Records* than in meditation. Who cares if someone is able to concentrate on his breath for thirty minutes? That is *not* meditation—it is boredom! To accomplish it, the mind has to be beaten into dullness. An effective meditation should never be boring, never dull. It should be an opportunity to respond to the most intelligent and inspiring levels of our consciousness. *It should consume our interest!*

Only a sufficiency of concentration is required for contacting the higher self—not the wretched excess generated by one-pointed thought on a single object of attention for long periods of time. In this regard, it is helpful to understand that true concentration never limits us to a *single* thought. The higher self does not think about one detail or one thought at a time; it entertains a whole universe of inspiration. Not even the subconscious is limited to one association; it regularly processes hundreds of details and images at once. The conscious mind is not equipped to work quite at these levels, but it can easily embrace many different thoughts without losing concentration. To work effectively in meditation, we ought to learn how to do this—not try to exclude all thoughts but one.

Some people have a hard time believing it is possible to think more than one thought at a time. They need to understand that it is quite common to walk and chew gum at the same time, while listening to a friend converse and observing what is happening down the block. We may even be able to think of what we are going to say in reply to our companion!

In meditation, we should train ourself to concentrate on the *themes* of what we are doing, more than the details. Each theme, such as contacting the higher self or improving some aspect of the emotions, will encompass a multitude of details and observations. We may have many of these details or ideas in focus at any one time, and yet we hold our concentration by continuing to be primarily interested in the work or theme at hand. We do not let ourself be unraveled by digressions into irrelevancies. Our basic interest in what we are doing holds our attention, comfortably and easily, so we can make sense of the complete activity.

A word of warning should be added to those who would continue to think of concentration as an enforced focusing on a single point or idea, emptying their minds of all other associations and considerations. This practice can seriously undermine the natural capacity of the mind to seize detail and manage thoughts. It is definitely possible to damage the associative mechanism of the mind by pursuing this type of concentration too long. In many cases, it is really a short-term venture into catatonic schizophrenia. It is both dehumanizing and anti-spiritual, because it disconnects the mind from the body and the higher self. *It is the antithesis of meditation.*

Fortunately, the average person who tries to concentrate in this perverse fashion will succeed for a while, then become terribly bored, and finally find his mind flitting all over the place. This is *not* a sign of an undisciplined mind, but rather a sign that the mind is just trying to work normally. It is bored and wants to get back to activity. We should heed its signal and abandon our misplaced attempts.

DETACHMENT

The steps of relaxation and concentration are purely preliminaries; actual identification with the higher self begins with a technique called *detachment*. Through this activity, we do the work of withdrawing our attention from the outer worlds of sensation and experience, so that we can refocus it on the more subtle realms of our inner life. As such, it is not really a withdrawal as much as it is a realignment. The purpose of detachment is *not* to make us indifferent to the mundane elements of life, although it may seem that way at first, but rather to expand our perspective on life to include more than the mundane alone.

There is nothing especially wrong or evil about our attachments to the world of form and experience—our likes and dislikes, our habits, our memories, and our possessions. For the most part, in fact, they are quite useful to us. It would be very hard to make our way in the world *without* habits or possessions. So it must be clearly understood that the purpose of detachment is not to divorce us from the usual concerns of the personality. We are not trying "to get out of the material world"; that would be mere escapism.

The reason for detachment is much more profound; we are trying to identify with the higher self. We are trying to make room in our awareness for the qualities of the higher life—love, courage, wisdom, joy, peace, and dignity. But if we do not believe ourself to be this higher self—if we believe ourself to be entirely defined and limited by the conditions of the personality—then we will never reach our goal. Thus, we must see our attachments for what they really are—matters of practicality and convenience allowing us to manifest more readily in the physical plane, not the end all and be all of our life and identity. We have the power and the ability to change our attachments and focus of concern at will, because we are greater than they are. We are a being of intelligence, will, love, wisdom, and divine origin. We are the higher self.

This line of reasoning is the heart of detachment. It leads us to the full realization that the personality is an *agent* of the higher self.

IN CONTROL

Of all meditative practices, detachment is perhaps the most readily and commonly distorted. It is easy to forget the basic goal of identifying with the higher self, and simply practice a technique of withdrawing from the personality. Such a practice can lead in many directions, none of them healthy:

1. It can lead to a state of dissociation or disconnection from the personality. We simply practice a studied indifference to the needs and demands of life. This may be useful for a turnip, but it is hardly an advanced stage for human beings. We cannot learn about the divine love and goodwill of the higher self by teaching ourself to care less. We cannot learn about the intelligence and wisdom of the higher self by teaching ourself to think less. We cannot learn about the active nature and stewardship of the higher self by cutting off our involvement in life.

2. It can lead to a denial of the value of the personality, an

attempt to slay it or vanquish it. We must remember that the personality is the child of the higher self, and should be respected as such.

3. It can lead to an attitude of escapism which actually has the effect of emphasizing our problems all the more. We become obsessed with our problems and escaping from them—and forget that the higher self is our source of solutions.

4. It can lead to a state of "spacing out," in which we go into trance and become absorbed in the bliss of our higher emotions—not the true power and support of the higher self.

None of these distortions of detachment will cause us any real difficulty, however, if we keep ourself focused on the basic theme of this practice—the realization that we have a body, emotions, a mind, and many memories and attachments, and they are basically good. But we are more than these things; we are an agent of the higher self. As such, we are able to control and direct and enlighten all of these elements of our personality, for our benefit. We are able to identify with the higher self—and assert dominion over the personality.

In no way is detachment a denial of any of our thoughts, feelings, or intentions—positive or negative. Instead, it is a careful and reasoned reflection on the fact that we are endowed with an extra dimension of wisdom, compassion, and strength which *transcends* our personality, its experiences, and its reactions. We have the opportunity to use these riches to discipline, heal, and enrich our personality and its self-expression.

WHO WE ARE

It is in the practice of detachment that we begin to truly benefit from an understanding of the difference between sensation and consciousness. We come to appreciate that while the personality is primarily focused in sensation, the higher self lives and moves and has its being entirely in consciousness. We therefore need a mechanism for detaching from sensation and refocusing in consciousness.

What is sensation, what is consciousness? Sensation is the capacity for awareness in the personality. It could be the pain we physically feel when we stub our toe, or the annoyance we emotionally feel as we react to it, or the sense of unworthiness we mentally feel when we decide this is God's way of punishing us. Consciousness, by contrast, is the capacity for knowingness in the higher self—our awareness of the intelligence, love, and power of God, and our divine origin. A practical example may help elucidate the difference. When we are tired, we feel sleepy and possibly irritable. We want to stop our work and rest. We are fatigued, discontented, sore, and dulled. All of these are sensations. But if at the same time we have an awareness of the purpose of our work and the knowledge that it is important and meaningful to finish it now, that is consciousness. And we can draw from this consciousness the determination and strength to press on and complete our work.

It is unfortunate that so many people are mired in the world of sensation. It is considered very chic in some circles, for example, to concentrate on our physical sensations and our feelings as a means of self-discovery and enlightenment. But the glorification of sensation entraps us in the world of the personality; it ties us, hypnotically, to the robot of our subconscious. We become a victim of our reactions and our attachments. The person who has glorified his sensations would simply give in to his distress and fatigue, and overreact to them—not attempt to rise above them. He would pamper himself. But even though it is often labeled "self-nurturing," self-indulgence is still self-indulgence; it leads us back into childishness and weakens our ability to act. It leads to overreactiveness and addiction to the physical plane.

This is not to be construed as an argument for stoicism

and self-denial, however. The key to detachment lies in recognizing that we have an alternative to both overreactiveness and indifference. We need not be a victim of every distressful sensation we experience; we can learn to identify with our purpose, our ideals, and our inner strength.

We therefore consider the idea that there is a *difference* between who we are and what happens to us, a *difference* between who we are and what we think and feel from time to time. We have the capacity to observe and intelligently direct our thoughts, feelings, and body, in whatever way will best fulfill our purpose and goals. We do not stop registering sensations—not in the slightest. We simply realize we can interpret the meaning of our sensations from a higher, more reliable perspective—and act instead of react. We are able to direct our body, speech, attention, thoughts, and emotions so as to express the best within us—and we are able to discipline and dominate the less than best which also exists within us.

Of course, the devotees of naturalness and spontaneity are appalled by this proposition—but they are merely victims of the nonsense that the personality is at its best when completely vulnerable to every stray impulse which happens along. They are quite adept at "going with the flow," but have no idea whither the flow goes. These unfortunate people are truly slaves to subconscious and unconscious impulses. The spontaneity they so prize has nothing to do with effective meditation.

Having recognized the difference between sensation and consciousness, we use the practice of detachment to identify more consistently with *who we are*. We rehearse the activities of transcending our usual personality reactions and mobilizing our more noble emotions, lofty thoughts, and better intentions. Detachment is not just a meditative process; it becomes an approach to living. But meditation is the focus for practicing and perfecting it—and without some use of the principles of detachment, there can be no effective meditation.

A DRILL IN DETACHMENT

These principles of detachment can be condensed into a very effective drill in consciousness, which can be reviewed at the beginning of a meditation as a means of identifying with the higher self. The drill should embrace the following ideas:

I have a physical body, but am something greater than the physical body. The body is important to me—it allows me to act in the physical world and be productive. The body can be tired or rested, sick or healthy, but I am able to observe these changes in the physical body—and even direct them. My higher self, the real me, is greater than the conditions of the physical body. It is the source of vitality within me.

I have emotions, but I am something greater than my feelings and emotions. The emotions are important to me—they help me express goodwill and interact with others. They can be sad or happy, selfish or cooperative, but I am able to observe these changes in my emotions—and discipline them. My higher self, the real me, is greater than the state of my emotions. It is the source of love and benevolence within me.

I have a mind, but I am something greater than my thoughts and memories. The mind is important to me—it enables me to make sense of life and express my talent and wisdom. My thoughts are sometimes destructive, sometimes constructive, but I am able to observe the changes in my thoughts—and guide them. My higher self, the real me, is greater than my thoughts. It is the source of wisdom and intelligence within me.

I have a personal will, but am something greater than this will. The will is important to me—it gives me motivation and intention. My intentions are sometimes defensive, sometimes purposeful, but I am able to observe the changes in my will— and use the will wisely. My higher self, the real me, is stronger than my personal will. It is the source of divine intention within me, and thus the true source of my personal authority.

My life also brings me many experiences, which allow me to learn and grow and serve. Sometimes I overreact to my experiences, and let them control me; at other times, I control them. But I am able to observe these experiences, see their value, and use them profitably. My higher self, the real me, is greater than my experiences.

Who am I? I am not my body, nor my emotions, my mind, my personal will, or my experiences, although I do have these things and they are valuable. I am the higher self, a center of pure love, wisdom, and power.

This is my true identity.

It is not necessary to memorize these words in order to use this drill; indeed, this is not recommended. It is much better simply to remember the sequence of ideas listed here and then *think* about them, one at a time. At first, entire meditations can be given over to contemplating and understanding these very important ideas. Later, they can be condensed and the drill can be used quite quickly—although it should never be rushed. Always, however, the ideas should be thoroughly thought through. The mere repetition of the words is almost worthless.

As we master this drill, and detachment becomes a familiar friend to us, we achieve a better grasp of the fact that we are *designed* to exert dominion over our personality; the higher self stands ready to add wisdom, discipline, goodwill, joy, harmony, and strength to our self-expression. And the personality is then able to act effectively as the agent of the higher self. The implications of this idea are immense—and worth the time it takes to explore them.

The fruits of detachment are well described in our essay, "The Practice of Detachment," in *The Art of Living, Volume I:* "The end result of detachment is a well-balanced personality which effortlessly and fully expresses the qualities of the inner self in daily life—the holistic qualities of love, joy, wisdom, strength, courage, and steadfastness. And because detachment leads to greater maturity, it likewise enables us to correct the weaknesses of our personality with intelligence and compassion. It frees us from the fears, worries, doubts, and frustrations that subvert most attempts at personal growth. Hence, the great importance of detachment is that it enables us to work in a state of relative objectivity and thereby create changes which are truly *improvements.*"

ATTUNEMENT

Once we have identified with the higher self through detachment, we are ready for the final step in entering the meditative state: fixing our attention on the power and benevolence of the higher self, so that specific activity can ensue. This step is called *attunement.*

Some may wonder why we wait so long to make attunement. Since this is the goal, why spend so much time with relaxation, concentration, and detachment? The answer is simple: we must transcend the bulk of the baggage in our personality before we assay this contact, lest we end up attuned to our fears, worries, or wish life. These elements may not be transcended entirely, but it is useful to set them aside as much as we can, lest we distort our intention to work with the higher self.

Attunement is the process of linking our personal strength to the power of the higher self, our emotions to the love of the higher self, and our mind to the wisdom of the higher self. The easiest way of doing this is to magnetize our awareness to these perfect qualities.

We are all familiar with the magnetic principle. If we want to find our direction through a forest, we use a compass with a needle that is magnetically attracted to the north pole. We do not try to use a knife or a stick or a butterfly. In consciousness, the most effective magnetic needle is the quality of love. It is highly magnetized and will orient us to the "true north" of our consciousness. This is because the higher self is continuously radiating its love and hope to the personality. Often, we may not be aware of this radiance, because we do not search for it within ourself—but it is there!

Attunement is very simple:

We magnetize ourself to the strength of the higher self by loving its power and authority. We trust in its capacity to support us and guide us, healing our weaknesses and enriching us with strength. We should not be afraid of this strength, because fear interrupts the expression of love; rather, we should be grateful for it and reverent toward it.

We magnetize ourself to the goodwill of the higher self by loving its benevolence and affection. We rejoice in its capacity to care for us, teach us, and enlighten us. We must be careful not to feel unworthy of this love, for that would diminish our receptivity; rather, we should sense the loving response of the higher self and increase our devotion to it.

We magnetize ourself to the wisdom of the higher self by loving its intelligence and knowledge. We celebrate the vast resources of understanding it has, and the capacity of our own talents, skills, and comprehension to grow in the loving aura of the wisdom of the higher self.

As we continue with this attunement, we begin to experience that there is something there, loving us in return; there truly does exist a great, benevolent intelligence within us, embracing us, helping us. It nourishes our ideals and plans, and heals our weaknesses and flaws.

It is important to be active in this work. It is very easy to sit back complacently and think that the higher self can just go ahead and love us as we are, and keep it up. If it is really all that powerful and loving, we conclude, what is it waiting for?

It is natural enough to think this way, but when we do, we are forgetting the obvious. The principle of magnetism can only help us find our way through the forest *if* we have a compass and are using it. It is the responsibility of the personality to attune itself to its inward dimensions. Just as the university and its full resources do not descend upon the home of a high school graduate and turn him automatically into an attorney or physician, our higher self cannot intrude into our awareness *until* we place our conscious thoughts, feelings, and intentions in harmony with it.

BRIDGING THE GAP

The work of attunement sometimes proceeds more smoothly if we learn to interact with the abstract forces and powers of the higher self in a symbolic fashion. The subconscious of the average person is focused in the material plane and the concerns of the relatively earthbound personality. This materialistic prejudice can make it difficult to accept or receive the forces and qualities of the higher self. Moreover, the untrained subconscious will tend to be unfamiliar with abstractions and subtleties. Much of this difficulty can be reduced, however, by working with proper symbols for the life and conditions of the higher self.

It can be helpful, for example, to regard the higher self symbolically as a benevolent, cosmic parent who loves us and understands our needs. To this benevolent parent we can then ascribe the virtues of the higher self we most need to attune to. Working with this symbol helps us realize that the personality does spring from the higher self and is taught, cared for, and supported by it. For individuals who have a hard time loving themselves, the use of this symbol can also aid in expressing a measure of love to the higher self.

It is likewise useful to think of our true essence of life as being a single, perfect idea in the mind of God or the universal life force. This complex blueprint or pattern is energized by the life force of the transcendent dimensions of life to vivify our personality and body.

Yet another good use of symbolism is to think of ourself as being bathed in a light which emanates from and incorporates the qualities and forces of the higher self's love, wisdom, and power.

In using symbols for attunement, however, we must take care not to slip into the bad habit of just watching pictures or thinking about concrete concepts. The power of attunement is the magnetic quality of love—not pictures or concepts. Symbols are used to give the subconscious a theme to relate to, but they are effective only if we concentrate on the love, the force, or the awareness which is associated with the picture. In using symbols, it is important to keep in mind that the higher self is alive and dynamic, actively nourishing us with vitality, ready to inspire us, and bathing us in love. *It is not a picture!* If we focus our use of symbols too concretely we can miss the real value of this contact.

THE BEST EVIDENCE

In working to make this contact with the higher self, the beginning meditator frequently wonders: "How do I know I am meditating?" In striving to answer this question, it is important not to give too much weight to relatively insignificant signs:

- The depth of relaxation.
- The ability to see white light—or any color of light.
- Changes in body temperature.
- "Alterations in consciousness," whatever they might be.
- Sudden changes in feeling.

- A sense of peace or bliss.

It should be remembered that all of these indicators are phenomena of the personality and can therefore occur without any contact whatsoever with the higher self. In actual fact, genuine meditation often occurs without any definite, unmistakable sign of change. It is only as our efforts to meditate build up, over a period of days, weeks, and months, and we begin to notice some subtle but very important changes occurring in our outlook and comprehension, that we realize beyond doubt that the contact has been made. Being a transcendent activity, meditation often has its initial effect on our unconscious and deep subconscious. It takes time for the results of our work to filter through the layers of the personality and emerge into conscious recognition. If we are patient, however, and continue to reinforce and repeat the contact we have already made, we will soon see the evidence.

Perhaps the best evidence is the growing realization that we are indeed loved and understood by a great, benevolent intelligence, which has always been in and around us and continues to be there, every time we reach out and contact it. It is a subtle realization, but as we become attuned to it, its presence becomes most real. This is an intimate experience, which goes beyond words or the need to doubt it. It is an inner knowing which comes in degrees, slowly building, sometimes fading. But as it builds, we identify more and more completely with the higher self.

THE TECHNIQUE FOR CONTACTING THE HIGHER SELF

For easy reference, the basic steps of entering a meditative state and making contact with the higher self can be condensed as follows:

1. Before we begin, we should focus on our purpose in meditation—to contact the life of our higher self so as to be nourished by its strength, wisdom, and love.

2. We should then relax the body and the personality to release excess tension and become comfortable.

3. Concentration is achieved by focusing our attention on the goals and themes we intend to pursue. These should fill our interest.

4. We identify with the higher self by thinking about the ideas in the drill in detachment, realizing that we are something greater than the aspects of the personality. We are an agent of the higher self.

5. We attune to the love, wisdom, and power of the higher self by loving its strength, goodwill, and intelligence and being thankful for its intimate involvement in our life. We look for some degree of its infinite, benevolent power embracing us and moving through us.

A Word From Herman

We had hardly finished the last chapter when Herman suddenly appeared again, this time with a loud thunderclap and an elegant flourish—as much of a flourish as an angel can make. He stood before us, more brilliant, more angelic, and more dazzling than ever before.

"I thought you'd like a confirmation that your method works," Herman announced.

"A sign from heaven, eh?" said Bob.

"I like what you wrote on the evidence that meditation is working," Herman complimented. "Maybe you ought to add that most signs are nudges."

"Nudges?" inquired Carl.

"Sure—little jabs pushing you in the right direction. I've got a nudge for the two of you right now."

"Uh-oh," groaned Bob.

"Now that you've brought your readers through the front door, when are you going to tell them about the *real* work of meditation?"

"You've seen the outline, haven't you?" said Carl. "The next eight chapters are all about integrating the higher self with the personality. That should be the real meat of meditation."

Herman grimaced—as much of a grimace as an angel can make. "I'm not sure I approve of your metaphor."

We chuckled politely—as politely as the two of us could.

"Yes, I've seen the outline, and I know you plan to write a great deal about using meditation to add the light and the love of spirit to the personality. Lord knows a lot of people need to learn those techniques. But have you considered the possibility that it may be a tiny bit materialistic to stress self-improvement so much?"

"I suppose in a way, it is," replied Bob. "It does bring heaven down to earth. But we have no intention to encourage people just to float off into a whacked-out, mindless stupor so they can pretend to be spiritual. That's just a way to escape responsibility and the dullness of life. And it's probably more materialistic than a lot of the lifestyles these people are trying to escape. It's motivated more by their disgust for the mundane than by a true reverence for life."

Herman nodded sadly. "Sometimes people do reject the things of the earth for the wrong reasons, and in the wrong way. But there is a time and a season for adoring God quietly and facing the light. Not all people who enter into the silence are becoming mindless, you know. Some of them know that their home is in God's mind and heart, and they are returning for a visit. They are fondly remembering their divine heritage. And there's a real value to that which cannot always be set down in black and white."

"Well, we don't want to make *everything* black and white," Carl teased.

Herman was in the mood to tease as well—as much of a tease as an angel can muster. "You humans in the West are always rushing off to do this, that, or the other thing," he said. "Occasionally, you might find it helpful to pause and recollect yourself—and reconnect to the source of life. If that means becoming a tiny bit 'passive,' don't knock it. When you get exhausted, you have to stop and take some time to face the light and recharge for a while. This is how you dip your thought toes back into the pool of universal life. It may be passive for a moment, but it enables you to become active again.

"Contacting the higher self is a little like breathing. You must breathe in the divine life and then exhale it through your self-expression. You inhale a fresh breath of wisdom and goodwill and courage, and then breathe it into your daily behavior. You can't just breathe in, you can't just breathe out—there has to be a proper balance and rhythm between both activities."

"I thought that's what we were advocating," Carl said quietly.

Herman looked thoughtfully, first at Carl and then at Bob.

"Are you sure? Maybe you'd better think about it. You can take that as a sign. But I have to fly. I'll eavesdrop on you from time to time. Bye."

And with that Herman withdrew into the next dimension. We were left in ours.

"Well, what do you make of that?" asked Bob. "I'm not sure I like *that* nudge. I've always been strongly impressed to demonstrate that meditation should be a means of releasing the life of the higher self for practical work in spiritualizing the personality. That's not materialistic! It's simply working to assist the great Divine Plan for evolution."

"I'm not sure Herman was saying that *our idea* of Active Meditation is materialistic," mused Carl. "You know, the Western bias *is* to tear into some project in a fury of busy-ness, without adequate preparation or a true grounding in purpose and perspective. Maybe Herman was warning us about that risk—that some of our readers might interpret our comments a bit too enthusiastically. We don't really want anyone to rush off to do God's work full of wrath, zeal, ignorance, and platitudes—but it does happen. All the time."

"You may be right," said Bob. "I do like Herman's notion about balancing the process of exhaling the divine life with adequate inhaling. It's too bad so many people confuse this lovely concept with actual breathing exercises. It's almost as if they believe that God has asthma and hyperventilates."

"The danger seems to be that we can scoff too much at the passive aspects of meditation, and some good people might get confused. They might think that we are putting down the importance of the quiet adoration of the inner life. And that would be unfortunate."

"Yes," Bob agreed. "We can't leave the impression that you just plug into God for a few seconds and then rush back into the physical world and serve, serve, serve. Meditation must be used to center ourselves in God, and then practice the presence of God in our daily activities and all our waking states of consciousness. I guess that's balance, too."

"You know, I have a sneaking suspicion," Carl added. "It's probably the time we've spent in adoration of God and the whole of heaven that set things up for Herman to visit us."

The lights flickered a moment, but that was all.

6

The Skills We Need
To Meditate

INTELLIGENT COOPERATION

Many people, unfortunately, believe that making contact with the higher self is the entire purpose and work of meditation. Once this basic contact is achieved, they then "rest" in a state of identification with the higher self, in the expectation that the higher self will take care of everything else. It will automatically enlighten them, heal imperfections, and lift them up into heaven. This kind of belief, however, is no more reasonable than the expectation that we can enroll in a course of study at the university and the university will do all the work for us, as long as we believe in its capacity to do so. No one has yet earned a college degree through "effortless effort." The university does not take our exams for us; it expects us to demonstrate our competence. The university does not study for us; it expects us to apply ourself to the learning process with self-discipline and intelligence, mastering the subjects required for our degree. Nor is this an issue of faith and devotion. No one can expect to become an engineer by *believing* that his professors are wise and competent, or expect to become a mathematician by worshipping the principles of mathematics, or expect to become a psychologist by sitting at the feet of a learned professor and adoring his insights. The mastery of these studies requires hard work, applied intelligence, and growth.

The same is true in meditation. No one has yet achieved enlightenment solely by sitting back and expecting the higher self to do all the work. Meditation is a time for active interaction with the higher self, enabling the personality to partake of the higher self's wisdom, power, and love. We do not become wise simply by adoring the mind of God, nor compassionate simply by believing that God loves us. We do not even become strong simply by surrendering to the will of God. We earn our degrees in spiritual mastery in much the same way that the college student earns his—through hard work, applied intelligence, and growth. Meditation is a process which supports and augments such sincere effort.

The philosophy of the Western tradition of Active Meditation can be encapsulated in three major principles. It is useful to understand these principles and keep them in mind as we enroll ourselves in the university of the higher self:

1. There is enormous power in the higher self to heal and enrich the personality and body.

2. The personality can learn how to tap this enriching power of the higher self through intelligent cooperation.

3. Intelligent cooperation becomes possible as the personality models itself after the design, intelligence, attitude, and activity of the higher self.

When meditative work is based on these three principles, it becomes genuinely integrative, tapping the life of the higher self and focusing it into the fabric of the personality, for enlightened change and self-expression. Because the higher self is more wise and powerful than the personality, and is designed to have authority over the growth and self-expression of the personality, it makes sense to cooperate intelligently with it. It makes sense to learn as much as we can about the higher self and find ways to focus its power, wisdom, and love into our own self-expression.

THE GREATER AND THE LESSER

To cooperate with the higher self, we must be willing to confront the problems and responsibilities of our own life. We must be willing to develop new skills as needed and learn to work with the love, power, and wisdom of the higher self. Our challenge in this regard is much like the work of a graduate student at the university, who is assigned a specific project or independent line of study to complete. Once the assignment is made, the graduate student is basically left on his own; he can consult his professor, but is expected to develop his own method of approaching, understanding, and resolving the problem. In a very real sense, he must be both teacher and student, inasmuch as he must act on the best of his ideas and plans and discard the lesser ones. He must learn to take himself beyond his current abilities. As he does, his creativity is stimulated and his courage is evoked, and he learns far more than if the professor were instructing him in the conventional manner.

Those who would cooperate with the higher self must come to appreciate this analogy. We do not cooperate intelligently by becoming passively dependent on the higher self, believing that it is magically working behind the scenes to remove all hardship from our life. We cooperate by striving to *integrate* the power of the higher self into the potential of the personality, thereby growing into new abilities, wisdom, and activities. We cooperate by striving to become an apprentice to the master of life—our higher self—and by working to harness the best within us while transforming our weaknesses, flaws, and deficiencies.

Since meditation is designed to promote integration, it is essential that the Western meditator comprehend that he, too, is supposed to serve as both teacher and student as he strives toward his goals. To make Active Meditation work, he will have to define the ideals he will pursue, assign himself projects in which he can learn about the higher self, and monitor and discipline his efforts to become a more intelligent apprentice. Indeed, he will have to be *more* than teacher and student; he will have to be healer and patient, parent and child as well. This is the heart of effective integration.

The work of spiritual integration can be summed up in a single maxim: *the greater takes care of the lesser.* The teacher takes care of the student. The healer takes care of the patient.

The parent takes care of the child. By activating this principle, we set the stage for the integration of the personality, for as the mature elements of the personality learn to take care of the naive, lazy, ignorant, and selfish parts, replacing them with something more noble, the personality is healed. Intelligent cooperation becomes possible. We also set the stage for the integration of the healed personality with the higher self, for only the greater power, love, and wisdom of the higher self are adequate to provide fully the guidance, strength, and love which the personality needs in order to complete its tasks with dignity and nobility.

The greater takes care of the lesser. This is a great truth, but relatively meaningless unless activated. If we just spend our time in meditation blissing out or pursuing pleasant fantasies, the greater will never be brought into contact with the lesser, and no transformation will occur. The great potential of the higher self will remain abstract, unexpressed. And so, it is the duty of the personality to *find* its hidden strengths, talents, and capacities—and, having found them, *learn to use* these strengths, talents, and capacities effectively.

It is unfortunate that this obvious tenet of common sense is so frequently neglected by individuals working on self-improvement, as well as professionals in medicine and psychology. We are not empty slates, waiting to be written on. Most people are mixtures of mature and immature elements. They have a capacity for goodwill and tolerance, but also a potential for resentment and intolerance. In some aspects of life they are skilled; in others, awkward and untrained. When motivated, they are capable of ambitious work, self-discipline, and thoroughness, but at other times they are lazy, self-indulgent, and careless. In some modes, they are cheerful and confident, but there are also dark portions of the personality which are sad and insecure. The average person is usually unaware of these contradictions in his character, and could care less. When crisis arises, however, he is swept into the unpleasantness of the problem and his reaction to it—his annoyance, anger, frustration, and anxiety. Instead of the greater taking care of the lesser, the lesser panics and loses control. Such a reaction generally blocks access to the very strengths and capacities which could enable the personality to overcome the crisis and triumph.

The person who takes time in meditation to discover the mature elements within his character, however, will be largely immune to such uncontrolled reactions. He will be able to:
- Approach the difficulties of life as a problem solver.
- Heal ruffled emotions.
- Discipline frustrations and anxieties.
- Mobilize courage to soothe doubts.
- Maintain a cheerful attitude in the face of adversity.

But the work of meditation must not be limited just to *finding* the noble and mature elements within our character; we must also learn what to do with them. It is one thing to be in touch with intelligence, goodwill, and courage, and quite another to be able to *act* wisely, compassionately, and steadfastly. Until we learn to act in these ways, our noble aspirations will constantly be in jeopardy from the less than noble departments of the personality. The child within us will want gratification, even while the adult would prefer that the child learn self-sufficiency. The student within us will want ready-made answers and pat solutions, even while the teacher within us will want the student to learn how to evaluate and solve the problems and questions he faces. The patient within us will want relief of distress, even while the healer within us will want to cure the underlying problem or conflict, not just relieve symptoms. It is therefore not enough to observe that there are greater and lesser elements within us; we must learn to use the greater to take care of the lesser. Only then does integration become a reality.

We learn this lesson first within the context of the personality, as we focus our meditative efforts to heal its deficiencies and solve its problems. As we become proficient at this level, however, we also learn to apply the same principle to the greater elements of the higher self, using them to take care of the lesser needs of the personality.

Meditation is not a game, to be played out as a luxury of our leisure time. Its work and goals are noble, and enable us to enter into the presence of the authority and wisdom within us. It is then that the principle of the greater taking care of the lesser reaches its zenith. But possibly the most significant applications of this principle lie in learning to trust and cooperate with the greatness within us.

THE POWER OF MATURITY

The integrative work of the greater taking care of the lesser cannot be effectively approached as a mechanical exercise to be performed by rote. The mature elements within us must be activated, so they embrace the immature elements within us, cleansing and healing them and nurturing their transformation. For this reason, the nurturing parent who involves himself with warmth and affection in the life of his child makes an especially good model for the work of integration. When the child is filled with fear, the parent rushes to explain, reassure, and soothe. When the child is confused and bewildered, the parent offers advice and guidance. When the child is unhappy, the parent endeavors to set a more cheerful tone.

Meditation is not designed to be a time when we forget our troubles and immaturities by pursuing fantasies of angels and a paternalistic God who will soothe away all our woes. Rather, it is meant to be a time when we draw the negativity or conflict of a problem or immature element of the child within us into the compassion, strength, and wisdom of the parent within us. This is not done by just observing that there is a problem and assuming that it will now "drop away," since we have observed it; it is not done by shouting platitudes that the child is really perfect. Nor is it done by criticizing the weak elements of our personality and feeling sinful and inadequate. It is accomplished by acting as a responsible, loving parent toward the childish aspects of our character.

There are tremendous measures of joy, wisdom, hope, compassion, courage, and peace which the higher self patiently and tenderly radiates into the personality, day after day. Most people are unaware of this constant expression of support and love, and therefore do not receive the full benefit of it. They do not trust the higher self as a loving parent or make any effort to cooperate with it, and therefore cheat themselves of much of the richness of life. They remain focused in their childishness and immaturity.

The individual who learns to act with the maturity of the parent within, however, is able to take advantage of these spiritual resources and put them to work to correct his immaturity and childishness. He must do more than just play with nice ideas, soothing words, and pretty images, of course; he must actually tap into the *force* of the spiritual ideals of compassion, wisdom, and power and focus them constructively. Tapping into the forces of these ideals is accomplished by trusting in the higher self and seeking to cooperate with its intent and design. Focusing the forces constructively is accomplished by acting to correct the weaknesses and problems of the personality with goodwill, forgiveness, affection, encouragement, and common sense.

As we activate the parent within us to operate in this way, we gradually establish a relationship which permits:

• The confusion of the personality to be drawn into the intelligence of the higher self, where it is cleansed and healed.

145

- The problems of the personality to be lifted into the wisdom of the higher self, where the solution can be discerned.
- The sadness of the personality to be raised into the joy of the higher self, renewing the personality with cheerfulness.
- The anger of the personality to be embraced and overwhelmed by the forgiveness of the higher self.
- The fears of the personality to be drawn into the strength of the higher self, producing the power to be courageous.
- The fatigue of the personality to be lifted into the aura of the higher self, leading to revitalization.
- The indifference of the personality to be raised into the compassion of the higher self.
- The sickness of the personality to be embraced by the ideals of the higher self, creating health.

The ability of the greater life and power of the higher self to reach out and heal the weaknesses and deficiencies in the personality is not a lovely fable or promise; it is an established fact. But the process does require the active cooperation of the personality—the willingness to treat itself as a loving, nurturing parent would treat a fussing child. Until the parent-teacher-healer capacity within the personality is activated, the child is essentially left on its own.

The implication of this idea is quite clear: at least to some degree, we must learn to take care of our own needs. We cannot remain the child; we must start viewing ourself primarily as a responsible adult who can parent the child within. We must become an agent of the greater life of the higher self. It is for this reason that passive surrender to God and blind faith in the higher self just do not make sense; they do nothing to support the parent within. They keep us perpetually in spiritual childhood.

God gives us the wisdom, but we alone can use that wisdom to solve our own problems.

God gives us compassion, but we alone can use that compassion to forgive those who harm or offend us.

God gives us strength, but we alone can use that strength to act with courage.

The higher self has designed the personality to be successful, healthy, and competent, but we must learn how to fulfill this design. We must become an agent of the higher self.

Of course, there will always be some who will fail to see the importance of activating the parent within. They will insist that they can fulfill *their* spiritual design just by loving God and surrendering to divine will. It may be helpful for such people to keep in mind, however, that *any* child can quietly fall into a swimming pool. The ones that do not drown are the ones who learn to swim. By learning to swim, they are doing something more than just believing that their parents will always be there to rescue them if they fall in. They are actually learning to take advantage of the purpose of the swimming pool—and their own arms and legs.

Others will claim that the strength, power, and abilities of the higher self can be activated simply by affirming them. While an attitude of positive expectation is always helpful in any endeavor, it does not make sense to reduce the need for spiritual integration to wishful thinking. Just as the child who falls into the pool cannot make the water hold him up and propel him across its surface through positive affirmations, neither can we expect the higher self to support us unless we first learn to cooperate with it intelligently.

HELPING THE CHILD GROW UP

In Active Meditation, therefore, two major assignments are given to the personality: to identify the genuine needs for growth of the child within, which will become center stage for the work of integration, and to activate the parent within, which will make it possible to focus the greater strength, love, and wisdom of the higher self into the personality.

Defining the genuine needs of the child within is a bit tricky. Too often, "needs" are simply confused for "wishes" and "wants"—the things the personality childishly craves for. Such things are generally tainted by escapism, hedonism, pettiness, and selfishness. A person who has difficulty establishing fulfilling and healthy relationships, for example, will tend to believe that what he needs most are friends and lovers who are more on "his" wavelength. What he genuinely needs, however, is to replace his selfishness, capriciousness, and pettiness with the greater love, affection, and compassion of his higher self, and learn to express these qualities as he deals with friends and lovers.

In striving to understand "needs," therefore, we must learn to recognize the distinction between the symptoms of our problems and what is needed to solve them. If we have been embarrassed, for example, the anger or resentment we may be feeling only *describes* the problem; our *need* is for the courage and cheerfulness of the higher self—and for using these qualities to dissipate and replace the anger and resentment. The belief that we "need" to find relief from our anger and resentment is erroneous. In the same way, if we are indecisive about the solution to a complex problem, our confusion only describes the nature of our reaction; our need is for discernment, wisdom, and the ability to think the problem through. The quest for ready-made answers or "easy solutions" is too simplistic. In other words, the genuine need of the child within is always for those qualities, strengths, or talents of the higher self which, if applied to the difficulty, *would help the child grow up.* It is surprising how seldom this simple approach is taken to solving personal problems, but nothing makes better sense. It is the way in which the greater takes care of the lesser.

Once the personality has learned to recognize its immaturity, and has decided to do something about it, we then face our second assignment: to activate the parent within and put its maturity and nobility to work applying the appropriate qualities, strengths, and talents of the higher self to resolve the problems of the child within. This is neither an overnight nor a magical process; it requires persistent and disciplined effort over a substantial period of time to effect permanent changes in ongoing habits of anger, self-deprecation, prejudice, selfishness, or pettiness. To be successful, we must constantly reinforce the authority of the parent within (recognizing that this authority is drawn from the power of the higher self) and restrain the natural tendency of the child within to rebel against it. Instead, the child within must be encouraged to trust and cooperate in the changes being made.

Throughout, we must keep in mind that both the child within and the parent within are aspects of the personality. The child within represents our immature, self-indulgent, and selfish elements. The parent within is the part of us which is mature, responsible, and willing to make sacrifices in order to grow. As such, the parent within is the ideal agent to focus the greater love, wisdom, and power of the higher self into the immature elements of the personality. Activating the parent within the personality is, therefore, the most efficient way to pursue the work of integration.

It is possible, of course, to make these changes without the use of meditation, but a regular practice of the techniques of Active Meditation is ideally suited to enormously accelerating the work of the parent within. This is just a matter of common sense. Meditation is designed to improve the relationship between the higher self and the personality, so the qualities and strengths of heaven can be brought into full flower on earth. What better way to fulfill this design than by using meditation to bring *our own* personality to full flower?

THE SKILLS OF MEDITATION

To use meditation effectively in this way, however, the activities of meditation must be focused. Certain meditative skills must be developed. Little good will be served simply by contacting the higher self and then spending thirty minutes feeling good about God. The resources of the higher self must be tapped, directed into the personality, and used to transform habits, attitudes, methods of thinking, and priorities. Those portions of the personality which have been torn apart by distress must be lifted up into the love and compassion of the higher self, cleansed, renewed, and given new definition. The problems of daily living must be solved. None of this occurs simply by hoping that it will. It requires the development of specific meditative skills.

Those who are accustomed to passive meditative systems may object to this premise, but it should be kept in mind that a general needs his officer corps and troops to win a battle. The sales manager needs his sales force to sell his product. Just so, the God within us needs a well-trained, competent, and active personality to parent and guide the day-to-day work of the outer life. It is perhaps enough for the child within the personality to go on belief and adoration alone, but the parent within needs effective skills in order to fulfill his duties and honor the intentions of the higher self.

The skills of meditation are practical abilities which are meant to be developed by the personality as it seeks to interact with the higher self. They enable the work of spiritual integration to proceed much more rapidly than would otherwise be possible. The ones we will deal with in this book are all skills that can be used to develop meaningful techniques for healing and enlightening the personality, and preparing it for greater partnership with the higher self.

Let us become acquainted with these skills.

TAKING CHARGE

Nothing much ever happens in a meditation when the person who is meditating simply makes contact with the higher self and then waits for it to do something. The personality is meant to assume responsibility for its behavior and activities and initiate meditative contact. Meditation is intended to be a very active time, with the meditator choosing themes to focus on, asking questions, pursuing hints and suggestions, attuning to selected qualities or forces of the higher self, directing them where they are needed, and so forth. This work can only proceed, however, if the person is able to take charge.

Actually, the skill of taking charge is an ability which embraces a much wider circumference than just meditative work. It describes an ideal approach to living. The personality is designed to be alert to what is happening in life and understand it, evaluating what is helpful and what may be harmful. It is expected to do the basic homework of successful living—getting involved in opportunities to learn and grow, searching for the undeveloped potential within, taking risks, experimenting with new ideas, and initiating sensible projects.

In Active Meditation, the meditator is expected to be a director of the action which unfolds. In this way, he begins to come into closer harmony with the higher self, which is the real director of all the action of our life.

WORKING AS A MULTIDIMENSIONAL BEING IN A MULTIDIMENSIONAL UNIVERSE

We are not just flesh and body. Our being extends through a number of dimensions, not all of them visible. In addition to the space we act in physically, we live in the dimensions of our emotions, the mind, and the higher self. The average person tends to think and act largely in the physical dimension, and believes the personality to be a manifestation of the physical body. In meditation, however, we must work multidimensionally, becoming aware of the higher self, our thoughts, our feelings, and the expression of these elements in physical activity simultaneously.

This is not as difficult as it may seem at first. In walking down the street, we can be aware of our body, the clothes we are wearing, the direction we are heading, and the reason for going there, all at the same time. Working multidimensionally in a meditative state is no more complex. But because not all of these dimensions are visible to us, we must make a concentrated effort to recognize and respond to them.

It is the ability to work multidimensionally, for example, which enables us to understand a person who is trying to cheat us and deal with him more effectively. We are able to see the many levels of this event simultaneously:

• The words and deeds which have occurred physically.

• The emotional reactions of both of us.

• His motivations for behaving in this way.

• The consequences of the different ways we might respond to his deceit.

• The values, dignity, compassion, and purpose in living which ought to guide our behavior.

The person who responds to such a circumstance one-dimensionally is likely just to become angry. But if we are able to work multidimensionally, we can respond instead with tolerance, compassion, and wisdom, even while standing firm and not permitting him to cheat us—and letting him know his behavior is unacceptable. Understanding the multidimensional nature of ourself and of reality, we know that our thoughts and attitudes do not have to be determined by physical events. They can be guided from other levels, in a way which honors the life of the higher self.

DIVINE ARCHETYPES

One of the great skills of Active Meditation is the ability to work with divine archetypes. Divine archetypes are patterns of perfection which God has created to assist in bringing the life and glory of heaven into manifestation on earth. These patterns are the design and living force from which all of life has been created—humanity, civilization, nature, and the universe. They serve as the seed and inspiration for all creativity, enlightened self-expression, and growth. The divine archetypes exist at the level of the higher self, not the personality, and therefore are not to be confused with Jungian archetypes, which are usually the creations of human thinking.

Divine archetypes serve as reservoirs of divine force; they are aspects of God. Examples of divine archetypes would be the power and pattern to be cheerful, to lead, to build, and to organize. A person with advanced skills in meditation is able to contact these archetypes directly, at the level of the higher self, and focus their force and quality into his creative work. They are invoked by being aware that they do exist as the literal environment of our higher self, by being devoted to their emerging potential in our life, and by being dedicated to working with their inspiration and power. Beginners are able to deal with archetypal forces, too, although not directly, by invoking the perfect divine pattern for some aspect of their work or self-expression. A mother, for example, could invoke the perfect pattern of dignity and courage in helping her child overcome strong fears. By working repeatedly to invoke this perfect pattern, she would gradually become familiar with its nature, its power, and how to express it.

Many practical examples of working with divine archetypes can be found in the essays "The Act of Human Creation" and "Becoming Graceful" from *The Art of Living* essay series.

SPIRITUAL IDEALS

Another kind of pattern of perfection which plays an important role in Active Meditation is the spiritual ideal. Spiritual ideals are aspects of our own higher self which serve as blueprints for our individual self-expression—the ideal way to think, feel, and act in any circumstance of daily life, past, present, or future. Many of these spiritual ideals can be observed in partial states of manifestation in our character, but to be appreciated fully, they must be traced back to their origin, the higher self.

The process of using spiritual ideals is similar to using divine archetypes. Having recognized a genuine need in the personality, we invoke the spiritual ideal of the higher self which we lack. If we are angry with a friend, for example, it would be the ideal of forgiveness. If we are irritated by delays, it would be the ideal of patience. Once we have linked our attention to the ideal, we would then consider how its force and perfection can be expressed, mentally, emotionally, and physically. In this way, we infuse elements of the greater into the lesser.

SYMBOLISM

A symbol is a visual image, memory, feeling, thought, event, or phrase which represents something in addition to its literal meaning. The use of symbolism can be an important meditative skill, if we keep in mind several principles:

• The symbol has no value except to the degree that it reveals or represents something more profound. We must not get trapped, therefore, in the *appearance* of the symbol, but look beyond it, to its life and power, and appreciate its capacity to stabilize and organize various levels of consciousness.

• Some symbols lead us back to the higher self, perhaps even to archetypal forces and spiritual ideals. But other symbols represent the forces and contents of the subconscious and unconscious portions of our personality—as well as mass consciousness. A symbol arising in a meditation (or a dream) must therefore be evaluated carefully, because we would want to deal with a symbol of the higher self differently than a symbol of the subconscious. A symbol of an archetypal force, for example, could be used repeatedly to help us reestablish contact with the power of that archetype. We would want to explore it thoroughly. A symbol representing a repressed emotion buried in the subconscious would never be used in this fashion, however; it would be used to search out the repressed emotion, so it could be cleansed and replaced by something healthier.

• Symbols can also be created by the meditator as needed. In working to establish a new habit pattern, for example, we might find it useful to create an appropriate symbol which will be specifically associated with the new habit. Using symbols in this way helps us organize the subconscious better.

SEED THOUGHTS

When a spiritual ideal is verbalized, it becomes a seed thought—a succinct phrase, a brief sentence, or a word which embodies a complex set of insights, motivations, thoughts, and qualities. Seed thoughts are activated in the meditative state. While in contact with the higher self, we fix our attention on the seed thought and enrich it with our devotion and our intention to honor it in our self-expression. This action creates something like a "psychological battery" charged with the spiritual force of the ideal we are contemplating. As we work repeatedly with the seed thought, this battery becomes a reservoir of power in our subconscious, energizing our aspirations, expectations, and intentions to act this ideal way in daily life.

An example of a seed thought would be: "I am the power to forgive." By holding this seed thought about forgiveness, we gradually build up our faith and determination to be truly forgiving in our relationships with others.

Seed thoughts differ from ordinary types of positive thought and self-hypnosis in that they infuse the subconscious battery with the higher dimensions of spiritual force. This can come only from contact with our higher self, and so must be energized in the meditative state. Ordinary positive thought does not achieve this, despite the confidence of the positive thinker and the fact that the intention is similar.

It is possible to energize a number of seed thoughts in a single meditation, but it is helpful to pause briefly between each one. At first, it is recommended that only one seed thought be charged per meditation, until expertise is gained.

MENTAL ROLE PLAYING

In translating a spiritual ideal or divine archetype so that it becomes an active part of our character, we must give it focus and definition. One of the best ways of accomplishing this is through mental role playing—for example, imagining ourself to be a wise and nurturing parent to the child within us, explaining the value of new ways of acting and demonstrating what this entails. Other roles that can be played for the same effect would be the inner teacher or compassionate healer.

Mental role playing can also be most helpful in focusing spiritual force into our subconscious and rehearsing the ideal way in which we should act in a variety of circumstances or conditions. In this way, we give our thoughts and feelings a trial run in handling a new ideal or power of the higher self.

BLESSING

Genuine blessing occurs as the higher self radiates its love and light toward an aspect of the personality or its daily life, for the purpose of nurturing it. The meditator can develop skill in blessing by cultivating a reverence for the life of the higher self and by trying to think and act as the higher self does. By blending a refined quality of devotion, trust, and dedication to the higher self, the meditator invokes its love and light, directing it toward some aspect of the personality's character or activity, past or present. The key to mastering this skill is learning to focus the blessing on the *potential to grow:* our potential to become more tolerant, our potential for greater health, society's potential to resolve its conflicts, and so on.

Because true blessing is an act of spirit—not just a benevolent attitude of the personality—it is one of the safest and most healing activities we can engage in, when confronted with imperfection, adversity, or difficulty. In addition to accelerating the development of inherent spiritual potential, it has the effect of neutralizing that which opposes and resists the life of the higher self. It charges the seeds of nobility within our character—our best plans and goals, our emerging genius, and the strength of our convictions—thus helping them grow. Blessing is an active expression of the greater taking care of the lesser.

PERSONIFICATION

The device of imagining the personality to be two people, the parent within and the child within, is an act of personification. It enables us to deal more readily with the concept that there is a mixture of both mature and immature elements in our character, and harness the power of the mature elements so they can take care of the immature parts.

This same device can be used in many other ways meditatively, too. Divine archetypes can be personified as muses, graces, or other figures from mythology. Our spiritual ideals can be embodied in a personification of "the saint within." This kind of personification makes it easier to contact and communicate with abstract forces and qualities, by giving them a concrete focus.

Personification can likewise be used to deal more effectively with problem areas of the subconscious. If we are rebellious and petulant, these traits could be personified as a spoiled child who is then firmly but lovingly disciplined by our inner, nurturing parent. Anger could be personified as a hothead who is then taught the lessons of self-restraint, tolerance, and benevolence by the teacher within. In using personification in this way, however, it is important to keep in mind that we are not just indulging in melodramatic games which will *reconcile* us to our petulance or anger; the object is to help us *grow away from* our immaturity and become more adult in our behavior.

THE HEART AND SUBSTANCE

These are the basic skills we need in order to meditate effectively. But meditation is not just a collection of skills. It is a program of self-improvement, in which we seek to integrate the power, love, and wisdom of the higher self into the life of the personality, thereby transforming the personality and enabling it to become an agent for the light and love of God.

In Active Meditation, therefore, we use these skills as the basic building blocks for constructing specific techniques which will help the personality grow and achieve the goal of enlightenment—an enlightened consciousness and an enlightened self-expression.

There are seven such techniques, and these will be explored, one at a time, in the coming seven chapters. These techniques are:

1. Creating an enlightened self-image, which will help us establish a correct awareness of identity.

2. Defining intelligent goals and values, which will give us a proper focus for our self-expression.

3. Cleaning the mental household, which will enable the personality to become a more effective partner of the higher self.

4. Healing the emotions, which will help us develop the right attitude.

5. Invoking the wisdom of the higher self, which will bring us guidance and enrich our understanding of life.

6. Applying the wisdom of the higher self to solve problems, enabling us to become more effective in our self-expression.

7. Exploring the themes of creative self-discovery, leading to a more enlightened role in life.

By no means are these the only ways in which contact with the higher self can be used in meditation. But these seven techniques do represent the heart and substance of Active Meditation and its primary goal: spiritual integration.

7

Establishing An Enlightened Self-Image

A WINDOW TO THE LIGHT

"Mirror, mirror, on the wall, who's the fairest one of all?" the wicked queen was wont to ask. As long as her subconscious was strong enough to distort the oracle, the answer always was, "Why, you are, darling." But the moment a ray of truth was able to slip through, the answer became: "Snow White."

We often distort the mirror of our self-image this way. The patient-student-child within us longs to believe that it is all right, that it is the rightful heir to the higher self, and that everyone in the world adores it. And yet, if it is not told this, it begins to believe quite the opposite: that it is a miserable wretch, unworthy of success, and despised by all. In both cases, we displace the best within us and block our access to the higher self. All we can see is the mirror reflection of our own beliefs.

We need a better pathway to the higher self than belief. Belief does play an important role in our life: a belief in our essential goodness as a human being is quite necessary, as is the belief in the presence and power of the higher self. But beliefs are easily twisted into fantasies, fears, and childish expectations; we can be led into believing things which are not true. When this occurs, we end up in contact only with our beliefs— not the higher self.

In order to receive the power, light, and love of the higher self, there must be a place in our subconscious where these qualities can enter and take up residence, without being distorted or diminished. Esoterically, this is the function of a *healthy self-image*. Without a basic self-respect and a conviction that some part of us is worthwhile and stands for something noble, the resources of the higher self will just remain a lovely vision or beautiful potential. And potential wealth pays no bills; potential courage cannot help us in time of need. But if we are convinced that a part of our personality—the doctor-teacher-parent within us—stands for the worth and dignity of ourself and our work, then it will be possible to activate the strength and support we need in times of crisis.

This is just common sense. The bum on welfare has his dreams and his dole to placate him, but the hard-working person with a good job has ready access to a decent income. The person with an unhealthy self-image must be satisfied with his beliefs and fantasies, because he has compromised his ability to contact the higher self. But the one who has carefully established a proper self-image has a basis for acting effectively in life. The active meditator understands this principle, and views the creation of a healthy self-image as one of the first priorities of his work.

It must be understood that this is not an exercise in narcissism. An overly-confident self-image is just as distorted as a "poor me" self-image. Both block off the light of the higher self and keep us surrounded by mirrors of our own creation. Rather, it is a technique for establishing a point of access in the personality that can be used by the higher self.

Unfortunately, very few people who have an unhealthy self-image actually recognize it as such. Instead, they are blinded by a pleasant self-deception: they assume that what they would like to believe about themselves is their real self-image. Thus, if they like to think of themselves as humble, they are able to cover up very pompous and arrogant ways of acting. Or, if they like to think of themselves as competent and wise, they are able to disguise serious deficiencies in intelligence and skill. It does not work this way in real life, however.

In truth, our self-image is what we honestly think and feel about ourself. It is revealed in how we typically react to challenge, success, and crisis—and in how others react to our customary behavior.

Some might here object: "If I want to engage in this kind

of self-deception, what of it? What harm is it?" The answer is that the harm can be great indeed. If a person drags with him through life a chronic inferiority complex, guilt feelings, or intense discouragement, little room will be left in the personality for the possible expression of the optimism and joy of the higher self. Even the seeds of these qualities may be killed by the blight of pessimism and negativity. Just so, if a person bullies his way through life projecting an image of hostility, defensiveness, and a need to dominate others, there will be little room left for the kindness, sympathy, and cooperativeness which might be tapped in the higher self. In either case, the best within us has been squeezed out.

The personality is like a household of consciousness. If the windows in a house are kept shuttered, no light can come in. Just so, a person who is dominated by pessimism, depression, hostility, or inferiority is like a household filled with darkness, because all the windows are covered. The light of the sun cannot penetrate the gloom.

It is not always gloom that covers the windows, of course; sometimes our fantasies and foolishness become so opaque that the light of the higher self is all but blocked. If we are attentive to maintaining a healthy self-image, however, we can remove these coverings and reopen a window to the light.

Still, it is amazing how many people look to the light of the higher self for help, but forget to raise the blinds of their own self-image. As a result, they do not understand how much they are missing in the way of peace, joy, insight, or courage. They believe in the treasures of heaven, but do not experience them. Yet the fault lies not in heaven, but in ourself.

This should not be a difficult principle to grasp. If we try to comfort someone steeped in grief, we often find our efforts rejected—not because this person does not need our help, but because the depth of the grief is so great it blocks off everything that could relieve it. There is no room for help.

It is our responsibility to make sure the window to the light of the higher self remains open; that we honor and welcome the riches of heaven we need. It is therefore important to take the time to establish a healthy self-image.

A BASIS FOR ACTING

A healthy self-image is far more than an occasional good feeling of confidence, or a visualization of success. It is designed to be a vessel for the life of our higher self, a fixed representative of the best within us that can guide us in our daily activities, both consciously and subconsciously. It can serve as the protector of our ideals and our most cherished qualities, talents, and plans. It should be the staging ground for our noble endeavors—a center of awareness from which we can go forth into an imperfect world, interact with it, and then return, with the certain conviction that this part of us is never damaged by outer circumstance or failure. In this way, the healthy self-image is meant to be our basis for acting maturely and responsibly in all that we do. Instead of reacting thoughtlessly to the events of life, we are able to respond in a manner which will be more in harmony with our higher self than the negativity and adversity of outer circumstance.

The healthy, ideal self-image is that point where our spiritual nature meets and can interact with our human nature. To put it in religious terms, it is a place in consciousness where we can receive the wealth of the kingdom of heaven and the blessings of the higher self. And it is the place from which we focus these qualities and blessings into the rest of our personality.

Each individual will naturally have his or her own special virtues, talents, and strengths featured in the healthy self-image. But there are certain components in *every* proper self-image. These are:

1. Our most idealistic views on life, people, duty, opportunities, and ourself.

2. An enlightened appreciation of the most important roles we play in life—parenting, work, community and religious involvement, and so on.

3. An intelligent appraisal of the talents and qualities of consciousness we can mobilize to fulfill our duties.

4. A basic decision to play the role of the doctor-teacher-parent within the personality, rather than indulge the patient-student-child within. A healthy self-image will never lionize illness, immaturity, or imperfection. It respects the ideal of growth.

DIRTY DISHES

Indeed, it is impossible to build a healthy self-image unless we learn certain basic lessons of coping with the constant imperfection in the world—not to mention the elements of imperfection we find in ourself. If this core area of conflict is ignored or not handled appropriately, the entire issue of integrating the higher and lower selves can be placed in jeopardy. The very heart of this integrative work involves the continual struggle to knead the pure life of the higher self into a human nature which may be barely adequate in some areas, mediocre in many, and outstanding or competent only in a few. And so, it is important to cultivate a proper perspective on interacting with imperfection.

A good analogy for this perspective can be found in washing dishes. Years of personal experimentation have revealed to us the persistent and annoying tendency of dirty dishes to stay dirty. They do not wash themselves! And frequent exhortations notwithstanding, we have not been able to coax either fairies or elves into attending to this problem. Instead, we have had to wash our own dirty dishes. We have tried many techniques, but are able to report now that the best is integrating the dirty dishes with warm, soapy water, combined with certain scrubbing and drying exercises. The result: clean, dry dishes. The dirty water runs down the drain.

For quite some time, we were offended by the messiness of these plates and glassware—until we realized that it was only natural for remnants of food to cling to dishes after they have been used. Now, we see it is a perfectly normal part of dinner for dishes to get dirty—and for us to clean them once we are done. Sometimes we even enjoy it, although a neighbor thinks this is outrageous. "I don't care how detached you are," he cries, "the only proper way to regard dirty dishes is with disgust."

Nonetheless, we do not find it necessary to take our dirty dishes to a "plateologist" or a "dishiatrist" to have the dirt analyzed, so that we can better understand the nature and origins of the dirt. We do not go off to a house of worship to listen to sermons about the virtues of being squeaky clean and the sinfulness of dirt—or to be told that all we need to do is believe in "Gawd" and He will cleanse our dishes for us. We do not even feel especially guilty when a few dirty dishes pile up, as they occasionally do. We simply do the dishes when they need it, and are done with it.

Just so, we should regard our imperfect attitudes, false perspectives, secret sins, and the imperfections of others and the world at large as nothing more than "dirty dishes." They must be cleaned regularly and as completely as possible, but there is no reason to accompany the process with hysteria, anxiety, guilt, or gnashing of teeth. There is no mysterious reason why our thoughts, feelings, attitudes, and beliefs get dirty from time to time; it is just a natural phenomenon of using them. We pick up bad habits here, become a little tired there, and soon the dust begins to accumulate. But the remedy is obvious and easy. We simply integrate these imperfections with a little "warm and soapy water"—the love, wisdom, and strength of our higher self. The scrubbing is performed by the higher aspect of the personality—the doctor-teacher-parent within us. The result is a healthy self-image—and the understanding that Archimedes is not the only one who can have an eureka experience by getting into hot water!

We must take care not to let our dirty dishes pile up, however, or we may find the task of cleaning them monumental. In this regard it is wise to remember that although dirty dishes are a natural byproduct of eating, it is not desirable to leave them dirty. So also, such imperfections as negative attitudes, selfishness, pessimism, fear, doubt, and prejudice may be natural to our human nature—but they are not desirable. They should be cleansed as quickly as possible, without overdramatizing their significance by reacting emotionally to them. There is absolutely no reason why we should impair our effectiveness as a human being by blighting ourself with confusion, fear, guilt, or depression, just because imperfection happens to exist. None of these reactions is in harmony with the life of the higher self.

Still, many serious problems, individually and in society, do result from the unenlightened way in which we cope with imperfection. At times, our perception of imperfection becomes far more debilitating than the problem or fault itself. Every serious meditator, and everyone who strives to live a spiritual life, should therefore learn to work with imperfection, wherever it exists, without hating it, glorifying it, or ignoring it. Hating our flaws and failures leads to self-rejection and self-contempt—eventually, to a denial of the higher self. Glorifying our flaws leads to a martyr complex and the parasitic manipulation of others—not better spiritual connections. Ignoring our flaws creates a psychological state of estrangement from the higher self.

The dimensions of this problem are enormous, although

they need not be; the difficulty is fed by the exhortations of the ignorant and malicious, who are intent on preserving, if not enshrining, our human imperfections. To quote the essay "Becoming Graceful," from *The Art of Living, Volume V:*

"The roots of this condition lie primarily in the Western tradition of puritanism, which made it a principle of 'spirituality' to remove all elements of style, art, color, joy, and fun from living. Puritan sects dressed in blacks, grays, and whites and deliberately maintained a grim, spartan lifestyle. They championed a work ethic which was so severe it has soured the enthusiasm of many people toward work. Above all, they promoted the notion that happiness is something evil—that a person who seems happy must be doing something immoral; a person who is friendly must be trying to manipulate others; a person who is optimistic is not sufficiently sensitive to the suffering of the world. These ideas have now crept into mass consciousness, influencing virtually everyone in our society in one way or another. They have been seized upon and elaborated, to the point where anyone who finds delight in what he does is somewhat suspect. The patient person is thought to be apathetic; self-confidence and a decent self-image are construed as signs of haughtiness and vanity; good humor is believed a sign of silliness.

"In modern society, the philosophy of grimness is perpetuated by sour, dried up, joyless people who take refuge in it as a justification of their own spiritual emptiness—their lack of goodwill, affection, and wisdom. Not knowing how to enjoy themselves, they are threatened by those who do, and so condemn them and accuse them of being unspiritual. Not knowing how to be friendly, they try to intimidate others into being unfriendly, too. Not knowing how to celebrate life, they try to make everyone who does feel guilty. They preach that the 'true' spiritual life is one of sacrifice, hardship, misery, sadness, groveling, and submission. As a result, they manage to suppress the life and thoughts of others to a startling degree."

What we must understand, before we pursue the integrative work of meditation, is that our primary responsibility in dealing with imperfection is not to reject it, but to *heal* it as best we can. If we are too hostile, we should cultivate affection. If we are too anxious, we should cultivate confidence. If we are too discouraged, we should cultivate enthusiasm. If the dishes are dirty, we should wash them.

Effective meditation is a powerful tool for cleansing the personality—and a powerful opportunity for healing the mind and emotions. The work of meditation does not unleash a storm of guilt, anxiety, misery, and discontent, as so many people fear. To quote "Becoming Graceful" once again:

"In enlightened living, a measure of the optimism, dignity, and cheerfulness of the higher self is always bursting through into practical expression. The enlightened individual knows pain, sorrow, and suffering as much as anyone else—perhaps even more—but is never far from the inner life. This inner life steadfastly lifts him above the unpleasant aspects of life he must deal with and allows him to act with joy, kindness, and enthusiasm, no matter how depressing outer circumstances may appear. Truly, only pompous and artificial people ever feel the need to present themselves in sober, joyless, and grim ways to the world—the enlightened person does not. Only spiritual hypocrites take themselves so seriously that they believe their works and efforts to be threatened by good humor, enjoyment of life, and simple human charity. Only those who have no contact with the life of spirit are arrogant enough to use their suffering and sacrifices as justifications for demanding attention, loyalty, and submission from others. Behaving in these ways is incompatible with the enlightened life—it betrays a consciousness of smallness and poverty which excludes God and His universe of power, intelligence, and goodwill."

THE HIGHER MEETS THE LOWER

In this context, we can observe one of the basic tenets of the activity of integration—that strength overwhelms weakness. When the higher meets the lower, it transforms the lower into a more perfect expression of the higher.

Courage overwhelms discouragement.

Forgiveness overpowers anger.

Enthusiasm conquers pessimism.

Joy defeats grimness.

Order overwhelms chaos.

None of this can occur, however, unless these qualities are focused through skillful activity. The infinite qualities of life will remain infinite until we give them finite focus. Then and only then does the above principle begin to help us clean our dirty dishes. It is nice to talk about the joys of "unconditional love," but it is even more powerful to give that unconditional love expression in the conditions of our life. This is when we discover that we can "move mountains."

This basic principle is most useful in building a healthy self-image. It serves no purpose to attack and blast away at the problems and flaws of the personality; rather, we want to recognize that the mature elements within us are fully capable of quietly infusing our character with superior strengths and qualities, gradually replacing or dissolving the negative elements within us.

TAKING INVENTORY

In building a healthy self-image, it is important to keep in mind the dual nature of the personality—the distinction between the doctor-teacher-parent within us and the patient-student-child within us. While it is currently very chic to chat about oneness and the presence of God everywhere, differences do remain:

Between our intentions and our behavior.

Between our understanding and the actual events of life.

Between our conscious awareness and our sensory perceptions.

Between our higher self and our personality.

The healthy self-image is meant to bridge this gap, not emphasize it. There are always those who love misery, however, and they have been quite diligent in emphasizing the differences. There are plenty of differences, to be sure, but they are meant to be *complementary*, not divisive and destructive. There are differences between warm, soapy water and dirty dishes, but the differences are not harsh; there is no need for alarm. The dishes do not burst into flame or crumble into fragments when inserted into water; they simply come clean, so they may be used again. The enlightened washer of dishes sees the different characteristics of the water and the dishes, but also fully understands how they can be used together, harmoniously, for productive work. Just so, our higher and lower natures each have their distinct duties to perform—but they are meant to perform them in healthy relationship to one another. It is the goal of Active Meditation to establish this healthy relationship.

As this concept applies to the work of building a healthy self-image, we look to the ideals, values, and goals of the doctor-teacher-parent within us and from this study realize that there are many good elements within us. The patient-student-child within us may have distorted these good elements to some degree, but the good has not perished. It is still there.

In other words, we take inventory of the cherished principles we stand for, the goals we have set for ourself, the noble attitudes we value, and the other good aspects of our mind, emotions, talent, and ideals. We look for the elements of the personality which can serve as a basis for the expression of health, strength, ability, goodwill, and constructive ambition.

In no way, however, does this include compiling a list of our problems, sins, weaknesses, and miseries—even though those who are used to dwelling on their problems may find it difficult to resist the temptation. Some people do not believe that they have very many elements of goodness within them. But it is important for such people to keep in mind that we are not just looking for actual expressions of these values, goals, and ideals, but also the *seeds* of them. Everyone has these seeds, and so we must continue to look for them and begin to appreciate them. We must spell out our strengths and affirm them!

Once we have identified our strengths, there are three specific meditative techniques we can use to energize them with the life and power of the higher self: the practice of self-respect, the practice of self-esteem, and the creation of a mental symbol. Self-respect is the approval we give to the goodness in our character and higher self. Self-esteem is the approval we give to the accomplishments we have made. The creation of a mental symbol enables us to focus this approval in our daily thoughts and feelings.

SELF-RESPECT

The fundamental premise of the practice of self-respect is accepting the higher self as our real nature—not our imperfections and difficulties. At the same time, however, it must be emphasized that it is *not* the object of this technique to practice self-deception. We are not pretending that our imperfections are just an illusion; it is a matter of common sense that the results of bad manners, apathy, incompetence, and fear are *not* illusory! Nor are we pretending that now that we are sounding the magic word, the full force of the virtue and wisdom of the higher self will immediately take charge of the whole scope of the personality. Again, common sense tells us that no such instant changes are likely to occur; the path of self-improvement is trod step by step.

Instead, the practice of self-respect in Active Meditation is meant to be the *affirmation of our intention* to behave as the higher self would have us behave, to think as the higher self would have us think. In the presence of our higher self, we declare, mentally, that our most cherished values and talents are to be the dominant qualities and intentions of our thought and self-expression. This is not a casual declaration, but a commitment to the best within us. It may have to be repeated many times, but each time we do, we are in fact creating a vessel in consciousness that is filled by the power, wisdom, and goodwill of the higher self.

Done in meditation, this activity is far more powerful than the average practice of affirmative thinking, although the intent is similar in both cases. The ordinary practices of positive thinking rarely go beyond the level of the personality. They have their value, but the type of affirmation being advocated in this technique is more akin to the act of a skilled engineer seeking employment with a large manufacturing firm, so that his work will be supported by the vast resources of the company. He recognizes that the total resources of an international firm will provide a potential for inventiveness and experimentation far greater than what he could do in his own basement or garage. Applying to such a firm, therefore, would be an act of self-respect—an act of taking his talent, discipline, genius, and ambition and committing them to a larger enterprise.

In exactly the same manner, we have the opportunity to take the best of our talents, genius, values, ideals, and qualities, limited though they may be, to the infinitely more powerful wisdom and resources of the higher self. By pledging them to the larger enterprise of the higher self, we build self-respect. Working together, our genius can become inspired, our strengths augmented, our attitudes repaired and healed, and our dedication blessed. As we declare our intention to be a noble person and do what is correct and proper, the higher self can invest itself more fully in our daily activities. In this fashion, our self-respect grows, and with it, our healthy self-image.

The actual steps to be followed in cultivating self-respect in meditation would include:

1. Entering the meditative state and contacting the higher self, as described in chapter five.

2. Affirming our worthiness as an individual who is seeking to be a noble person and do the right thing. This involves identifying with the higher element of the personality, the doctor-teacher-parent within us, and affirming that we want to do what we can to help this part of the personality to grow and become stronger.

3. Affirming the value of the major roles we play in life—for example, parent, spouse, worker, and citizen. We have the opportunity to make a contribution through these roles—and the opportunity to touch more of the life of the higher self by meeting them responsibly—and so they are worthy of our respect.

4. Affirming our interest in nurturing various qualities of the human spirit in our own life—for example, integrity, forgiveness, patience, courage, or endurance.

In applying this formula meditatively, it is important to dwell on each affirmation thoughtfully—not just repeat it by rote. We can be aware that even as we make this affirmation, the higher self is responding by charging us with new love, power, and wisdom. Often, this charging occurs unconsciously, but it does occur. The actual details of this formula can be varied as necessary to meet our own individual needs.

Above all, whenever we use this technique, we must set aside our concerns about our imperfections and our selfishness. Without denying that we do have flaws and weaknesses of character, we must concentrate on *strengthening* the idealistic skills, traits, and qualities within us. We align ourself with the best within us and charge it with the life of the higher self.

SELF-ESTEEM

The second major meditative technique for building a healthy self-image is the practice of self-esteem. To properly understand the role of self-esteem, however, we must carefully distinguish it from self-confidence and mere arrogance. Self-confidence, while useful, is too easily generated through self-deception; some people simply declare that their life, their career, and their personal relationships are perfect—even when they clearly are not. Arrogance is the attempt to build self-esteem by putting everyone else down while carefully preserving the illusion of superiority; it is based on a very pessimistic attitude about our own weaknesses.

True self-esteem, on the other hand, is a quality which is generated out of a healthy appraisal of our accomplishments and our competence—not as a result of self-hypnotic babblings or egotism. Just as we receive our paycheck for work accomplished, not work yet to be done, so also self-esteem is a reward which can be claimed only after we have actually made some kind of achievement. It is therefore real and substantial, not illusory.

The value of a meditative practice of self-esteem is that it builds a habit of periodically reviewing our progress and achievement in life. Far too many people go through life modestly accepting most of the good that they do without fully appreciating it—but spending a great deal of time fussing over difficulties, failures, and adversities. If they spent an equal amount of time considering the value of their accomplishments, their self-esteem would be much higher. As it is, they are doing a great deal of good work but forgetting to pick up the paycheck—the paycheck of self-esteem.

The meditative practice of self-esteem is designed to reverse this situation, by blessing the good achievements we have made and the skills of consciousness we have acquired. In addition, it gives the personality an opportunity to recognize more completely that the higher self is the source of our ultimate strength and contains the power we need for self-expression. It improves our self-image.

This technique is also very powerful in overcoming the negative effects of criticism—especially self-criticism and self-condemnation. We all make mistakes from time to time, but it is vital to keep a healthy balance on our score sheet of success and failure. *It is absurd to think that anyone is ever a total failure;* we all manage to do some things well and successfully, even if they are only simple acts of self-sufficiency and personal affection. Whatever we do well is the basis for building our self-esteem.

Therefore, we should take the time to review the good things we have done—help we have extended, projects we have contributed to, kindness we have projected. They may be great, they may be almost trivial, but these are the achievements of daily life which make us feel rightfully proud. Then, as we review them, we should meditatively bless each one of these achievements.

Blessing is more than feeling good about what we have done. It is the act of radiating goodwill and joy into the whole of our being, in recognition of the significance of these worthwhile achievements. By blessing our legitimate achievements, great and small, we add new life to our good habits and thoughts, we boost our self-esteem, and we affirm our general usefulness in life.

In addition, we should also remind ourself of the talents and qualities of consciousness which helped us in performing these good works. We should be thankful for these skills and strengths, and for the support of the higher self, and bless them so that they, too, become charged with the energy of our self-esteem. Just as the technique of self-respect protects our basic identity and our ideals, so also the practice of self-esteem becomes the armor which protects us from the negativity in which we may have to live or work from time to time.

It is unfortunate that many people seem to rely on hostility, sarcasm, indifference, rudeness, prejudice, or bigotry in order to protect their values and their way of life. These defense mechanisms do work, at least to a certain degree, but the price we pay in setting up these shields is enormous. We lose the most valuable parts of our humanity. Self-esteem, by contrast, helps protect us against the adverse conditions of life while strengthening the best within us.

The meditative technique for the practice of self-esteem includes the following steps:

1. We begin by entering the meditative state and contacting the higher self as described in chapter five.

2. We *review* a number of achievements, recent or remote, which we know to be worthwhile. These do not have to be spectacular; they can be simple events, such as keeping our temper under control when provoked, living up to commitments we have made to the higher self, or making valuable contributions to a project at work.

3. We *approve* of these achievements, knowing they have helped us bring some of the light and power of the higher self into manifestation on earth. They are therefore worthy of approval—and every part of the personality which has helped in accomplishing these good things deserves our gratitude.

4. We *bless* these achievements, by radiating our goodwill and joy into the whole of the personality. This blessing flows from the higher self into the personality as we continue to concentrate on it.

5. We then reflect on the talents and qualities we had to mobilize in order to make these achievements. Before we could make these good contributions, we had to be a good person in some way, and we should recognize it—and bless these skills and strengths as well as the achievement itself.

As with the technique of self-respect, it is important to take enough time in meditation to perform this exercise properly, thinking each step through carefully. Our achievements are one of the most important assets we have, and they deserve proper attention.

They deserve to be approved.

VISUALIZING AN IMAGE

It is also possible meditatively to create a mental image which symbolically represents our ideal self-image. In doing this, however, it is important to understand that the image itself is not nearly as important as the values, the attitudes, and the ideals we associate with it. If we cannot approve of ourself or respect ourself, creating a flashy visualization will do little to help us. This may come as a shock to those people who believe in the total power of visualizations and mental imagery, but it is just common sense.

The value of creating a specific image for ourself is that it can help remind us of the need for self-respect and self-esteem. It can remind us of the values we hold and our intention to act in certain ways. At times, the higher self may even be able to use such a symbol to jog our memories and not allow ourself to be overwhelmed by imperfection or negativity.

In creating a symbol for our healthy self-image, we must take care not to dip into the fantasy department of our subconscious or of mass consciousness as a whole. It might please us to think of ourself as Superman or Wonder Woman, but such an image is not likely to remind us of our responsibility to practice self-respect and self-esteem. It is more likely just to space us out in a fantasy we cannot fulfill, thereby serving to injure our self-esteem, not increase it.

Instead, we should draw our visualization from such basic themes as the doctor-teacher-parent within us. An excellent image, for example, is that of the loving son or daughter of God, possessing a rich heritage and blessed by wealth and intelligence. Appropriate images can also be drawn from scriptural sources, such as the Good Samaritan, but the most serviceable images are usually those we create for ourself. This is done by visualizing ourself acting in ordinary circumstances of our life, but imbued with certain qualities of the higher self, as appropriate—great courage, a deep compassion, a strong faith, or inspired wisdom. Such a visualization can be quite specific, and the more often we call it to mind, the stronger it becomes in consciousness. In this way, we join the commonplace—our ordinary circumstances of life—with the noble—the qualities of the higher self.

Regardless of the image chosen, it should always be carefully linked with the power of the higher self—not the whims and urges of our wish life.

A KEY TO SUCCESS

Every time we attempt to think and act as the higher self would have us think and act, we strengthen our self-image. Every time we consult our higher self for guidance on how to view some situation of life, past, present, or future, we add to the quality of our self-image. Every time we rise above the pettiness and negativity of our personality and impose our higher life on our attitudes and habits, we reinforce our self-esteem.

There will always be aspects of our personal life that cannot be changed. Tragedy, accidents, and misfortune come into the life of everyone. Some events which seem to be tragic eventually turn out well; others do not have a happy ending. But the person endowed with a healthy self-image has the advantage of a good relationship with the higher self. He has the strength of self-esteem to protect him from the pain of adversity and the common sense to make sure that defeat or failure does not become a roadblock. He will recover from such circumstances by calling on his optimism and resourcefulness to initiate new projects and explore new possibilities.

It is a little known but true fact that successful people generally experience even *more* defeat than unsuccessful people—because they are oriented toward trying more and doing more. They simply know how to handle the setbacks and criticism they encounter, and are therefore able to press forward until they do succeed. Lack of success is caused more by our own reaction to failure than it is by the failure itself.

A LINK TO HEAVEN

Creating a healthy self-image is the first step in establishing a full partnership with the higher self. It is unfortunate that many good people assume that they are supposed to think of themselves as inferior in the presence of their higher self. Mass consciousness has been terribly infected by an overdose of contrition; anything we can do to improve our self-image will in turn contribute to the healing of this problem in humanity as a whole. And it is a problem—a most undesirable one, both spiritually and psychologically. We need to realize, as it is stated in the essay "Inspired Humility" from *The Art of Living, Volume III:*

"We are a divine creation, designed to become perfect even as our Father in heaven is perfect. We must therefore not deny our worth, or grovel in unwholesome contrition, or quail at the thought of our imperfections. There is no doubt that the personality makes mistakes from time to time; it is a necessary part of evolution. But even though the personality is not yet perfect, there is a part of us which is! There is a part of us, the higher self, which is awesome in its talent, love, compassion, and wisdom. Our duty as a human being is to put on our 'robe without any seams' and express our innate love, compassion, talent, and wisdom in every department of life. We are called to act with inspired humility.

"The robe without any seams is a marvelous garment. It fills us with reverence for the presence of divine life wherever we may encounter it—in others, nature, the affairs of nations, the work of civilization, and all noble endeavors. It motivates us to engage our personality in the active expression of the very best elements within us. The more we wear it, and honor its purpose, the more we evolve into the kind of person who is *able* to contribute creatively to humanity and civilization, through our genius, love, and patient understanding."

A healthy self-image allows us to mirror the ideal strengths and qualities of the higher self in our personality. It helps us correct that which is improper, and also provides a basis for noble achievement and success. This kind of self-image becomes a vital part of the basic mechanism we need in order to enable our spiritual nature to triumph over our negativity, peevishness, and ignorance. It is a basic ingredient in the work of *practical transcendence.*

Transcendence does not occur by becoming so indifferent to the needs of the personality that we simply float to heaven and drift on out to the stars. It occurs in practical ways, as we patiently lift the lower elements of our nature into rapport with the higher elements, cleanse them, and then set them to work.

In this sense, the healthy self-image becomes a permanent part of our human nature which never leaves the grace and love of our higher self, even in the midst of the most unfavorable circumstances. It becomes an actual link to heaven, which helps us preserve the sanctity and purity of our highest talents, attitudes, and values.

A healthy self-image is our way of revealing heaven in the way we act and think and feel.

THE TECHNIQUES
FOR ESTABLISHING A HEALTHY SELF-IMAGE

The three techniques for establishing a healthy self-image can be summarized as follows:

Cultivating Self-Respect

1. We enter the meditative state and make contact with the higher self, as described in chapter five.

2. We affirm our worthiness as an individual who is seeking to be a noble person and do the right thing.

3. We affirm the value of the major roles we play in life.

4. We affirm our interest in nurturing various qualities of the human spirit in our daily life.

Cultivating Self-Esteem

1. We enter the meditative state.

2. We review a number of achievements which we know to be worthwhile.

3. We approve of these achievements and are thankful for the contributions made by every aspect of the personality in achieving them.

4. We bless these achievements and the contributions of our personality.

5. We reflect on the fact that these worthwhile achievements and contributions have enriched the value of our life.

Visualizing An Image

1. Having completed the work of cultivating self-respect and self-esteem for one phase of our life, we use the skill of visualization to create a mental symbol which will represent our ideal self-image. The image can be based on literary or religious sources, or our own rich associations.

2. The symbol should be active. In other words, we visualize ourself acting in ordinary circumstances of life, but imbued with specific qualities of the higher self.

3. We charge the symbol with the power of the higher self.

8

Defining Values
And Goals

A STABLE STRUCTURE IN CONSCIOUSNESS

One of the great tragedies, both in meditation and in daily living, occurs when people embark on noble endeavors without the capacity to complete them. It happens in meditation when we resolve to change a bad habit into something more enlightened, but then succumb to internal resistance. It happens in daily living when we make certain promises and commitments, only to be overcome by frustration and opposition. We call upon our inner strength, but cannot harness or sustain it. And so the opportunity slips away.

Some people think that the only key to tapping their inner strength is to believe in it—or hold an affirmation of great power in their mind. Yet a belief in tolerance is usually not enough to enable us to confront strident criticism with dignity and forgiveness. The "strength" of an affirmation that all will work out well may wither in the face of opposition. What belief and affirmations do not give us is a stable structure in consciousness from which to act.

They give us hope, but not direction.

They give us a sense of comfort, but not stability.

They give us confidence, but not the power to act.

Yet if belief and affirmations do not give us a stable structure in consciousness, what does? What gives us the ability to master internal resistance and persevere against great odds?

A combination of things—the purpose of the higher self and the values and goals of the personality. By harnessing the purpose of the higher self and translating it into a system of noble values and goals, we organize our character with structure, stability, and direction.

This is a matter of common sense. The person who knows what he stands for and has carefully organized his talents and ideals in the pursuit of specific goals makes a valuable partner for the higher self. It is through such a personality that the higher self can achieve meaningful expression on earth. And so, the greater responds to the readiness of the lesser by flooding it with a proper measure of the power and the intelligence to act.

Unfortunately, not all people are ready to act in harmony with the higher self. They may have a sense of direction, but it is not the direction of the higher self. They may have a measure of organization, but it serves only to preserve the status quo—not the noble purpose of the higher self. In fact, the majority of people are much more aware of what they do *not* want than what they do. They spend the bulk of their time fighting off that which they hope to avoid, rather than defining the contributions they hope to make to society or the ways they could express their inner potential. When at work or in a public place, they are more concerned with what others think about them than with making intelligent decisions which will honor the wisdom of the higher self. They subscribe to values which will be approved by others—and goals which have been structured by their peer group. As a result, they do not have access to the life of spirit within them. They must derive all of *their* direction from the approval of others and the goals of their peer group.

Such people have very little stability. Because they are primarily concerned with the opinions of mass consciousness and the approval of others, they are easily swayed by the criticism, advice, or opposition of friends, neighbors, and colleagues. They are often uncertain about where they stand in life, what they ought to be doing, or how they should behave. They are accustomed to having others tell them what they ought to do, directly or indirectly, and therefore have not made the effort to define their values and goals. They lack a consistent set of purposes for living. Their focus is diffused, which means that life is frequently confusing to them. Consequently, they miss many opportunities for achievement and success and waste much time on activities which are neither constructive nor productive.

Quite often, these are good people who truly want to be the right person and do the right thing. But they do not know how to go about it; they are not linked with the genuine resources of direction, stability, and power within themselves. They seek these stabilizing qualities instead from others and from society. And yet, they cannot find them there. So they slowly become frustrated by their failure to achieve.

Some adjust to this frustration by immuring themselves in a state of resignation, deciding it is not possible to achieve more than they have, and so they must be satisfied with it. Others, more resentful, grouch and complain, blaming those who have held them back—and society itself. The most pessimistic conclude that their empty life is the result of exploitation and oppression by others—primarily those who *have* achieved success. They find a kind of destructive power in anger, and set about protesting and attacking whoever appears to be the greatest villain. They still have not achieved anything, but they have learned to be obnoxious, and this gives them a certain tawdry satisfaction. And yet, not even that is always enough. Some become predators, believing that the only way they can get what they want is by stealing it.

In each of these cases, the real problem is a simple one. These people have not taken the time to find and harness the power of enlightened purpose. They have not defined the values which would give them structure, or if they have, they have not honored them. They have not defined the goals they seek to achieve, or if they have, they have not worked persistently toward them. They may be angry at the immorality of others, but anger toward the lack of virtue is no value. They may have dreamed of what they want—but a dream is a wish, not an intelligent goal. Anger and dreams cannot link us with the power of the higher self.

It must be understood that the higher self does not idly dream about the future, about what might be nice to attain. It has a clear understanding of its purpose and a clear definition of its destiny or goals. It knows whither it is going and what it needs to accomplish. The time schedule for these achievements is somewhat flexible, as it depends on the cooperation of the personality, but the purpose and destiny are *not* variable. They are clearly laid out.

If we coordinate our efforts, both in meditation and in daily living, with the purpose of the higher self, we will establish an enlightened structure of direction, stability, and power. But this means aligning ourself with something greater than our dreams, fantasies, and emotions.

To build this enlightened structure, we must carefully define our values and goals.

UNABLE TO GROW

The need for this definition is clearly illustrated by the plight of the typical married couple. In our society, marriage is set forth as the fulfillment of fairy tales and fantasies. A strong romantic feeling for one another is considered an ideal base for marrying. To make it even more appealing, this strong emotional reaction is labeled "love"—which it is not—and is credited with the power "to conquer all" in popular songs, movies, cheap paperback romances, and television.

In spite of all the hype, however, the emotional reactiveness of physical passion notoriously does *not* have the power to conquer all. Once the sensations of fun and bliss, which are all the average person expects out of marriage, wear thin, and the husband and wife begin to confront real problems, most have little understanding of why they *are* married. They are unsure of their purpose for being together, and do not have a strong sense of either values or goals for their marriage. Vainly, they try to put the "magic" back into their marriage—but they have no idea what the magic is.

There will be some who will instantly cry foul—that such a description of marriage is unromantic. But true romance is not found in passion and emotional reactiveness. It springs from the capacity of a man and a woman to share in mutual endeavors, to help each other grow, to create an enlightened home environment, and to make a healthy contribution to community and society. It should be an expression of maturity, not immaturity.

Unfortunately, immaturity is one of the most prevailing problems in humanity. It is, of course, natural for all of us to have weaknesses and deficiencies—but it is *not* natural to glorify adolescent values and goals and pretend they are adult. We are meant to grow into greater maturity, to cooperate with the parent within and help it take care of the child within, so that we more rapidly leave our childish ways behind.

If we are the kind of person who listens only to his feelings in deciding what to do in life, however, we will not be able to grow. We will remain in a state of perpetual adolescence, psychologically. We may mean well, but the ideals we claim to follow become tarnished by our intense desire for immediate gratification and pleasant sensation—or the desire to avoid the opposite. The only power we have to pursue achievement and sustain our efforts is desire. And while desire is generally quite enough to get us launched in activities and relationships, it is seldom enough to see us through to successful completion.

The inadequacy of desire is that it breaks down in the face of stress, conflict, and frustration. Romantic passion, after all, is known to disintegrate into petty accusations once the character flaws of husband and wife begin to grate on each other. Unless there is some sense of value and purpose beyond the desire to be with each other, the marriage will not endure that stress. The same pattern is repeated in any endeavor motivated and sustained by desire.

If we have properly defined our values and goals, however, and thereby linked ourself with the higher self's power of self-expression, the times of stress and conflict will not be excessively difficult. We will be well prepared to meet them, and will use these occasions to reinforce our capacity to act with our inner power. This principle is well demonstrated in the life of Sir Winston Churchill, who was one of the few people in England who had anticipated the threat of Hitler and had clearly defined how England should respond to it. As everyone else panicked in the aftermath of the failure of appeasement, unsure of what to do next, Churchill stepped boldly to the front, able to act dynamically and effectively—and lead England to its finest hour.

An individual's inability to handle challenge, conflict, and responsibility becomes a grave limitation restricting the unfoldment of the plans of the higher self. It means that the person is unable to channel the power of self-expression effectively, and this affects the whole scope of his performance in life.

The crippling effect of this limitation on self-expression can be compared to the restricted conditions which arise during a natural disaster. When an earthquake strikes, for example, the devastation it produces is often tremendous. There is a desperate need among the survivors for food, clothing, shelter, medical aid, and funds for rebuilding. Generally, there is a massive outpouring from other sectors of the world to meet these needs, but the aid does not always reach the stricken area. The ordinary lines of communication and most transportation routes have been greatly disrupted, making it very difficult to transmit the needed resources to those who could use them.

We limit ourself in much the same way when we fail to define our values and goals properly. When crisis strikes, the established lines of support—which run to our emotions and desires—are disrupted. The higher self has the direction, stability, and power we need, but we cannot tap them. We become a victim of our own failure to be ready to act.

STABILIZING FORCES IN CONSCIOUSNESS

A readiness to act is not a gift of serendipity; it is the result of careful reflection upon our values and goals. This reflection, properly handled, links us with the will to act of the higher self, so it can be summoned and employed at a moment's notice—even during crisis.

Our **values** are what we stand for, the principles we guide our life by. Anything we might readily abandon as a matter of expediency, convenience, or compromise in the face of pressure is not a value. A value can never be something we merely wish for or hope to avoid. It is much more than that; a value is an idea, commitment, promise, or principle we have chosen to cherish and cultivate. We are willing to work for, fight for, and defend a genuine value.

An example of an enlightened value would be a high regard for integrity and personal honor, so strong that we cannot be corrupted by any offer of money, position, advancement, fame, or personal favors. Another would be a commitment to helping and encouraging our children to grow into intelligent, compassionate, and ethical adults, so strong that we do not hesitate to make meaningful sacrifices when circumstances call for them. A third might be such a deep awareness of the benefits of spiritual service that we do not allow personal desires and frustrations to divert us from offering the help we can give.

The power of such values is that they stabilize our state of mind and feeling from day to day. Having carefully defined our value of integrity, for example, we know how we intend to act when confronted with temptation and corruption. We do not have to weigh the options at that point; our respect for our personal honor is so great it cannot be weakened.

Many people experience substantial conflict because they have not defined their values—or placed them in a meaningful hierarchy. If helping their children conflicts with something they want to do, they are caught in a terrible dilemma. But the person who has already defined his or her commitment to helping the children grow, and places great value in it, has little trouble in "sacrificing" personal desire.

Obviously, the more a value reflects and embodies the wisdom and light of the higher self, the more useful it is. Values derived solely from the experiences and beliefs of the personality are transitory at best; eventually, we will grow out of them. Therefore, they are limited in their usefulness as a stabilizing force in consciousness. But values based on the qualities and principles of the higher self will be permanent; we grow *into* them, as we discover more about them.

Our **goals** are what we hope to achieve, the specific objectives we strive toward in personal growth, work, self-understanding, service, relationships, and responsibility. Like values, the noblest goals are those derived from the purpose and destiny of the higher self. Our goals should therefore be defined in terms of our intention to *contribute* to life, rather than our desire to *consume* more of life. This is just a matter of common sense. If our goals are defined in terms of amassing more money, inducing others to do our work for us, or establishing that society owes us certain "rights," they will orient us toward the pursuit of material satisfaction, not enlightenment. Such goals are built on consuming life, not enriching it. In the short term, they may seem attractive, but in the longer perspective, they will undermine our self-expression. By contrast, if our goals are defined in a context of making a more intelligent or powerful contribution to life, to improve the quality of our community, environment, and civilization, they will stabilize us in the life of the higher self.

The function of our goals is to give direction to our day-to-day activities. Without goals, we tend to wander aimlessly through life, accomplishing very little. With unenlightened goals we will accomplish more, but much of it may be counter-productive. Spurred on by enlightened goals, however, we will be able to move forward in life in harmony with the basic purpose and destiny of the higher self.

Goals are not the same as purpose—purpose is the general urge or power to do something, whereas a goal is the objective which will be reached by harnessing that impulse—but they are a necessary part of the activity of establishing a structure of direction, stability, and power in our consciousness. They insure that the power of the higher self will be used properly, and not diverted into meaningless activity.

Some people, of course, decry goals and denounce them as "mechanistic." They believe that goals are traps which grossly limit our creativity, sensitivity, and enjoyment of life. Instead of setting goals, they emphasize the moment-to-moment experience of being human. But what these people need to realize is that goals are not antithetical to the quality of human life. Enlightened goals, based on enlightened values, provide a *structure* in which we can express our human qualities. This structure is never a simplistic focus on a single goal; rather, it is a rich and multidimensional hierarchy of many different goals, embracing every level of life. Some of these goals pertain to work, some to creativity, others to relationships and our self-fulfillment. *Together*, they give our consciousness a holistic structure for thinking, planning, feeling, and acting.

Our values and goals are the tools we use to manage power, coordinate the activities of our life, and sustain useful work. They are a necessary part of our humanity.

ASKING QUESTIONS

The ideal time for defining values and goals, of course, is during meditation. While using the techniques and principles of Active Meditation, it is much easier to understand the purpose and destiny of the higher self upon which our values and goals ought to be based. In addition, it is also far easier to energize them while in meditation, so that they become legitimate channels for the power of our will to act.

This work will utilize a number of meditative skills, the most fundamental being our capacity to invoke spiritual ideals. This can be done by posing questions to be answered. In determining our values in life, for example, the primary question might be: "What kind of character do I want to build?" In defining our goals, the primary question could be: "What do I want to accomplish with my life?" Our intention is not to answer these questions as the average person in the street would answer them, but rather *in the context of our spiritual ideals.* The process of answering them ought to include a review of our experiences in life, what has worked for us and what has not, our beliefs and aspirations, our intentions, and our highest inspirations.

Some people, however, have trouble asking and answering such abstract questions in meditation. It is therefore helpful to enrich this process with the meditative skill of personification. In this case, it is the wisdom of the higher self we wish to personify, so we can more easily contact it for the answers we seek. An excellent way to achieve this result is to personify the wisdom of the higher self as a very wise counselor with whom we can consult, ask specific questions, and obtain helpful answers.

In working with such a personification, it is important to keep in mind that not every random thought which passes through our awareness is necessarily a message from the higher self. It is possible to color personifications with our wish life—or just the desire for spectacular results. But if we are working in a meditative state with the focused intention to tap the guidance of our higher self, then the majority of impressions which arise within us will probably be helpful. In sorting out the impressions which do arise, common sense will be our best guide.

It is easy to work with the personification of the wise counselor; we simply ask the basic question we have in mind, pause for an answer, and then follow up with as many secondary questions as are appropriate, until we have obtained the new understanding we seek. The wise counselor will not initiate this process for us; we must be willing to take charge and ask questions and pursue hints. But if we are, a good flow of ideas will develop, in the form of mental impressions, images, flashes of insight, or possibly even conversation.

DEFINING VALUES

The key question for defining values is: "What kind of character do I want to build?" As we ask this question, it will lead us to pose other questions about how we want to behave and our attitudes toward various responsibilities in life. A partial list of these subsidiary questions, by no means complete, would include:

How do I want to respond to opportunities for growth?

What should be my attitude toward authority? How should I respond to people in positions of authority? How should I respond to different sources of authority—male, female, older people, younger people, traditions, government, and the higher self?

What should be my ideal response to failure?

What should be my ideal response to criticism?

What should be my ideal response to discouragement?

How should I respond to the temptation to cheat, tell white lies, or take advantage of the naiveté of others?

What qualities of consciousness do I cherish and want to increase?

What weaknesses of character do I need to correct? What priority or importance do I give to correcting them?

What should be my attitude toward people I work with?

What should be my ideal response to the attempt of others to force me to accept their values and beliefs?

How do I view the commitments, promises, and pledges I have made?

For this process to be worthwhile, we must answer these questions in the context of our own life experience. It is not enough just to think abstractly about our attitudes toward authority and cooperation; we must also consider our actual behavior toward supervisors and colleagues. Nor is it enough to blithely "accept responsibility," unless we are also willing to make binding commitments—either to ourself or to others—and follow through on them.

A modest amount of effort to review our values and attitudes in this way will reveal dozens of insights into the nature of our character and help us see more clearly what we need to strengthen, as well as what is crying out for revision. We will also begin to see the need to relate each of our values to all of the others, thereby creating a hierarchical structure which enables us to deal consistently with complex issues.

The object of this kind of review in meditation, however, is not to dig at old emotional wounds in a frenzy of self-condemnation. This is never healthy. Nor is it our purpose to wallow in guilt or remorse, although it is possible that we may occasionally touch the fringes of such feelings. Our intent, in all cases, should be to define *the ideal qualities which should be in charge of our self-expression.*

DEFINING GOALS

The primary question for defining goals is: "What do I want to accomplish with my life?" Pursuing this question in meditation will naturally prompt a number of others, which should also be carefully examined in conference with the wise counselor, who embodies the wisdom of the higher self. Some of these questions would be:

What contributions do I want to make in my life—and in what priority?

What are the best ways to honor my skills, talents, abilities, and inspirations through active self-expression?

How can I do this through my work?

How can I do this through my relationships?

How can I do this through my growth as a human being?

In what ways do I want to help others?

What are the most important projects I am involved in? How well am I expressing this priority?

What am I looking for in terms of emotional fulfillment? How do I define that?

How do I define physical comfort and security? What priority does this have in my life?

Invariably, this kind of review leads us to a consideration of unfinished business, half-filled dreams, and partly completed projects. When reasonable, we may decide that it is proper to revive the interest we once had in some of these projects. At the same time, we are likely to come up with some new ideas. Regardless of the type of idea being considered, we should make sure that it is consistent with the fundamental direction of our life before committing a fresh measure of enthusiasm, time, and energy. This is not the time to be seduced by enticing ideas which are actually digressions from our basic purpose.

While it is never easy to be objective about our life and

work, the more frequently we reflect on our goals in this manner, the more we will improve our ability to define our major objectives without serious distortion. As a result, we will become more adept in expressing the purpose of the higher self in all that we do.

IN THE DARK

It is not enough, however, just to define our values and goals; we must also add strength to them—the direction, stability, and power of the higher self. Otherwise, our values and goals will simply remain at the level of personal desires and aspirations. We will aspire to be honest, helpful, and kind, but not have the power to be honest, helpful, and kind. We must therefore *energize* our intention to act.

Some people have a difficult time understanding the distinction between desires and intentions. A desire is an emotional craving to acquire or avoid some condition or object. An intention, by contrast, springs from the will-to-act of the higher self; it is the basic power or impulse of enlightened self-expression. It is through our intentions that we tap and channel the power of purpose.

Harnessing the power of our higher self can be compared to the generation and distribution of electricity. It is only recently that mankind has begun to generate and use electricity, even though it has been in existence since the dawn of creation. Until we found practical ways to generate and distribute electricity, we could not tap its enormous power, even though there were sources of electricity all around us. We were in the dark.

Much the same can be observed in human self-expression. Tremendous resources of power are available to every human being, but very few people have learned to tap them, and even fewer have mastered the expression of this power. The majority of people are still in the dark, but this does not mean that the power is imaginary. It is quite real. It is our own failure to develop proper values and goals and charge them with the intention to act which prevents us from using this great power.

The higher self is the generator of our power.

The only way this power can flow into the personality is in tandem with the higher self's purpose. Power and purpose are linked together as inseparably as the voltage and amperage of electrical current. To tap this power, therefore, we must act, think, and feel in harmony with the purpose of the higher self.

Purpose can be translated into the personality through the medium of values and goals. These values and goals would correspond to electrical motors, appliances, and light bulbs.

The wires which connect these "motors" and "appliances" to the generator would be our own dedication and intention.

When the whole system is complete, the power which can be expressed through the personality is tremendous.

THE INTENTION TO ACT

The meditative skill which is most effective in charging our intention to act in harmony with our values and goals is the use of seed thoughts. In this case, the seed thought represents the basic purpose of the value or goal, and our capacity to express it wisely.

Any value or goal can be energized in this way. If, for example, we have been reviewing a lifelong tendency to procrastinate and miss opportunities, we obviously need to put a higher priority on the value of acting with efficiency and diligence, and the goal of taking greater initiative in life. To charge our capacity to fulfill these intentions, we then meditatively reflect on a seed thought which captures the essence of our intention and the ability of the higher self to support our new endeavor. *We do not dwell on the problem of procrastination, however!* That would be using the seed thought to energize the wrong thing. Instead, we dwell on our intention to work and act diligently in all that we do—to work with perseverance and thoroughness, starting our tasks promptly and completing them quickly. Examples of seed thoughts which would serve this purpose would be:

"The readiness to act."

"Enthusiasm for timely action."

"I do my work with thoroughness."

In working with these seed thoughts, we hold the expectation that the higher self is supporting us with the perfect measure of power and strength we need. We hold this thought with trust in the benevolent power of the higher self and knowledge of the fact that it truly *is* our partner in our efforts to improve and strengthen our values, goals, and intention to act.

By holding our attention on this seed thought for a minute or two meditatively, we charge the battery of our ability to act in these new ways, without procrastinating. We are literally adding to our subconscious the power we need to implement our ideals and values.

It is important to stay mentally active during this process of dwelling on the seed thought. There is a great temptation at times just to casually dream about being successful, instead of actually energizing our intention to act. Some people may also fall into the habit of fantasizing or visualizing the intended result. But looking at an image of success is not the same as energizing our *dedication* to expressing ourself in an enlightened, mature way!

In working to energize our intention to act, we must keep in mind that this stage of the meditative work is no time to battle the negative. We must keep our concentration focused on the constructive value or goal we are seeking to establish.

CHANNELS FOR GROWTH

The work of defining and energizing our values and goals is an important part of integrating the higher self and the personality. The definition of values and goals is not a technique which needs to be repeated every day, but the process of energizing them should become a regular habit in our program of self-development. As we put these skills to work, we build a more powerful character. We attain a better definition of what we stand for and where we are heading in life.

Esoterically, as we work with invoking and defining a sense of purpose, we create channels for our own growth. We tap the will-to-life of the higher self and establish lines of force between this source of power and our self-expression. In this way, we prepare ourself to receive and contain more of the tremendous power of our higher self.

We tap the abundance of life.

THE TECHNIQUES
FOR DEFINING VALUES AND GOALS

The three techniques for defining our values, defining our goals, and charging our intention to honor these values and goals in our daily self-expression can be summarized as follows for easy reference:

Defining Values

1. We begin by entering the meditative state and contacting the higher self, as described in chapter five.

2. We focus our attention on the wisdom of our higher self, personifying it as a wise counselor we can question.

3. Asking ourself the basic question, "What kind of character do I want to build," we explore the nature of our spiritual ideals and how we intend to express them through our be-

havior, thoughts, commitments, duties, and responsibilities.

4. This meditation should be repeated periodically, with a record kept of the results.

Defining Goals

1. We begin by entering the meditative state and contacting the higher self.

2. We focus our attention on the wisdom of our higher self, personifying it as a wise counselor we can question.

3. Asking ourself the basic question, "What do I want to accomplish in life," we explore the trends and directions of our life, looking for insights into how we can add greater meaning, talent, and productivity to our activities, by defining more enlightened goals. The goals we set should honor the purpose of our higher self and its will-to-life.

4. This meditation should be repeated periodically, with a record kept of the results.

Charging Values and Goals With Power

1. We begin by entering the meditative state and contacting the higher self.

2. Selecting a value or goal we wish to energize, we rest briefly in the faith and trust that the higher self has the perfect measure of power to support us in our efforts to express it.

3. We then use the meditative skill of working with a seed thought, which we activate by concentrating on our *intention* (not just our desire or thought) to express the particular value or attain the particular goal we have in mind.

4. This concentration is held for a minute or two, with the expectation that the purpose of the higher self is being embodied in this value or goal. As we concentrate on this seed thought, we should be aware that the higher self is a senior partner working with us, both in meditation and in daily life.

9

Mental Housecleaning

OUR MENTAL HOUSEHOLD

As people begin exploring the nature of their consciousness, they often confuse themselves unnecessarily. Being accustomed to thinking in terms of objects and things, they encounter difficulty in fitting together all the invisible and somewhat abstract "pieces" of consciousness. They would like a picture or map which would clearly show the relationship of values, ideals, self-image, the higher self, the subconscious, the unconscious, thoughts, emotions, and habits. Not having such a map, they struggle to make sense of these many elements as best they can.

This confusion can be reduced somewhat by thinking of consciousness as a mental household, a rather large home with many rooms. The inhabitants of this home are our self-image, values, sense of purpose, and talents; it is the sanctuary of the light of the higher self on earth. There is a living room where our conscious thoughts and feelings are expressed, but also many other rooms—a study where we reflect, plan, and formulate our goals; a nursery where we tend our newly-born thought children; a dining room where we take nourishment; and bedrooms where our subconscious and unconscious memories "sleep."

Ideally, this mental household is tastefully decorated with lovely patterns of beauty and joy, and kept in good repair. It is meant to be a stronghold for our heavenly treasures of talent, quality, and inspiration; a haven in the midst of the pressures and stress of daily living. And yet, it is not always easy to keep this mental household in perfect condition. It is not a museum, after all; it is an active center of life. We occasionally track in mud or pile up too much junk in the closet. Old furniture wears out. The contents of the basement become a fire hazard. Appliances break down and must be replaced. From time to time, the whole place needs a fresh coat of paint.

In other words, we get careless in how we treat our mental household. The mud we track in might be elements of crudity and materialism. The junk in the closet could be useless feelings of anger or rage that we feel we need in order to be a "whole person." The old furniture would be worn-out habit patterns which served us well many years ago, but no longer. The contents of the basement would be repressed thoughts and emotions in the subconscious. The broken appliances might be skills and talents we have failed to keep up-to-date. The need for a fresh coat of paint would represent a general condition of immaturity.

If we are aware of the problem of carelessness, and make a regular effort to keep our mental household in good repair, our household in consciousness will serve us well. But if we let conditions slide, we may put our mental household in jeopardy. A closet filled with immature attitudes can seriously befoul the atmosphere of the whole household and distort our self-expression. A materialistic or selfish lifestyle can impair our ability to honor the spiritual destiny of the higher self.

One of the great uses of the techniques of Active Meditation is to help us become more familiar with the mental household in which we live, and to make those renovations which will permanently improve the structure and quality of our consciousness. In this way, we establish effective control over our behavior, character, and reactiveness, thereby setting the stage for a more enriched self-expression.

MENTAL HOUSECLEANING

The process of keeping our mental household in good repair is called, appropriately, "mental housecleaning." It involves recognizing the areas of weakness, imperfection, and deficiency in our character, feelings, and habits, and using the power of the higher self to cleanse and update them—replacing them with something new and better, when this is appropriate.

Underlying the idea of mental housecleaning is the fundamental premise that this is *our* household, and we have a responsibility to act as an intelligent steward or caretaker of it. If we ignore the inevitable problems which arise, we are not taking proper care of our house. If we try to absolve ourself by insisting that the problems which arise are all the fault of someone else, or society, then we are missing a very important point. This is our household. We have it the whole of our life. We cannot move out of it or trade it in for a new one. Nor can we reasonably expect anyone else to come in and do our work of renovation for us. It is our responsibility, our personal domain. So we ought to take good care of it.

The conditions of our mental household directly affect the quality of our life. If we harbor hostility and rage toward others, we will have to live in the squalor of our anger and resentment. Our acquaintances will begin to find it less than pleasant to "visit" our mental household, and we will slowly become a friendless person. If we fill our house with competitiveness and greed, we will have to dwell in the atmosphere of jealousy, suspiciousness, and fear these conditions create. If we are arrogant and rude in dealing with others, we will find that our mental household is under constant attack from without, as people try to tear us down in reprisal for the way we treat them. In such circumstances, it is not rational to expect anyone else to protect us from these psychological assaults; our only protection is to adopt a more wholesome way of living.

By contrast, if we act with integrity in all that we do, even when it is convenient to act otherwise, we will find that our mental household is well lit by the presence of high ideals. If we act with consistency and self-discipline at work, we will discover new talents and skills growing in the "sun room" of our mental household. If we approach life with a basic willingness to grow, we will constantly be finding new rooms in our mental household we did not even know existed—rooms filled with treasure and promise.

Fortunately, very few people have allowed their mental household to become so overrun with laziness, crudity, rage, or selfishness that it is no longer fit to live in. But almost everyone does have a number of problem areas in need of major repair and cleaning, many of which keep reappearing, year after year, always bringing with them fresh issues of frustration and disappointment. To the degree that such chronic disaster areas exist in *our* mental household, they block our better efforts to integrate the higher self and the personality. It is therefore important for any serious student of Active Meditation to learn the basic principles of mental housecleaning.

And take broom and dustpan in hand.

INSPECTING THE PREMISES

The first step in effective mental housecleaning is to inspect the premises of our mental household and find out what is there—what is useful and healthy, what is old and worn out, and what is soiled and needs cleaning. It does little good to dust off the basically healthy attributes of our character while ignoring the portable disasters which really need our attention, and then believe that we have been hard at work on mental housecleaning. Self-deception is still self-deception, no matter how noble the intent.

It is not always easy to remain objective while inspecting our own mental household, however, for the very simple reason that we are both the examiner and the examined. Nevertheless, a strong intention to be an ethical person who acts in intelligent ways will protect us from much of the temptation to cover up immaturity and difficulty. The manner in which we pursue our inspection of the premises will also have a great deal to do with the objectivity and usefulness of our findings. If we distort this examination into a witch hunt, in which we are looking for reasons to dislike ourself, we will do more harm than good. Likewise, if we approach it apologetically, always finding some excuse for our behavior, we will not make very much progress.

The recommended way to proceed is to try to determine the *source* of our thoughts, habits, feelings, and memories, *why* we established these patterns in the first place, and whether or not they serve a useful *purpose* at present. By understanding the source of any given pattern of behavior or attitude, we will be able to see whether or not it is actually a pattern of our own creation, something which crept in the back door when we were busy elsewhere, or something which was tracked in by visitors and left behind. By understanding why we accepted or created a pattern of behavior in the first place, we will be better able to judge if this kind of behavior is still serving its intended purpose. We will also come to appreciate that many attitudes, habits, and thoughts which once were quite useful to us have lost their importance over the years, and need to be revised or eliminated.

There are seven major sources of the contents of our mental household. The first three are all of our own making. They are:

Our childhood experiences. At birth, our mental household is virtually a "blank slate," empty of any significant personality patterns, attitudes, or habits. Almost immediately, however, we begin to construct the foundation of our character, modeling ourself on the examples of our parents, siblings, and anyone else who is close to us during our early childhood. What we experience as a child, and how we respond to it, therefore, becomes one of the main sources of the contents of our personal household as an adult.

In order to put our childhood experiences in a proper perspective, however, it is important to remember that childhood is a time of immaturity and naiveté. As a child, we were prone to misunderstand the full implications of what we were told or what was happening to us. As a child, we did not have the intelligence, competence, or independence to choose our responses to life with wisdom or self-discipline. Consequently, habits, attitudes, beliefs, convictions, and feelings which have been left intact since childhood may no longer be appropriate. As an adult, we need maturity, self-reliance, and a sense of responsibility in order to fully meet the opportunities and challenges which come to us. If we are still clinging to childish preferences, immature reactions, and infantile grudges, we are not satisfactorily honoring the adult within us. We are playing the games of children.

While most adults have revised a substantial portion of their childhood programming, there is frequently an amazing amount of childish nonsense which the average person has not touched. It can be found in the tendency to fantasize, to make and break commitments lightly, to be excessively oriented toward seeking pleasure, to want to avoid work, and to be easily distracted from purpose and goals. As we uncover these residual influences of our childhood experiences, it is important to update them and replace them with more mature patterns of behavior. One never becomes an adult by clinging to the child within him.

Our adult experiences. Every adult has tasted a wide range of experience, some pleasant, some unpleasant; some helpful, some frightening; some educational, some frivolous. Many of these experiences have had a powerful impact on our attitudes, habits, beliefs, convictions, and behavior. In some instances, this impact has been constructive, helping us to grow and stretch our humanity to greater dimensions. In other cases, however, it has undermined our self-esteem and blunted our enthusiasm for living. We may have even become embittered.

Often, the changes in attitude and behavior which we make in the aftermath of a certain experience make sense only in the narrow context of that one event—not in the context of our whole life. As we become aware of such cases, it is important to restore a proper sense of balance, so that we do not let any one circumstance or experience cripple the rest of our self-expression—or block out the light of the higher self.

Our hopes, speculations, and dreams about ourself and our life. We tend to spend a lot of time ruminating on what has been, what might have been, and what may yet be. Sometimes, this is time well spent, as we review the past and our prospects and define more enlightened ways to act. Much of the time, however, it is just idle speculation. We worry that events are not unfolding as they should be. We imagine all manner of terrible things to fear. We fantasize ourself in completely illusory circumstances. Often, this dream world becomes a more powerful influence on our thinking and behavior than even the experiences of daily life. As a result, we become obsessed with certain pet theories or ideas, or paralyzed by certain private demons. Obviously, such influences on our attitudes and behavior are not healthy. As we encounter them, we need to dispel them with common sense.

Each of these three categories represents mental furnishings and goods which are our own to keep or discard. We have "bought them and taken them home," and so they have become our full responsibility. If in reviewing them we discover they are no longer useful, then it is up to us to replace them with something better. This is the essence of mental housecleaning.

The next two categories are from sources not of our own making. As such, they will have to be handled somewhat differently than those goods and contents which are truly ours.

These two categories are:

The thoughts and feelings of people we have known. No man is an island unto himself. All of us are constantly influenced by the habits, attitudes, prejudices, and beliefs of the people we associate with. Sometimes this influence is direct, as in the case of an employee who adopts the philosophy and work habits of a supervisor he admires—or another employee who rejects the philosophy and work habits of a supervisor he despises. At other times, it is indirect, as in the case of being subtly influenced by the negative, pessimistic attitudes of people we happen to be around a great deal. A surprising amount of our thoughts, feelings, and beliefs is shaped by this kind of "osmosis"—and it must be understood that it is a very pervasive influence, extending even beyond the range of our physical contacts with people. The psychic influence of the thoughts, feelings, and attitudes of others upon us can be as powerful as the physical influence—sometimes even more so.

The problem with recognizing these external influences is that they emerge in our own feelings, thoughts, and urges, and *appear to be our very own!* They cannot be recognized and dealt with, therefore, until we have established a coherent "baseline" which represents our personal attitudes, convictions, beliefs, and habits. Once this baseline is well defined, it becomes possible to monitor the thoughts and feelings which arise in our awareness and spot those which are alien to our normal pattern of behavior. We can also review the patterns of attitude and belief we have accepted in the past, and recognize which ones have been poisoned by others with unpleasant results.

The influences of mass consciousness. Our psychic susceptibility to the influences of other people also repeats itself on a larger scale, as receptivity to the forces of mass consciousness. Mass consciousness is the collective power of thought, feeling, opinion, attitude, and habit in the whole of humanity, and it tends to play a very large role in conditioning the attitudes and behavior of anyone who does not have a well-defined sense of individuality, a good self-image, or a mature, thoughtful mind. The person who finds it easiest just "to go with the flow," for example, is like a bobber floating in the sea of mass consciousness.

The difficulty of dealing with the influences of mass consciousness becomes especially acute for anyone who is attempting to pull away from the general trend of opinion and behavior in the masses. There are very powerful tendencies toward laziness, immaturity, and intimidation in mass consciousness, and the one who would tame these influences must expect to have them magnified in retaliation for his audacity. Once again, therefore, it is most important to know what our baseline of attitude and values is, so that we will not be confused by the impact of mass consciousness on our mental household.

The final two sources of the contents of our mental household are from deeper levels within ourself—levels we are not normally aware of. They are:

The contents of our unconscious mind. Many people mistakenly assume that the unconscious portions of our being are filled only with repressed memories of unhappy experiences of life—the graveyard of misery and disaster. This is a very unhealthy and incomplete portrayal of the unconscious. In point of fact, there are many levels and departments in the unconscious mind. Some of them do contain repressed memories, but the higher levels serve as repositories for our noblest values, qualities, convictions, talents, and urges. It is in the unconscious mind that the basic *patterns* of our character can be found, both good and bad. The unconscious is designed to keep automatic functions of the personality, such as fully perfected skills and talents, operating smoothly. A musician with "natural" talent, for example, draws on many skills stored at unconscious levels. Unfortunately, some of our well-practiced "skills" can be rather immature, such as the tendencies to be disruptive, rebellious, or the perfect parasite.

For the most part, these patterns and capacities are already present in the unconscious at the time of physical birth, as latent or potential influences which do not become apparent consciously until the personality matures and begins to act and react in life. To become aware of the content of the unconscious, therefore, we must look for attitudes, habits, and patterns of behavior which are part of the very *structure* of our mental household. This is not an easy process, but much can be learned by using the skills of Active Meditation to reflect on the most fundamental core of our character strengths and weaknesses.

The ideals and qualities of the higher self. These should be the most prized possessions of our mental household—the power to heal, the wisdom to solve problems, the compassion to forgive, the strength to act with courage, the power of inspiration, and the benevolence to act with kindness and charity. These qualities represent our ideal way of thinking, feeling, and acting in any circumstance. As such, they should be thought of as fine jewelry and elegant *objets d'art*. Unfortunately, many people do not handle these ideals and qualities with quite this level of respect. Instead of putting them on display for everyone to see and enjoy, they hide them in a closet and replace them with the paste jewelry of religious righteousness, self-importance, and illusions. In fact, they are often most uncomfortable and edgy in the presence of genuine spiritual ideals, because their ordinary ways of thinking and acting are so gravely out of harmony with them, In some cases, of course, these treasures have not even been discovered.

The purpose of mental housecleaning is to harmonize our household of attitudes, memories, habits, and feelings, so that the ideals and qualities of the higher self can be expressed without serious distortion—consciously, subconsciously, and unconsciously. Our goal is *not* to make the subconscious blank and start all over again—which would be impossible, even if we wanted to—but to gently repair the damage that has been done and correct the deficiencies which exist, so that order is restored and the whole of the house is filled with light.

Each of the seven sources of contents in our mental household represents a valuable element of our self-expression. They are meant to serve us well. But we have a responsibility in return—to make a regular habit of inspecting the premises of our awareness for weaknesses and signs of disrepair.

If we do not, we may eventually find that we are carrying with us our own portable disaster. And that would block our efforts to become a better agent of the higher self.

TAKING BROOM IN HAND

Having identified areas of deficiency or distortion in our mental household, we must do something more to get rid of them than just opening the front and back doors and waiting for the wind to blow them out. The wind is far more likely to blow new dust in than it is to blow old dust out. Mental housecleaning is an activity which requires skill and dedicated effort.

The first step is deciding to take charge of the contents and the quality of our mental household. Recognizing that nothing will happen to improve the quality of our life until we initiate action to change it, we set ourself to the task of cleaning up our problems and repairing whatever damage has been done. The strength of this decision can be greatly augmented by remembering the basic principle which underlies all successful work of integration in Active Meditation: *the greater takes care of the lesser.* There is a part of us which has the maturity and ability to supervise the work of mental housecleaning. Not only that, but we have already defined this "greater" part within us to a certain extent, through our work to improve our self-image and define our values and goals.

Indeed, it is very important to have spent a sensible amount of time clarifying the basic issues of self-respect, self-esteem, and what we stand for *before* we launch into any major effort of mental housecleaning. In this way, we establish the baseline of what is acceptable and what is not which will be so important in discerning what needs to be kept, what needs to be strengthened, what needs to be purified, and what needs to be removed altogether. It also gives us a reservoir of direction, stability, and power to draw from to assist us in our work of transformation—the direction of our purpose, the stability of our values, and the power of our inner strength. And it keeps us focused in constructive work while proceeding with our efforts to clean house, instead of becoming trapped in defensiveness. Far too often, people who embark on the work of mental housecleaning lose sight of what they really want to accomplish, and simply become tangled up in avoiding what is undesirable and worrying about their imperfection. No real transformation occurs.

Thus prepared, we are then ready to take our broom in hand and begin the actual work of cleaning house. The skills of meditation we choose for this activity, however, will vary with the particular category of problem we are dealing with. Difficulties generated out of our own experiences and attitudes must be treated differently than unwanted conditions tracked in by others—or problems from the deeper levels of the unconscious. Of course, some problems will naturally be combinations of different sources; there is always a certain amount of overlap. Our own conscious and subconscious attitudes of fear, for example, will tend to be fed and exaggerated by the strong currents of fear in mass consciousness and repressed elements of fear in our unconscious. To completely heal this kind of problem, we would have to deal with it at all three levels.

THE WISE AND BENEVOLENT PARENT

To correct problems of our own making, the best meditative skill to use is role playing. We imagine ourself to be a wise, benevolent parent who is seeking to help a child improve his behavior and attitudes. The role of the wise, benevolent parent, of course, represents the force of "the greater" within us, and is in harmony with our higher self. It serves as an ambassador-in-residence of the higher self within our personality. The child is a symbol for the character flaw or deficiency we are seeking to correct. In playing this role in our mind, we begin by gently explaining to the child that its behavior is no longer appropriate, although it may well have been in the past. We ask it to cooperate with the new directions we are establishing, and explain briefly how much more productive and helpful the new line of behavior will be. As we do this, we project certain key thoughts into the attitudes of the child, drawing the child to us and completely enveloping it in our arms, as though we were healing it, which we are. We focus the power and authority of the higher self lovingly upon the ability of the child to respond to our new direction and guidance. Once this stage is completed, we then spend a few minutes mentally rehearsing the ideal new pattern of behavior or attitude, so it becomes firmly impressed in the mind of the child—and our own subconscious.

In working to treat a problem of shyness, for example, we would begin by playing the role of a wise, benevolent parent who was perfectly at ease in acting with confidence, courage, and a sense of dignity and poise. These are the qualities of consciousness which neutralize shyness. So, we recognize that there is a part of us which already knows how to express these qualities, and we play this part.

Having identified with the confidence, courage, and dignity within us, we then begin instructing the timid child within us about its need to become more confident and poised as well. All of this is transpiring as a mental dialogue in a light meditative state. We briefly demonstrate to the child the opportunities it has missed because it was too shy, and then explain how much better life will be as it is lived with confidence and dignity. This part of the process need not be drawn out excessively—a couple of minutes will do. Then, continuing to play the role of the wise, benevolent parent, we draw the child to us, embracing it with the healing power of our love and concern, and project to it a number of reassuring, cleansing thoughts. One might be that the child's fear of embarrassment is greatly exaggerated; that he has many skills and talents well worth expressing, and he should be confident in what he does. Another projected thought might be that the companionship of others is a great treasure to be enjoyed, and the child should relax and be comfortable in dealing with others. The power of these thoughts, and others like them, should be radiated toward the child for quite some time, until there is an awareness of a proper response. The new patterns of confidence and poise should then be reinforced by mentally rehearsing the ideal way of acting in the key events of the next few days.

One of the reasons why the role of the parent counseling a child is useful in mental housecleaning is because it emphasizes the compassion and intelligence which is needed for this work. And so, even if our image of "the parent" has habitually been distorted by negative experiences of intimidation, criticism, and neglect, it is important to work with an ideal image of a benevolent, wise, and concerned parent. The subconscious is not a machine; it is a vital part of our humanity. It has values and feelings. It has common sense and knows when it is being fooled. It understands hypocrisy and will not cooperate unless instructions are given with sincerity and commitment to change. It is therefore imperative to work with the subconscious in the context of striving to nurture the ideals of the higher self, not just put a stop to conflict or avoid further difficulty. Dramatics, such as kicking, screaming, or condemning, are not only unnecessary but very definitely harmful. Nothing is gained by being defensive or antagonistic; we must harness the inner life and our impulse to grow.

It is also useful to work in a detached state, so we do not get pulled down into the problems of the subconscious. Playing the role of a wise and compassionate parent helping a confused and distressed child is an excellent way of achieving and maintaining the necessary detachment. Moreover, it allows us to work easily in more than one dimension of consciousness at the same time, being in touch with the authority of the higher self even while correcting the problems of the personality.

Throughout this process, we should remain alert to clues and signals which may lead us on to a more complete understanding. In working with the shy child, for example, we might get a brief intuitive glimpse of ourself as a very young child, being told by a parent or teacher that we were worthless and good for nothing. Such a flash might well indicate that the real cause of our shyness is this childhood event, which we had repressed, and that it will have to be dealt with as well. As necessary, therefore, we will want to feel free to explore and investigate greater implications to our problems. But this activity of exploration and investigation should *never* be permitted to become a distraction from the real work of healing the difficulties. Some people, unfortunately, become obsessed with probing for new insights and analyzing their woes, without ever getting around to doing anything to correct them and heal them. This is self-deception, not self-discovery. The bulk of the time we spend in the work of mental housecleaning should be devoted to healing and enriching our mental household— not discovering what needs to be done.

At all times, the communication between parent and child should be kept as simple as possible. Ideally, it should be the *force* of our convictions, attitudes, and intentions that we communicate, more than words and images. In other words, it is not enough just to go through the motions of forgiving the child for indiscretions of anger or selfishness; we must endeavor to touch the spiritual ideal and archetypal force of goodwill which powers all forgiveness, and express it. It is not enough just to instruct the child not to misbehave again in the future; we must tap the authority of the higher self and our spiritual purposes and impress upon the child, kindly but firmly, the need to cooperate and be obedient.

The secret lies in the step of drawing the problems and deficiencies of the child into the loving aura of the parent, where they are purged and repaired. Cultivating a positive, healing state of consciousness into which we draw our problems is the heart of this technique of role playing, and the reason why it is so suited to a meditative state. Just throwing light on our problems is not enough, but if we absorb our problems in the light of our higher self, the difficulties and distortions will be dissolved. The darkness within us will be extinguished.

The wholeness of our household will be restored.

THE FORCE OF CONVICTION

To correct problems we have picked up through osmosis, from others and from mass consciousness, the best meditative skill to pick would be the use of seed thoughts. From the very beginning, however, it is important to realize that we are not on a crusade to reform our friends, enemies, or mass consciousness—or looking for an excuse to avoid responsibility for our problems by blaming others. We must be responsible for our own mental household. In other words, our problem is not that others are guilty of polluting our thoughts and attitudes, but simply that we have been polluted. Being defensive about the problem will therefore do us no good; in fact, it will probably aggravate the situation.

Instead of fighting the negativity of others, therefore, our most effective approach is to strengthen our own expression of good. Having discovered the pollution of our attitudes or moods by someone else, or mass consciousness, we take the time in meditation to carefully establish or restore our own alignment with archetypal forces and our spiritual ideals. We then focus the power of these forces and ideals into the thoughts, feelings, and moods of our subconscious through the use of seed thoughts, holding each seed thought for several minutes so it saturates our consciousness. The seed thoughts, of course, would reflect the primary thrust of the archetypal forces and spiritual ideals we have contacted, and would express how *we* intend to act in the face of opposition, intimidation, or whatever the problem is.

As an example, if we have carelessly allowed our attitudes to be influenced by the incessant whining and complaining of someone we work with, to the point where we have begun to whine and complain ourselves even though we do not approve of such behavior, we would not want to focus very much attention on the actual problem. It is not really our problem, after all, so why give it any measure of legitimacy? Instead, we should align ourself with the spiritual ideal of contentment and the archetypal force of perfection, filling our awareness completely with these qualities. We should then rest in the seed thought that active, enlightened work toward proper goals is the force which eradicates imperfection, not complaining. In fact, there is no room in our attitudes and behavior for complaining, because we are so completely oriented toward working to make improvements. The force of this conviction, focused in our seed thought, will drive away and disperse the power of the thought which has polluted us.

PENETRATING THE UNCONSCIOUS

Persistent problems from the unconscious levels of our mental household are most effectively purged by using a combination of these two techniques, role playing and seed thoughts. Just relying on role playing is usually not enough, as we are trying to penetrate to levels of awareness not generally responsive to conscious command. But it is a good starting place, because these unconscious patterns *are* patterns of our own immaturity. Once we have reached the stage of drawing the immaturity of the child into the loving aura of the parent, however, we must spend extra time flooding the moods and attitudes of the child with well-directed seed thoughts based on the spiritual ideals of the higher self and divine archetypes. The principle that the greater takes care of the lesser still remains effective; we just have to work a little harder to dislodge unconscious patterns. We must respect the multidimensional nature of their origin.

If, for example, we have been self-centered and demanding since early childhood, we are probably dealing with a pattern of arrogance rooted in unconscious levels. We would therefore play the role of the wise, compassionate parent healing a bossy, spoiled child, penetrating the resistance of the child with a strong but benevolent conviction that it is time to grow up and honor the wisdom and power of the higher self with a proper measure of inspired humility, concern for others, and cooperation.

It is in the work of revising and reforming the patterns of the unconscious that the tremendous power of Active Meditation can be most appreciated. In a very real sense, effective meditation deals simultaneously with transcendent and personal elements of consciousness, while psychotherapy, positive thinking, and hypnosis generally fail to harness the transcendent levels.

A DAILY PART OF LIFE

The starting point of all self-improvement is the realization that the way the world treats us depends largely upon how we treat the world. And we cannot treat the world wisely and ethically if our own mental household is in disrepair. The work of mental housecleaning may not eliminate all conflict and difficulty in our life, but it will free up the power, courage, intelligence, and goodwill of the higher self so that we can act maturely in all we do. As a result, the life of our higher self will have a better residence here on earth to dwell in, our thought children will be raised in a healthier environment, and our light will shine on earth all the more brilliantly.

The work of mental housecleaning is meant to be a daily part of life. It is an illusion to think we can use these techniques three or four times and then be done with them. Just as a physical home must be dusted and swept on a regular basis, so must our attitudes, habits, and feelings be monitored regularly. Mental housecleaning should be a daily meditative routine—and a lifelong habit. No one can afford to neglect it.

THE TECHNIQUE
FOR MENTAL HOUSECLEANING

The technique for mental housecleaning can be summarized as follows:

1. We begin by entering a meditative state and contacting the higher self, as described in chapter five.

2. We identify the source of the problem or deficiency we seek to repair and clearly define in our mind the constructive traits or positive qualities which will heal it.

3. If it is a problem of our own making, we play the role of the wise, benevolent parent who seeks to help his child grow up and become more mature. We explain the value of the change to the child and then draw the imperfections of the child into our loving aura, projecting the strength of the ideal way of behaving into the attitudes of the child, to heal them.

4. If it is a problem resulting from pollution by others or mass consciousness, we dwell on the appropriate spiritual ideal or divine archetype which will neutralize the difficulty. From this ideal or archetype, we generate a seed thought for how we generally want to think and behave. As we saturate our awareness with the force of this seed thought, it expels the pollution which is troubling us.

5. These techniques generally need to be repeated many times to achieve full effectiveness.

10

Healing The Emotions

IN SICKNESS AND IN HEALTH

In medicine, the most dreaded of all diseases are those which are difficult to detect until they are so far advanced that treatment may be too late. This is why cancer and heart diseases are so feared. But what the majority of us have not yet learned is that the most insidious diseases which afflict us are not physical ones at all—*they are emotional!* As a result, we allow them to fester and spread—sometimes until they have almost destroyed us—before we take any effective action to contain them or heal them.

These are the diseases of immaturity, anger, rage, selfishness, grief, jealousy, pessimism, fear, guilt, and cruelty. They are so intensely destructive that people suffering from them ought to be quarantined until they recover. Yet incredibly, many people accept these diseases as valuable parts of their humanity. They wear their immaturity as a badge of honor, rather than seeing it as a blight. They make important decisions on the basis of how they "feel" about their options, ignoring the fact that their likes and dislikes may reflect highly irrational prejudices. They claim they would be less of a person if they got rid of their anger, because "being angry is a part of being human." Such people might as well claim that if they caught the flu they should do nothing to heal themselves, because being sick is part of the human experience.

It is startling to what degree our culture has enshrined the sick and distorted use of the emotions. High achievers who are confident and proud are set forth as role models, when many of them are really nothing more than arrogant, greedy, and smug. Individuals who know how to "take care of themselves" by being aggressive and intimidating are thought to be strong. Anyone who complains loudly and bitterly enough about government and society is accepted as being an expert voice of authority, even though he or she may have demonstrated nothing more than a capacity for faultfinding, cynicism, and paranoia. Outpourings of sentiment and sympathy are taken to be signs of compassion and caring for the problems of others, even though they are often just projections of neurotic self-pity and anger. A lack of guilt and inhibition is widely regarded as a sign of emotional maturity, yet is often nothing more than a pretty mask for massive selfishness. It is commonly assumed that anger is a proper response to criticism, that grief is a proper response to any loss. Woe to the person who fails to respond in those ways, for he will surely be accused of being emotionally repressed!

These cultural perspectives on the emotions are reinforced in movies and television, where the "heroes" are often self-centered, stubborn, and aggressive, and in popular fiction, with its heavy emphasis on probing the agonized feelings of highly reactive people. This is understandable, of course, because the vast majority of people live in an emotional state for essentially the whole of their lives. They make decisions, act, move, plan, react, and behave on the basis of how they *feel*, instead of how they *think*. It is understandable, but not especially healthy. Due to the heavy domination of feelings in our culture, the correct uses of the mind and the spiritual will have been smothered in sentimentality. Creativity has been crippled. Human behavior has been trapped in a continuous time warp of adolescence. And the true value of the emotions is yet to be discovered by the average person.

This true value will never be discovered by psychologists who merely observe the way most people react emotionally to the events of their lives, or survey the feelings of a random sample of people on different issues. At best, such efforts end up *describing* emotional states; they are far too limited to produce any enlightenment on the subject. To understand the purpose and correct use of the emotions, we must consider them from the point of view of the higher self, the agent which seeks to use the emotions, the mind, and the physical body for creative self-expression. This is just a matter of common sense.

From the point of view of the higher self, the purpose of the emotions is to serve as a vehicle for the expression of spiritual love in daily life. In practice, this lofty purpose translates into using the emotions to:

• Touch others with kindness, compassion, gentleness, forgiveness, hope, and nurturing support.

• Aspire to the best—whether it is the highest level of competence we can achieve in our work or the noblest ethics and ideals of life—and be devoted to whatever is good.

• Keep faith in our humanitarian values and goals.

• Form a bond of goodwill and kinship with others, with society, and with humanity as a whole.

Ideally, the emotions should be kept free of pettiness, selfishness, anger, guilt, fear, sadness, and jealousy. This is not always an easy ideal to keep, especially in an atmosphere where these emotional diseases are accepted as commonplace and healthy. But to the degree that we let our emotions slip into these negative conditions, we compromise their ability to express spiritual love.

Properly used, the emotions enrich our self-expression. It must be understood, however, that this definition of the emotions is radically different from that of the ordinary person, who attempts to use the emotions to generate motivation, evaluate conditions and make decisions, and set goals. From the point of view of the higher self, it is the will which is designed to generate motivation—never our cravings or desires. It is the mind which is designed to evaluate conditions and make decisions—never our likes and dislikes. And it is the higher self which sets goals—never our personal thirst to experience new sensations and thrills.

The work of the emotions is to create a climate of benevolence, compassion, and grace in which our relationships, creative efforts, and self-expression can blossom. This work cannot proceed as scheduled, however, if our emotions are ill and contaminated.'

TREATING MORE THAN SYMPTOMS

To make much progress with our emotions, we must begin by realizing that there is a significant distinction between relieving symptoms of distress and actually curing fundamental flaws of consciousness. Far too often, when people do set themselves to the task of improving their emotions, all they are interested in doing is relieving the symptoms. As a result, they try to resolve their conflicts by avoiding them or running away from them, instead of changing those elements within their emotional makeup which precipitated the conflict in the first place. Indeed, most people blithely assume that they did not contribute in any significant way to the problem—it was all the other guy's fault.

This is a theme with many variations. If we are frustrated because our wishes and lusts go unfulfilled, we tend to assume the problem is our frustration, and seek other outlets for gratification. It seldom occurs to us that the root of our difficulty lies in our wishes and lusts, rather than our failure to gratify them. If beset with fears, we usually try to deal with them by avoiding the conditions we fear, rather than developing the courage to confront them maturely—or the wisdom to see that our fears are inappropriate. If we allow ourself to become morbidly dependent on someone else, or on society, we generally try to rationalize our habit of dependency, and perhaps even claim it is our "right," rather than develop self-sufficiency. If we have hurt feelings, we tend to nurse them and exaggerate the damage that has been done to us, instead of trying to increase our tolerance of others and our self-respect.

Unfortunately, the tendency to seek relief from the symptoms of emotional distress, rather than work to heal the root causes of the problems, is so ingrained in mass consciousness that it is not really useful to approach the healing of anger, grief, jealousy, or selfishness directly. Most people immediately assume that the only way to heal these difficulties is to give vent to them! As that approach produces the exact opposite of genuine healing, a different tack will be taken. We will examine the five major areas of difficulty *leading to* emotional distress, and the adjustments which will be required in each in order to achieve a greater state of emotional well-being. These five problem areas are:

1. The lack of ethics and a goal-centered life.
2. The lack of self-control and self-restraint.
3. Obsessions and addictions.
4. Congested self-expression.
5. The need for positive spiritual qualities.

THE LACK OF ETHICS AND GOALS

The emotions have no inherent stability of their own. They are highly fluid and easily influenced by external conditions and the moods of others. As a result, it is not possible to achieve continuity of character and purpose through our feelings. What is needed is a well-defined core of ethics and goals, which will serve to give our emotions focus, so they can be used in noble self-expression, not reactiveness.

Unfortunately, most people have done little to build up this kind of central core of ethics and goals. They are like a toy boat on a river, able only to drift with the current. Lacking any drive or direction of their own, they become the victim of an endless sequence of emotional reactiveness. Their opinions tend to reflect the beliefs of the people they have spoken to most recently. Their moods usually reflect the moods of the people they happen to be with. Their ethics are either borrowed from the cultural subgroup they belong to or are shaped by the expediency of the moment. They mimic heroes, friends, and family. As a result, their behavior is more a reflection of what they like and experience than it is a product of genuine self-determination. Even when they begin to recognize that they have become trapped in external influences, they continue in the reactive mode. The only difference is that they now *rebel* against these influences instead of reflecting them. From the point of view of the higher self, this is no change at all; they are still governed by their reactiveness.

A person who has failed to define his values and goals tends to express his emotions thoughtlessly, selfishly. To such a person, anger is expressed as easily as affection; jealousy is no different than love. Self-expression becomes nothing more than the expression of whatever emotion feels right at the moment—even though it may be inappropriate, harmful, or silly. The result is an infantile preoccupation with the lowest octave of emotional expression. The emotions are used exclusively to gratify desires, protect self-interests, and interpret sensations. They are marked by pettiness and petulance. They are never used to build a suitable climate of beauty, grace, and aspiration.

For many of us, of course, the problems resulting from a lack of ethics and goals are more subtle; we know what we are trying to accomplish, but we fail to pay enough attention to the tendency of the emotions to be caught up in the moods of mass consciousness. When this occurs, we end up reflecting attitudes which are inconsistent with our nobler purposes and goals for living.

Values and goals should never be based on the emotions; they must be built on the spiritual ideals and purposes of the higher self, as described in chapter eight. Until we have built an adequate foundation of values and goals, however, it would be fruitless to attempt to heal the emotions. We simply would not have the stability needed to do it.

THE LACK OF SELF-CONTROL

Even if we have established a good foundation of values and goals, we may find it difficult at times to mobilize them sufficiently to control our emotions. Good intentions can all too easily be overwhelmed by the force of old habits and reactive patterns; noble attitudes can be swamped in an instant by tidal waves of anxiety, guilt, or anger; a peaceful mood can be quickly shattered by any unpleasant intrusion. This is not because the emotions are designed to traumatize us, but because we do not always handle our feelings with perfect self-control or self-restraint.

In other words, we frequently react to insults with anger *before* we realize that we do not actually want to behave in this way. The strength of our value is not yet sufficient to counteract our lack of self-control. Or, we respond to opposition and criticism by losing heart and becoming disappointed *before* we remember that we have set a certain goal and ought to be busy pursuing it. The power of our goal is not yet focused well enough to keep the immature elements of our emotions from rebelling and distracting us from our work.

The problem of inadequate self-control is complicated by society's preoccupation with whitewashing the lack of self-discipline and making self-restraint appear undesirable. There are hordes of psychologists and therapists who have worked overtime to develop acceptable rationalizations for the lack of self-restraint:

• By relabeling it "the spontaneity of the moment" and setting it forth as something good.

- By encouraging their clients to "experience" their anger, dissatisfaction, or self-pity fully, thereby creating a "cult of hurt feelings."
- By promoting the use of fantasy as a way of releasing pent-up feelings.
- By helping us to "look back in heartburn" over the broken dreams of the past, as though life were nothing but a soap opera of self-gratification.
- By teaching us that selfishness is perfectly all right when hidden behind the label of "self-fulfillment" or the activity of taking care of our needs.

These are dangerous practices. The emotions are meant to serve the expression of spiritual love. Spiritual love is *not* permissive or undisciplined; it is not found on the wavelengths of spontaneity, hurt feelings, fantasizing, wishing, or self-indulgence. It can be expressed through the emotions *only* if our feelings have been aligned with our values and goals as well as with love, and are responsive to intelligent guidance and discipline from the mind and the higher self. Lacking a proper amount of discipline, the emotions become disorderly, unruly, and rebellious. They attempt to create the higher self in their own image, rather than cooperate constructively with it.

The correction of the lack of self-control lies in strengthening our capacity for self-expression, by increasing our detachment and self-determination.

The initial stages of detachment have been described in chapter five. These simple practices are useful not only in entering the meditative state, but also in learning to express the emotions with self-control. Detachment establishes the fact that there is a part of us, the parent within, which supervises the affairs of the personality and has the authority to correct and override childish reactions and desires. In no way does this involve repressing the emotions or creating a climate of emotional indifference; it simply means that we have chosen to express our emotions with common sense, purpose, and the guidance of the higher self. We will use them to enrich our life and self-expression, not detract from them; to help others, not to harm them; to cooperate with authority, not rebel against it. This level of detachment is cultivated by carefully observing what happens to us, thoughtfully reflecting on its significance, choosing the ideal way we should respond—and then behaving that way.

Self-determination is increased by taking the time to examine and reflect on the elements which actually lead us, push us, inspire us, or drive us to act, especially in the small and seemingly insignificant moments of life. It is possible to be motivated by the highest principles in the broad sweep of life, yet still be driven by pettiness, greed, anger, and competitiveness as we react to specific circumstances and individuals in daily living. A good way to conduct this examination is to take a few minutes at the end of each day to reflect on how often our actions were guided by intelligent decisions, and how often we simply let old habits and attitudes automatically condition our self-expression. It will be instructive—and perhaps startling— to learn how frequently we actually do lose control of our emotions. But being startled in this way is often enough to stimulate us to exert our self-determination more regularly. In addition, it can be helpful to consider, from time to time, the consequences of continually appeasing our petty wants and hurts, at the expense of more constructive behavior. If we can see that we will achieve much more in life by acting nobly and honorably, our motivation to act with self-restraint will be greatly strengthened.

Once we have discovered the major areas in which we lack control of our emotions, it is important to strengthen our self-determination, by:

1. Invoking the spiritual ideal we should have been expressing through our emotions at the time we lost control.

2. Dedicating ourself to expressing this spiritual ideal more consistently and effectively.

3. Meditating on seed thoughts that embody the strength of the ideal.

Throughout, we must recognize the value of taking charge of our life and our emotional self-expression.

OBSESSIONS AND ADDICTIONS

The emotions operate by building up a magnetic rapport with anything they happen to like, and a magnetic rejection of anything they dislike. When used constructively by the higher self, this feature of the emotions is quite effective in building an enlightened climate for relationships, work, and self-expression. But when used unintelligently by the average, reactive personality, it tends to lead to serious problems of imbalance:

• The compulsion to have a certain experience over and over again.

• A fanatical obsession with certain ideas or topics.

• Addiction to the gratification of specific desires or cravings.

Compulsions, obsessions, and addictions in any form are, by definition, a mistake, for they represent unbalanced states of thinking, feeling, and action. It is always easy to spot these unbalanced states in others, but surprisingly difficult in ourself. This is because the strength of our compulsion or fanaticism tends to hypnotize us and blind us to the lack of balance. Thus, we view our vanity as self-respect; our blind ambition as a noble drive; our lust to manipulate others as protecting our rights; and our righteous judgmentalism of others as a concern for justice.

The emotions will gladly cooperate with compulsive and addictive tendencies, because it gives them license to indulge in wild excesses. The childish elements of our feelings very much like this kind of unrestrained stimulation, and will feed it. The result, however, is not at all beneficial to the purposes of the higher self—or even the long-term prospects of the personality. Life does not support wretched excesses for very long—including our own. Our fanaticism will tend to draw to us fanatics of an equal but opposite persuasion, who will try to destroy us. Our addictions will lead us into slavery to the object of our craving. Worst of all, the work of maintaining these compulsions and addictions is so great that it quickly leaves our emotions exhausted, unable to serve their purpose. It can be extremely difficult to rebuild the emotions from this point of burnout.

Obsessions and addictions are healed by restoring balance to our understanding of the proper role of emotions. Balance is epitomized by what the Buddha called "The Noble Middle Path," which postulates that happiness can never be found through the pursuit of excess. Rather, it is achieved by looking for and finding those central values and principles which *define* self-expression, and being governed by them. In other words, a person who truly values his health will not be vulnerable to addictions which would destroy his health, such as drinking or smoking. A person who *genuinely* loves God with all his mind and heart and soul and might, and his neighbor as himself, will never become a religious bigot or self-righteous fanatic. His life and emotions are balanced by the spiritual ideal he serves.

Understanding the proper role of emotions continually reminds us that the emotions are designed to enrich life, not drain it. If we are always seeking the "ultimate thrill," however, our emotional priorities are upside-down. We will have to redefine them in order to escape the grasp of our compulsions and addictions. Such a radical change, of course, is not always easy. Our effort can be effectively supported by using the following meditative skills:

• Role playing, with the wise parent embodying the proper use of the emotions and working to correct the compulsive behavior of the child within.

• Seed thoughts, such as "the balanced expression of love" or "the dominion of my higher self."

CONGESTED SELF-EXPRESSION

The emotions are designed to contribute to the self-expression of the noble qualities, themes, and skills of the higher self in daily life. If we fail to mobilize and express our talents and capacities, through repression or inhibition of any kind, our life force will stagnate and become congested. If this problem is prolonged for any substantial period of time, the results can be quite devastating. Just as hardening of our arteries can dangerously reduce the flow of blood to our vital organs, so can a hardening of our self-expression curtail the natural flow of life force to our mind, emotions, and physical body. The result can seriously cripple our usefulness and achievements.

There are two major ways in which we congest our self-expression. The first is by giving an excessive amount of attention to behaving in negative ways, thereby excluding noble themes, qualities, and skills. The person who chronically resents the way he has been treated, or buries himself in guilt over the way he has behaved, or maintains a constant state of embarrassment regarding a flaw in his character gradually builds his whole life upon the foundation of his distress, to the point where anything more noble or healing is systematically excluded. His consciousness becomes "dammed up" behind his wall of negativity.

The second is by giving insufficient attention to expressing our values, our self-respect, and our dedication to our goals. Perhaps we are timid, or easily intimidated by others, or simply a bit too passive toward life in general, but we congest our self-expression by not making enough of an effort to honor it. We give up rather than persevere in the face of opposition, even though our goals are worthy. We appease those who intimidate us, even though we know their goals are destructive.

Regardless of the origin of congestion in our self-expression, its impact on the emotions is never favorable. Having been cut off from the capacity of the higher self to support and maintain them, the emotions become prey to the negativity of others and mass consciousness. The quality of life steadily decreases, and we become less responsive to the noble elements of life, such as beauty, faith, hope, and grace. Frequently, we even become parasitic.

The remedy for a congested self-expression is to break up the attitudes which are "damming" our consciousness and replace them with attitudes which will serve as a conduit for our self-expression. If our problem is the *presence* of the wrong kind of self-expression, such as chronic resentment, guilt, or embarrassment, we must draw these elements into the loving aura of the parent within and heal them, as described in chapter nine. However, if our problem is the *absence* of an affirmative self-expression, we will have to work to create one. This can be done by contemplating ideal ways of acting in various situations, and then charging these ideal ways of acting through the use of appropriate seed thoughts, such as "the dedication to act."

THE NEED FOR POSITIVE SPIRITUAL QUALITIES

Most people spend their lives consumed with the work of overcoming their problems, believing if they can just surmount this difficulty here and that one there, the rest of their life will fall magically into place. Most of the time, however, this attitude distracts them from the real difficulty underlying their problems: they have not established an effective base of spiritual qualities and treasures in their personality. Like some poor people, both their "bank account" and their capacity to "make money" are sadly deficient. They do not know how to generate good ideas, establish a healthy emotional climate, or initiate productive work in the physical plane.

This deficiency is perhaps more obvious in the emotions than in other departments of consciousness. Emotional problems cannot simply be removed; they must be *replaced* by a more spiritual option. If we have not taken the time to cultivate spiritualized emotional qualities, such as faith, goodwill, tolerance, joy, affection, generosity, and kindness, we will have no power to make improvements in the emotions. It takes the warmth of affection and forgiveness to melt away the coldness of bitterness and hate. It takes the glow of optimism to extinguish the darkness of despair. It takes the calmness of patience to neutralize the irritation of petty anxieties. Nothing less will work.

This news may come as something of a shock to those who have been eager to believe that good intentions, positive thoughts, and trust in God were all they needed for spiritual living. These are excellent starting points, but it is not enough just to know that God is perfect—or even to know that the higher self is perfect. We must convert the spiritual qualities of the higher self into skillful emotional expressions of our nobility, compassion, and dedication. Otherwise, our emotions will remain empty even while the higher self is full.

The spiritual qualities needed for an enlightened emotional self-expression are not developed overnight or by reading a book. They are refined through the effort to act in harmony with our humanitarian values and spiritual ideals. As we work with them, we begin to discover that they are very much different than most people suspect—far richer, more powerful, and genuinely creative. They grow as we grow. Some of the most important spiritual qualities to develop for an enlightened expression of the emotions include:

Devotion	Faith	Compassion
Cheerfulness	Charm	Caring
Tolerance	Forgiveness	Harmony
Cooperation	Affection	Sharing
Generosity	Goodwill	Tenderness
Enthusiasm	Optimism	Reverence
Aspiration	Gratitude	Patience

These qualities are all designed to be expressed *by us*, through our own emotional self-expression, not just occasionally but as a regular feature of daily living. As we learn to do so, the size of our "spiritual bank account" will steadily increase. And so will the quality of our life.

DIVINE LOVE

To be effective, a meditative technique for healing the emotions will have to address and repair each of these five problem areas. It cannot just be an exercise in feeling good about ourself, blowing off steam, or blissing out. Instead, it must gradually attune us to the abstract nature of divine love while keeping us focused in learning to honor and express the quality of love in meaningful ways in our relationships, our work, our attitudes, and our aspirations.

We must begin with a clear recognition of a fundamental principle: *the power to heal our emotions lies in the higher self—not in the emotions themselves.* We must therefore look beyond our hurt feelings and urges and be tutored by those qualities which can actually transform and heal the emotions.

We must acclimate ourself to the proper wavelength of healing, which is the love of the higher self.

Indeed, this is the wavelength of *all* successful healing, not just the healing of the emotions. The love of the higher self, however, differs considerably from the state of sentimental affection normally called "love." It links us immediately with the omnipresence of God, yet keeps us focused in repairing the imperfect conditions within our life—in our character, work, and environment. It lifts us into a divine state of wholeness, while teaching us to relate ideally to the many parts of the whole. It fills us with benevolence, compassion, and goodwill, so that we may go forth and express these same qualities in our dealings with others. It brings to us the patterns of health, the inspiration, and the power to act which we need in order to establish a proper self-expression on earth.

It may seem odd to some to discuss the patterns of health, inspiration, and the power to act in the context of love, for the mind, the will, and the body are generally treated separately from the emotions and love. But it must be understood that love is *not* an emotion; it is a spiritual quality. It can be expressed through the emotions, but also through the other aspects of the personality, including the mind. Indeed, it is through the cohesiveness and inclusiveness of divine love that all of these elements of self-expression are drawn into their intended wholeness. Until we understand love in this context, we will fall short of our mark in healing the emotions. We will be dealing with an imitation of love, not the divine quality.

The single most important element of healing the emotions, therefore, is to learn to practice the presence of divine love—to become attuned to divine love, to respect it as a motivating force of life, and to endeavor to honor it fully in our own self-expression. These lessons are learned as we develop three basic skills of love:

- The skill of *aspiration*, which teaches us to lift up our mind and heart and become filled with the omnipresence of divine love.

• The skill of *devotion*, which teaches us to love what God loves—to honor the potential of the ideal for perfection in all life forms, and to nurture that potential.

• The skill of *faith*, which teaches us to remain constant in our attunement to the divine presence of love as we work patiently to heal the deficiencies of our emotions.

It is important to appreciate the threefold sequence of aspiration, devotion, and faith. Many people have been taught only the first steps of love—of rising above the problems of the emotions and the physical plane and becoming completely absorbed in the abstract or transcendent love of God. While this is a valuable first step, it is not the complete activity of love. Divine love should always be seen in the context of creation and self-expression; what we learn at transcendent levels should then be brought back to mundane levels and integrated into physical living, to transform that which is imperfect.

To transform that which is imperfect. This is the work of divine love. And it should be the motto of our effort to heal the emotions.

HEALING THE EMOTIONS

These ideas can be condensed quite nicely into a very effective meditation program for healing the emotions. As usual, the technique begins by entering a meditative state and making contact with the higher self. Once the meditative state has been reached, we then proceed as follows:

1. We fill ourself with divine love through the practice of the skills of aspiration, devotion, and faith. Through aspiration, we lift up our heart and mind to be responsive to the wavelength of love. Through devotion, we identify with

divine love as the source of all life. We love love, adoring the perfection, compassion, and benevolence of God, both the God Transcendent and the God Immanent, the God of the universe and the higher self. Through faith, we increase our appreciation of the healing power of love.

This exercise of filling ourself with divine love is a simple one which should be a daily part of our meditative activity. Repeated in this way, it gradually magnetizes the whole of our personality to the perfection and wholeness of divine creation. It establishes the wavelength of healing, by aligning the personality with the higher self, thereby facilitating our access to all spiritual ideals and the seeds of perfection for every aspect of our character and our work. This first step is the cornerstone of an effective practice of the presence of divine love.

2. Once we have filled ourself with divine love, the next step is to focus its power for the specific act of healing. This is accomplished by choosing a spiritual ideal to love and, by loving, activate in our own life. Generally, the ideal we would choose would be related to one of the five problem areas described earlier (not the symptoms, but the actual problem). If our problem is a lack of ethics, we would focus our aspiration, devotion, and faith to loving the ideal of acting with a solid foundation of values and goals in life. If our problem is a lack of self-determination, we would direct our aspiration, devotion, and faith to loving the ideal of approaching life wisely, courageously, and with a strong sense of individuality.

This just makes good sense. To be an agent of divine love, we must learn to love what God loves and lovingly contribute to the unfoldment of the divine plan in civilization and human nature. We can only learn this lesson if we are willing to practice, in meditation and in daily life, a deep reverence for the underlying themes and ideals of life, recognizing that:

• There is an undercurrent of divine life throughout the whole of life.

• Nothing exists beyond the reach of God's benevolent influence.

• There is a divine purpose and momentum at work even in the most desperate of conditions.

• Goodwill is the natural force behind all correct human relations.

After we have become well-practiced in this step, there may be many times when this love for a spiritual ideal is not motivated by the need to work on one of the five problem areas of the emotions, but just for the sake of adoring the seed of divine perfection. This kind of work is highly recommended, as long as it is given practical focus through some aspect of creative work or service to civilization. The power of transcendent love is designed to be used for *healing*.

3. Having established our love for the ideal, we must then draw the imperfections and hurts of our emotions into the powerful aura of our spiritual love, to cleanse them and help them grow toward the ideal. This step can be patterned after the similar one in the technique for mental housecleaning, in which we play the role of the wise parent who compassionately draws the immaturity of the child to him, soothing and correcting the hurt. The parent represents the mature elements of our personality, connected with the divine love of the higher self, while the child symbolizes the immaturity within the emotions. The child sees only the symptoms of distress, but the parent remains focused in the inclusiveness of divine love, surrounding the child with the love of the ideal, until the child is filled with this greater awareness.

It should be understood that the ability to keep our nurturing love focused on the seed of perfection for any specific aspect of life is one of the strongest methods available for integrating the life of the higher self into physical life. As we learn to use love in this way, we *activate* our spiritual ideals in our regular self-expression. As these ideals come to life for us consciously, they automatically expel the negative conditions of fear, gloom, resentment, anger, pettiness, and selfishness. There is no need to vent these feelings or even imagine them being dissipated; our real strength lies in remaining focused in the love for the ideal. This is the perspective we should strive to maintain as we play the role of the compassionate parent healing the immaturity of the child.

The use of role playing in this way can often be augmented by meditating on appropriate seed thoughts, such as "the power to forgive," "the building of faith," "optimism," and so on. The key is to project the power of the seed thought into the awareness of the child, thereby filling the emotions of the personality with the strength to honor these ideals in actual behavior.

One of the common ways this technique might be used, for example, would be to heal a tendency to engage in angry outbursts. The angry outbursts, of course, are not the real problem—and neither are the external conditions which provoked them. The real problem is our lack of self-control and our lack of an appropriate spiritual quality that would replace the anger, such as goodwill.

Taking this problem into meditation, we would begin by filling ourself with divine love. We would spend several moments aspiring to a fuller appreciation of God's love, adoring it in all of its manifestations and building faith in our capacity to be an enlightened channel for it. This is much more than just "feeling good" about God; it involves filling our heart and mind with the momentum of love.

Once the proper measure of love has been tapped, we would then focus it on loving the ideals of acting maturely and compassionately in the face of pressure, of exerting control over our emotions when they are tempted to be reactive and angry, and of becoming a proper agent of goodwill in all that we do. This devotion could include the realization that neither

God nor the higher self finds it necessary to act with anger; it is the power of goodwill which helps build civilization, improves the quality of human relationships, and enables us to grow.

Having established a proper devotion to the ideals we ought to be serving, we then draw the reactive patterns of anger in the personality into the healing power of our love. Playing the role of the compassionate parent, we lift our childish anger up into the aura of our love, embracing it and filling it with the strength of our ideals. We can simultaneously project to the child seed thoughts such as "tolerance" and "goodwill," to help shape the proper response we are seeking.

The possible applications of this technique to healing emotions are, of course, unlimited. It can be used to improve relationships, create a more wholesome environment for our family, forgive our enemies, and in many other ways. No matter how we choose to use it, however, it will always have the benefit of helping us grow toward the light and love of God.

THE TECHNIQUE
FOR HEALING THE EMOTIONS

A brief summary of the steps in this technique for healing the emotions is included here for easy reference.

1. We begin by entering the meditative state and contacting the higher self, as described in chapter five.

2. We fill ourself with divine love, through the practice of aspiration, devotion, and faith. This should include a love of God in His abstract beneficence, a love for the whole of divine creation, including our fellow human beings, and a love for the latent perfection of life.

3. We focus this divine love more specifically, by loving a spiritual ideal we need to increase in our life. We seek to nurture this ideal in our own self-expression even as God nurtures it through the whole of creation.

4. We draw elements of our own emotional immaturity into the powerful aura of this love of the ideal, for the purpose of healing them. Meditative skills which can be used to facilitate this activity are mental role playing and the use of seed thoughts.

A Breath of Herman

We had paused to let the typewriter rest and to talk about the direction to take in the next three chapters.

"I think we've presented a good introduction to using meditative techniques for understanding and healing the personality," Carl said. "It's time to shift our emphasis a bit, though, and lead the reader to a deeper realization of the higher self."

"Yes, there's always the danger of becoming too stuck in the life of the personality," Bob agreed. "The personality has an enormous capacity to think only of its immediate problems, difficulties, traumas, hurt feelings, and fears. We can build up some very important meditative skills by managing these problems, but meditation should also lead us beyond them—to new and higher perspectives toward life. Sometimes, when people are just beginning, they forget that."

Apparently our discussion invoked interest in other dimensions. There was a slight tremor in the room, not enough to move the furniture, but enough to be noticeable. Slowly, the tremor became audible. Someone was quietly intoning the word, "OM." We suspected it was Herman. Soon, our friend from the angelic realms had reappeared.

"How are you doing, boys?" Herman inquired.

"You probably know the answer to that better than we do," Bob replied.

"Well, I'm an angel, not a critic," Herman protested. "I wouldn't want you to think I'm lying around heaven eating bon-bons and passing judgment while the two of you are slaving away down here on earth, trying to fit conjunctions and gerunds together and make sense out of all these complex ideas. A lot of people think of the higher self that way, you know— they think it is constantly judging and condemning the efforts they are making, as though the personality can do no good. This just isn't true."

"We certainly haven't found it to be true, at any rate," Carl agreed.

"It's a point you may want to stress," Herman continued. "You've been writing a lot about techniques for cleaning up the personality and transforming the quality of life. Lord knows there is a great need for this, but please be careful not to unwittingly convince your readers that the higher self is some kind of critic. It seeks to inspire the personality to grow and transform itself, not coerce it. There's a big difference."

"Yes, a lot of people seem to project their own tendencies to criticize and dominate others onto their conception of the higher self—or God, for that matter. Since they would behave in those ways if they had supreme authority, they assume the higher self works in that way, too," Bob commented.

"There's always a danger, whenever you start stringing techniques together, that people will begin to think that the techniques themselves are the alpha and omega of meditation. And if they have trouble mastering the techniques, they will start to worry that the higher self will be critical. But meditation is not *just* a series of techniques, as you well know. I like the way you put it a few chapters ago: that it is a method for strengthening the bond between the higher self and the personality. That's very good. But this means that if meditation is going to be useful, it must be a part of life—something that lives and breathes and becomes part of the rhythm of your livingness."

"Absolutely," said Carl.

"So don't let anyone get the idea that meditation is some kind of psychological obstacle course—duck this temptation here, jump over that resentment there, and crawl through the tunnel of narrowmindedness up ahead. Be sure your readers know the purpose of growing is to *grow toward the light!*"

"I really didn't think we were leading anyone on a steeplechase," protested Bob. "To bring the higher life into daily thought and behavior, you have to learn to clean up the mental household and remove the barriers to spirit. That's what makes meditation effective—and helps people realize that spirit can be brought into daily life."

"Yes," chimed in Carl, "what could be a better proof of the power of spirit than its capacity to transform an angry person into a forgiving one, or a sour, grumpy person into a joyful, cheerful agent of light?"

"Absolutely nothing," replied Herman, twinkling as only an angel can. "But I hope you are not going to leave it at that. Life is not just a matter of attacking our problems and conflicts. The spiritual life begins with resolving these difficulties, yes, but it must include much more as well. It must involve building a capacity to make some kind of contribution. What good have you gained if you have successfully fought off all of your anger and fear, but haven't also learned to express goodwill, patience, kindness, and faith? What good have you served if you have understood all that is wrong with your life—or even the world—unless you are able to participate in the work of healing and redeeming it?"

"Well, that's just what we were outlining for the next several chapters," said Carl.

"I'm looking forward to reading them," Herman replied, still twinkling. "Do put in a few words for me, though. Make sure everyone understands that the goal of meditation is to become enlightened—not just extra aware of their problems."

No one spoke for awhile. Herman hovered, gently chanting "OM." Finally, Bob spoke.

"It's a delicate balance, isn't it? Some people start meditating and end up floating in the clouds somewhere, totally spaced out. Others try to avoid that, but end up focused excessively in their problems."

Herman just had to interrupt. "Is there something wrong with floating in the clouds? I do it all the time!"

Bob and Carl laughed. "But you don't get spaced out, I'll bet," Carl teased.

"That's true," Herman agreed. "Well, as you said, it's a delicate balance. And sometimes you people in the West develop a real mania for fussing over every little thing. Sometimes, you know, it is possible to let a few of those problems just fall away and get on with the business of growing toward the light."

"Isn't that just common sense?" asked Bob.

"Sometimes common sense is not as common as you presume," Herman answered. "We call it *wisdom* up here."

"That's what we're writing about in our next chapter," exclaimed Carl.

"I'll see if I can't sneak in between the lines every now and then," Herman replied. "Well, I have to fly now. Keep up the good work."

In a twinkling—his final twinkling—Herman disappeared into a small, white cloud, leaving us only with the echo of "OM."

11

Invoking Wisdom

ADDING WISDOM TO LOVE

It is commonly thought that there are specific pathways to God: the path of faith, the path of good works, the path of devotion, the path of the will, and the path of wisdom. In India, for example, there are many different pathways recognized as separate forms of yoga. A guru teaches techniques which will enable his students to pursue one particular path, and no other. To a large degree, this practice has also been transplanted to the West. Often, teachers will instruct their students not to experiment with any meditative techniques other than their own.

Up to a point, there can be value in such specialization. An individual frequently needs to concentrate on one specific approach to God and the higher self, especially in the beginning stages of growth. Until one path is mastered, the effort to pursue many paths at once would be a distraction. Nevertheless, it is also important to see the need for balance in our approach to God and the higher self. The person who can only love God does not have a very complete relationship with God; he is in harmony only with the heart of God, and not with the mind, the will, or the plan of God. The person who has built great faith in the higher self, but nothing else, has likewise limited himself or herself to those facets of the higher self which are activated by faith alone. This is just a matter of common sense.

Most people choose either the path of faith or devotion when they first embark on the spiritual quest, and rightly so. Until we are properly imbued with an unshakeable love for divine life and a solid faith in the benevolence of God's design, the development of esoteric knowledge and skills might prove disastrous. Untutored emotions succumb all too easily to temptation, selfishness, and rebelliousness; the risk of entrusting an immature personality with the mysteries of life is great.

As a result, the major focus of spiritual teaching throughout history has been directed at instructing the emotions in the lessons of faith, love, and devotion. But once these lessons are mastered, we must go on and also learn the lessons of good works, the will, and wisdom. We must teach the mind *as well as the emotions* to become involved in contacting God and the higher self, translating the plan of God into effective service, the will of God into purposeful direction, and the light of God into individual wisdom.

The need to add wisdom to faith, good works to love, and the penetrating force of divine will to devotion is a fundamental tenet of the Western tradition of Active Meditation. And yet, strangely enough, most systems of meditation do not encourage the development of the mind. They are so intensely focused in the techniques of faith, devotion, and love that they view the mind as an enemy, a slayer, rather than a meaningful pathway to God and the higher self. They encourage their adherents to still the mind and view it with contempt—failing to see the inconsistency of holding in contempt one of the major creations of the higher self.

Because this blighted view of the mind and the role of wisdom in meditative practices is so widespread and poisonous, it deserves to be carefully examined and evaluated. If we allow erroneous concepts about the mind or wisdom to influence our thinking, we can undermine much of the good that Active Meditation is designed to do.

THE WISDOM FACTORY

The higher self is a repository of great wisdom—not just ideas, but also the meaning of those ideas and the power to act creatively with them. Being immortal, it has acquired a tremendous store of talents, powers, and knowledge from various dimensions throughout its long existence. Some of this accumulated wisdom has been extracted from life experiences on earth, some from its experiences in other dimensions. In addition, because the higher self is a divine creation, it also has access to the full wisdom and force of divine archetypes—the fifth-dimensional patterns of consciousness from which the forms of life are created. There is therefore enormous wisdom in the higher self.

To some degree, the emotions are able to reflect this wisdom, by learning to love truth and adore beauty. But the portion of the human personality which is designed to contact the wisdom of the higher self and become a conduit for it is the mind. The average human mind, of course, is largely unprepared to act in these ways. It is still enslaved by the emotions. When the mind is properly trained, however, it has the potential to become a miniature "wisdom factory," in which the power of the wisdom of the higher self is used to refine the experiences of daily life into common sense, insight, new skills, and greater intelligence. Such a mind will be a noble element of the personality.

As long as we remain obsessed with our emotions and the sensations of the body, however, we are unable to tap this potential—and this, unfortunately, is a real problem for most people. Instead of training the mind and using it to view life objectively and understand the events which occur, they choose the easier option of listening to what their feelings and their body tell them. As a result, they are focused almost wholly in their physical bodies and emotions, and the mind remains weak and undeveloped. This prevents them from understanding the events of life—but also from making contact with the wisdom of the higher self.

The problem is that when a person does decide, at last, to train and cultivate the mind, the early lessons to be mastered sometimes carry him into modes of approaching life which cause the typical spiritual devotee to recoil in utter horror.

In order to learn discrimination, so that we can separate the wheat from the chaff—or the goo from the guru—we must train the mind to make evaluations and judgments. In the beginning, it is easy to take this lesson to extremes, becoming harshly critical of others, ourself, and society. Yet eventually, our critical tendencies are seen to be destructive and we learn to use the skill of discrimination as a lens to the higher self, not a weapon.

In order to learn discernment, so we can embrace the ideals of the higher self, we must train the mind to reach out and discover what lies beyond itself. This can strain the willingness of the mind to accept new ideas, however, and it often retreats into skepticism and disbelief—until it becomes more comfortable with the basic purpose of thinking, which is to discover and expand.

In order to learn to work with knowledge, so we can translate the wisdom of the higher self into practical self-expression, we must train the mind to work pragmatically. At first, this may be disturbing to the individual who has had a long-standing habit of adoring the "unknowable, ineffable, abstract wisdom of God." It may also cause us to focus excessively in the mundane issues of life, ignoring the divine realities of the higher self. Eventually, though, we learn that we are a multidimensional being, capable of working pragmatically in daily life while remaining focused in our spiritual heritage.

In order to learn to work abstractly, so we can interact with the divine archetypes of the higher self, we must train the mind in certain intuitive skills. At first, this may lead to a preoccupation with low-level psychic phenomena and showy displays of psychic gifts. Sooner or later, however, we outgrow this mode of psychic work and begin using our intuitive skills to explore the abstract nature of life.

In order to learn to work with the power of thought, so we

can tap the power of archetypal life, we must train the mind to form convictions. In early stages, this lesson may go awry, and we end up becoming prejudiced and willful instead. Nevertheless, we eventually master these distortions and learn to use the mind as an agent of the higher self.

Because these lessons must be learned, the mind has earned a reputation of being critical, skeptical, materialistic, profane, and prejudiced. Yet the reputation is not really deserved. These problems are not actually inherent in the nature of the mind. They occur as emotionally-oriented people try to learn to use the mind—or even worse, try to use an undeveloped mind. Still, it is the mind which has taken most of the blame. It is the mind which has been labeled "the slayer" by a host of spiritual authorities, because they do not understand the phenomena they observe.

To believe that the mind is designed to be a slayer is tantamount to believing that wisdom kills. This is nonsense. Wisdom is the accumulated knowledge, insight, and power to act of the higher self. And it can only be tapped by us for use in our daily lives *if* we have trained and developed the mind.

Nevertheless, hordes of well-intentioned and dedicated people are convinced that they must bypass the mind in order to attain enlightenment. It is always pathetic to observe these people, as they try to pursue a life of goodness and spirituality without the benefit of wisdom. These are good people, filled with faith, devotion, and love, but their faith is built on belief alone, not a knowledge of what they believe. Their devotion is based on adoration alone, not on insight into what they idolize. Their love is guided only by their hopes, not a comprehension of life. They remain as little children who do not grow up.

This lack of comprehension can lead to serious distortions about the spiritual life, the higher self, and God. Sadly, much of what has been written on these subjects has been written by people who have scorned or ignored the development of the mind. Consequently, their descriptions of the spiritual life tend to be bland and filled with platitudes. Their analysis of the higher self is usually vague; frequently, they will simply state that these higher states cannot be described in words. This is not true. The problem lies not in the failing of words, but in the faultiness of the person using the words.

It is therefore important to realize that *ignorance has never been a spiritual virtue.* It is ignorance which destroys the spiritual life, not wisdom. It is the empty mind which is the slayer, not the active and enlightened mind. And those who label the mind the slayer and encourage others to view it as such are the ones who have done the greatest damage.

THE BEST SOURCE OF WISDOM

The skillful practice of Active Meditation illuminates the pathway between the intelligence of the personality and the wisdom of the higher self. This illumination generally does not occur as a sudden flash, but rather builds gradually over a long period of repetitive practice, as we focus our need to know and solicit the guidance of the higher self. To understand how this occurs, we must comprehend the following basic points:

1. Everyone is endowed with an enormous inner wisdom and the capacity to acquire greater understanding of life.

2. This wisdom is available to anyone who develops an effective and balanced working relationship with the higher self. In such a relationship, the physical body is attuned to the higher self's ideal of productivity, the emotions reflect the higher self's capacity to express love, and the mind is aligned to the higher self's resources of wisdom.

3. The nature of the wisdom of the higher self is abstract. As such, it defines principles, rather than the applications of these principles. The personality grounds wisdom in its con-

duct of daily living as it learns to formulate concrete applications for the abstract principles of the higher self.

4. The abstract ideas or principles of the wisdom of the higher self have three aspects—power, meaning, and pattern. Another way of describing these three aspects would be force, quality, and design. To learn to work with these abstract ideas and principles, therefore, we must train the mind to rise above its usual preoccupation with the *form* of ideas, and learn to work with the power, meaning, and pattern of ideas.

5. Access to the wisdom of the higher self is acquired by learning and practicing the skills of contacting and using abstract knowledge and intelligence. It is *not* learned merely by absorbing the predigested precepts of a guru, philosopher, or religion—or the traditions and opinions championed by mass consciousness. The statements of enlightened individuals can be useful guides to the abstract levels of wisdom, but the pathway to the wisdom of the higher self can only be illuminated through our own efforts. *In any circumstance, the most reliable source of guidance is always our own inner wisdom!* Cultivating it is therefore a matter of good sense.

A BRIDGE TO WISDOM

Many people know so little about wisdom, however, that they end up pursuing the wrong thing. Some people, for example, are convinced that wisdom and truth cannot be understood—perhaps not even experienced—because it is known only by God. Such dedicated nihilism is an anathema to wisdom. And what is truly remarkable is how these people can know so definitely that truth is unknowable! Others are equally determined to reduce truth and wisdom to the level of mere opinion. These people are offended by the suggestion that the inner life is structured on definite principles and laws.

They prefer to believe that "what you believe in your heart is true for you and what I believe in my heart is right for me." But truth and wisdom are not relative. If something is a principle of truth, it applies to all alike. It does not vary from individual to individual. The applications of wisdom may vary, but the principles of wisdom do not. They remain absolute.

The principles of wisdom and truth have an existence independent of our observations, senses, and understanding. They are the structure of intelligence of the fifth dimension. Or, to explain it in a different way, they are the structure of intelligence which is the mind of God. As such, they are knowable—and reliable. They are the one objective phenomenon of life. In other words, if one thousand enlightened individuals were to contact the same archetypal force of divine wisdom, they would all basically agree on their interpretation of it. Their interest in it and perhaps even their description of it might vary, depending upon their background, work, and cultural training—but they would all recognize that they were contacting the same archetypal force.

This is a powerful concept, because it confirms that divine wisdom is an absolute reality which can be known. It makes the process of cultivating wisdom much easier, because we can reasonably proceed on the assumption that the higher self and the universe in which it lives is already wise. Our task is primarily one of building a bridge between the personality and the wisdom of the higher self. As we do, we increase our capacity to become aware of and utilize the wisdom within us.

The bridge which links us with the wisdom of the higher self is built in five stages:

1. By cultivating a love of truth.

2. By training our mind to become responsive to wisdom and truth.

3. By learning to work intelligently with symbolic and abstract thought.

4. By focusing the intention to apply wisdom in the pursuit of enlightened living.

5. By developing the habit of exploring the higher realms of life.

Each of these five stages in building the bridge to wisdom will be examined in a section of its own.

THE LOVE OF TRUTH

The magnetic power of love is a tremendous asset in the effort to attune to the wisdom of the higher self. The love of truth is not just a platitude, but a dynamic concept. As our love of truth grows, our capacity to invoke inspiration, penetrate self-deception, and comprehend the ideals of the higher self also grows.

Like wisdom, truth is multidimensional. In physical life, we often think of truth one-dimensionally, as the accuracy of facts, statements, and statistics—or we personalize it, making truth subservient to our subjective beliefs, desires, and opinions. As we explore the inner dimensions of life, however, we will find that there is much more depth to truth than this. We must consider the meaning, design, purpose, and universality of truth as well as its appearance and application to us. After all, a "true" statement which is used to deceive people—as is so commonly done in advertising and politics—can hardly be thought of as embodying archetypal truth. In the same way, a concept about the power of God which causes people to grovel before God and think themselves worthless is surely not a part of divine wisdom, for it works against the purposes of both divine and human life.

If the concepts of wisdom and truth are to make sense, we must see them as derivatives of the divine archetypes of life. Any idea or concept which is in harmony with archetypal life and helps to fulfill its purpose is wise. Any statement or act which is in harmony with divine ideals and honors them is truthful.

We do not establish the wisdom or truth of any idea or concept, for wisdom and truth are inherent in the plan of God. But by loving truth, we master the first stage in building the bridge of wisdom. The love of truth consists of three elements:

1. Devotion to the divine origin of truth and wisdom.

2. Respect for truth and wisdom as the basis for conducting life—individually and collectively.

3. The effort to honor truth and wisdom and revise our thoughts, feelings, and behavior so that they become consistent with the divine archetypes of life.

Unless we love truth, we are likely to accept *counterfeit* insight and use it to guide our thinking and creativity. We will be too easily satisfied with superficial explanations.

Unless we love truth, we are likely to deceive ourself. As we explore the wisdom of the higher self, we begin to discover that some of the attitudes and beliefs we have cherished at the personality level are nothing but prejudices, attachments, and self-deceptions. It can be painful to make these discoveries, and even more painful to act upon them, unless we are sufficiently motivated to do so. The love of truth is the one force which can provide this motivation. It gives us the courage to risk being wrong, and learn from our errors. It likewise gives us the courage to risk being right—which to some people is even more frightening.

Unless we love truth, we will be constantly adrift in the sea of public opinion. We will be unsure and confused as to how to proceed—whether to be skeptical or enthusiastic, pessimistic or optimistic. We may even believe that we can serve truth by hating falsehood—which is perhaps the greatest deception of all. The love of truth helps us establish a proper posture toward the use of the mind and the wisdom of the higher self.

TRAINING THE MIND

The empty mind which some misguided spiritual authorities cherish is *not* a blank slate waiting to be written on—it is no slate at all! The mind is the primary staging ground by which the wisdom and creative inspiration of the higher self enters into the personality. A stupid, untrained mind is therefore a serious barrier to the development of practical wisdom, common sense, and truth. To build the bridge to the higher self, we must make it a constant habit to train and improve the quality of the mind.

These are some of the basic skills the mind needs to develop:

Concentration	Discernment	Discrimination
Logic	Analysis	Objectivity
Induction	Deduction	Planning
Evaluation	Organization	Creativity
Contemplation	Intuition	Integrity
Common sense	Adaptability	Harmony
Detachment	Association	Synthesis

None of these skills by itself would guarantee responsiveness to the wisdom of the higher self, as they can all be developed for the use of the personality alone. Yet until these skills are at least partly mastered, it will not be possible to become responsive to our inner wisdom.

How are these skills learned? To some degree, the conventional instruction of high school and college can provide an excellent basis for developing many of these skills. But the level of skill demanded by these institutions is not at present very high. So the intelligent person will see this instruction only as a starting point, and will work throughout his or her life to continue the education of the mind. This is accomplished by using the mind actively to pursue insight about our past, our relationships, our careers, the weighty issues confronting society, the new frontiers of mental discovery, and the meaning of daily events. When the mind is able to comprehend these issues, without coaching from others, then it can be assumed that it is well prepared to comprehend the guidance and wisdom of the higher self.

SYMBOLIC AND ABSTRACT THOUGHT

To go very far with Active Meditation, we must learn to view the world of ideas, events, and ourselves as *symbols* of wisdom and truth. These symbols are not wisdom and truth themselves, but have the potential to *embody* the richness and force of archetypal life. In time, the skill of recognizing the real within the symbolic becomes highly important to the meditator; it becomes the basis for comprehending the broad patterns, meanings, and principles within events, relationships, self-expression, and the unfoldment of consciousness. As Paul taught us, "Ever since God created the world his everlasting power and deity—however invisible—have been there for the mind to see in the things he has made." While inner wisdom does exist independent of the life of form and the personality, *the way to wisdom* is found by studying the outer appearances of life and then speculating on the laws, principles, designs, and ideas which gave rise to them.

A symbol is any concrete form which reveals the abstract essence from which it has derived. The symbol itself does not contain the power, significance, or intelligence of the abstract thought it represents, any more than a picture of a flower contains the fragrance, beauty, or life of the flower. The value of either the symbol or the picture is that it helps us become aware of the reality it represents.

272

Many people are confused by the value of symbols. They have been taught that symbols are images, and the ability to "think in images" is the same as working with abstract ideas. This is as silly as believing that a person who thumbs through a seed catalog, looking at all the pictures of flowers, is a gardener. And yet this misconception is widespread. An image is not a symbol at all until we go beyond the image itself and contact the abstract reality it represents. The mere observation of an image does not accomplish this.

If we can learn to use symbols to go beyond images, events, and other aspects of the form life and touch the abstract essence of archetypal life, however, they can be most useful to us—a doorway to inner wisdom. Working with symbols will help us learn that the mind is not limited to concrete intellectual analysis alone; it is capable of handling creative inspiration, abstractions, and insight. It will introduce us to a refined world of subtle qualities, meaning, and purpose. And it will greatly stimulate the power of our thinking. The person who has not learned to think symbolically will read a few paragraphs in a book and then struggle to comprehend its meaning. To a large degree, he will be limited to a literal interpretation of what he has read. But the person who has trained himself in symbolic and abstract thought will be able to read the same paragraphs and intuit the intention of the author in writing them, the value of these ideas to his own life, and the relationship between these concepts and others he has read on the same subject.

In working with symbols, however, it must be understood that there are both abstract thoughts and abstract feelings. A symbol can lead us to either one, depending upon our need and orientation. An abstract feeling would be the essence of a particular emotion. Goodwill, for example, is the abstract quality which is the essence of the practical expression of tolerance and forgiveness. It is experienced as a broad, pervasive feeling of love and respect for others. An abstract thought, by contrast, is the archetypal force which is the essence of a particular idea. It is experienced as direct understanding of the significance of an idea and how it relates to other ideas.

An example may help clarify this distinction. If we are unhappy in life, but manage to tap the quality of cheerfulness and joy in meditation, we would be touching an abstract feeling. If we then also touched an understanding of *why* we have been unhappy—that we have expected others to make us happy instead of accepting responsibility for our own happiness—this would be an abstract thought.

Abstract feelings are quite useful in our work to heal and enrich the emotions, expanding our expression of divine love. In the work of building a stronger bridge to wisdom and truth, however, we must focus primarily on abstract thought. We must seek to understand life and be guided by wisdom—not just feel good about life.

As we begin working with abstract thought, it will most commonly arrive in response to our efforts to understand a confusing aspect of mundane life, as described in the example just cited. But as we become more adept at interacting with inner wisdom, the focus of abstract thought will shift. More and more it will arrive in response to our efforts to be creative. While contemplating a set of ideas or possibilities, we will suddenly find ourself immersed in an awareness of what to do with these ideas, what they mean, and the purpose they fulfill. These will not be separate, finite thoughts, but rather the perfectly proportioned facets of a pure and clear diamond of thought—a thought which embraces the entire range of possibility and application and yet remains whole. Wherever we focus this diamond, we are able to understand how to proceed. We have tapped the basic design and power of this particular idea.

This kind of abstract thinking is experienced only by those

who spend large amounts of time in deep thought and have refined their skills in working symbolically and abstractly. Such experiences are almost totally devoid of mood or attitude; the meditator is entirely absorbed in the intelligence, meaning, and purpose of the thought he is contemplating.

When we reach this level of functioning, we are able to deal directly with the archetypal forces of divine mind. We are able to inspect the fundamental principles and patterns which serve as the ideal blueprint for all creativity, healing, and self-improvement. We do not have to speculate as to the nature of human psychology; we can examine the archetypes from which it derives. We do not have to wonder when creative inspiration will strike; we can go seek it out, rather than waiting for it to arrive. The capacity to operate in this way is one of the great fruits of Active Meditation.

In practice, the simplest way to develop a capacity for abstract thought is to search for the purpose or underlying themes behind any event, pattern, or fact in our life, our relationships with others, and the affairs of society. As this becomes a regular habit, we become progressively more attuned to the meaning behind the outer symbols of life.

THE INTENTION TO APPLY WISDOM

Within every archetypal idea there is not only intelligence and meaning but also a strong impulse to act. In order to work fully with the wisdom of the higher self, therefore, we must become responsive to the will-to-life it contains, as well as its inspiration and light. This is accomplished by cultivating the intention to apply wisdom in enlightened living. Without such intention, much of the value of Active Meditation is apt to be dissipated in idle speculation and otherworldly pursuits. It will lose its practical benefit.

The will-to-life is a powerful force which seeks to activate all enlightened elements within consciousness. The best way to harness this will-to-life is to nurture a personal determination to be the right person doing the right thing at all times. As this determination builds, we gain access to the force of will within wisdom. We can then use this force of will in meditation to *penetrate* the elements of ignorance, self-deception, and selfishness still in the character of the personality, while simultaneously strengthening the elements of intelligence, maturity, and discipline which can clear them away.

Many people fail to appreciate this active mode of wisdom. They believe that wisdom consists entirely of understanding life; if they understand their foibles and failings, then they are wise. And yet, this is not actually true. The person who understands his deficiencies and flaws and then fails to change them is hardly wise. Understanding must be translated into action before it becomes wisdom.

The intention to apply wisdom to the challenges of enlightened living creates a pathway for the light of wisdom to enter into our conscious thoughts, feelings, and behavior. It also helps provide a practical focus for the wisdom, qualities, and ideals we contact during meditation.

Some people, of course, would argue that giving meditation a practical focus destroys the whole purpose of meditation, which they think is to leave the physical plane behind. Yet the spiritual duty of the Western tradition *is* to give enlightened expression to the forces, ideas, and qualities of spirit, and not just passively adore God. If we can find no practical use for the love and wisdom of the higher self, either in ourself or in society, then there must be something missing from the "love" and the "wisdom" we have discovered. The need for the life of spirit is great. There is hardly an area of our character, our endeavors, or the affairs of society which cannot benefit from an extra touch of understanding and insight. The pursuit

276

of wisdom should never be limited to arcane secrets and religious mysteries alone. In most cases, it has a direct application to daily life, because *God is involved in every area of life!*

The wisdom and light of the higher self has the power to shine through *every* facet of our self-expression. But it cannot do so until we formulate the intention to take an active part in applying wisdom—to harness the illuminating light of the higher self to cast out ignorance wherever we find it.

This is what *enlightenment* means in the Western tradition.

EXPLORING THE HIGHER REALMS

The power within archetypal ideas affects us in another way, too. It stimulates our curiosity to explore the higher realms of mind and spirit—to not be restrained by the known and the familiar, but to reach out beyond the boundary of our thoughts and discover new dimensions.

The mundane focus of ordinary consciousness serves a useful purpose in helping us remain attentive to our duties and obligations. And yet, it can also serve to cramp our curiosity and limit our perspective on life. To complete our bridge to the wisdom of the higher self, it is therefore necessary to teach ourself to break free from the restrictions of ordinary consciousness and periodically explore the higher realms of life.

Many people—even meditators—simply become bogged down in narrowmindedness and limited perspectives. They value only the qualities and principles of living which are directly useful to them, and either ignore or reject everything else. As a result, they become mired in prejudice, fear, doubt, prohibitions, and misconceptions. In one who pursues the wisdom of the higher self, these traits can sabotage the entire effort.

There are three fundamental attributes to cultivate in

teaching ourself to explore the higher realms of consciousness:

1. Broadmindedness. Recognizing that a single archetypal force can give rise to thousands of different expressions, we begin to appreciate more fully the rich diversity of self-expression among the peoples and cultures of human civilization. We cultivate a more universal posture toward life, thinking in terms of the planet as a whole as well as our personal needs.

2. Speculation. We make it a habit to review situations from the past, present, and future and explore the possibility that there might be a better way—a more enlightened way—of managing problems, seizing opportunities, and fulfilling responsibilities.

3. Innovativeness. In dealing with problems and creative challenges, we strive to look for new ways of handling them. In this way, we invoke the guidance of inner wisdom to help us in our thinking, instead of merely relying on the traditions of the past.

INVOKING WISDOM

These five stages in building the bridge to the wisdom of the higher self can, of course, be translated into a meditative technique for invoking wisdom. While this technique, like all of the others in this book, begins with establishing contact with the higher self, it is designed to be used at light meditative levels as well as more profound levels. As such, it can be conveniently used whenever we have the *need* for wisdom—at work, while reading, while reflecting on the problems of life, and so on. It should not be limited to formal meditations.

The technique is also designed to be flexible and versatile. Routines and set formats can become deadening to the development of wisdom. So can rigid expectations. There are many ways in which the higher self can communicate with us—through mental impressions, images, a sense of rightness or wrongness, or specific words and thoughts. We should be flexible enough to perceive wisdom in whatever form it arrives.

Once contact has been established with the higher self, the next step is to take a moment to define our need to know. What is our need for wisdom? This could be a problem we need to solve, an area of confusion, an opportunity we want to evaluate, an aspect of character we want to review, a relationship we want to improve, a responsibility we want to better execute, or something else of this nature. In order to better understand this situation, we need guidance and assistance from our inner wisdom. The purpose of defining this need to know is that it gives us a starting point from which to proceed. We are not just waiting for a handout of wisdom from the higher self, but taking the initiative to invoke guidance to help us act more wisely in a specific way.

Having defined this need to know and given focus to our quest, it is then important to be flexible and choose the method of contacting the wisdom of the higher self which will best suit our purpose. There is an extensive "menu" to choose from:

1. **Invoking the ideal solution.** We can assume that the ideal way of handling this situation already exists in the understanding of the higher self, as a pattern or principle. All that we need to do is to transfer this existing wisdom into our conscious awareness. This can be done by thinking of our inner wisdom as a vast research library where information on every subject already exists—including the ideal solution to this particular line of inquiry. In our imagination, we can visit this research library and investigate the answers it already contains. Or, we might take advantage of a "meditative time warp" and assume this ideal resolution has already worked itself out in physical manifestation. By looking back over what has already occurred and reviewing the way in which the ideal

has unfolded, we are able to obtain valuable insights and clues as to how best to proceed.

2. **Discerning purpose and principles.** Since the abstract essence of an idea includes its purpose and principles, an excellent method for transcending the limits of mundane thinking is to seek to discern the purpose and principles at work in the subject of our inquiry. This must involve something more than just examining what we *want* from the situation, however—that would only reveal our personal motivation. Rather, we must endeavor to look at the situation from the perspective of the higher self, and how it views the purpose and principles being served. This process can be stimulated by asking our inner wisdom various questions: What forces are involved in this situation? What is their origin and intention? What lessons are being taught? Is this in harmony with universal principles? What is the best way to fulfill the purpose being served?

3. **Role playing.** We can imagine that we are a wise research scientist or an experienced investigative reporter seeking to discover the truth behind some phenomenon or aspect of life. Cast in one of these roles, we can reflect on the why, how, when, where, and who of the object of our inquiry. We seek this information from the vast resources of the wisdom of the higher self. Role playing is an excellent way to achieve a greater measure of impersonality and objectivity in our effort to invoke wisdom.

4. **Working with symbols.** It is sometimes quite useful to invoke a symbol for our object of inquiry from the higher self, and then ponder on the meaning, insight, and force which the symbol represents. This is done by dwelling briefly on the expectation that the higher self will subtly suggest to us an appropriate symbol. As our attention shifts from our need to the realization that the higher self is capable of doing this, and we adopt a receptive, listening attitude, the invocation is answered

and the symbol comes into focus. In specific, there are a great many esoteric symbols which can lead to much insight into the wisdom of the higher self as they are contemplated and examined. Nevertheless, it is always important to remember that the purpose of symbols is not fulfilled merely by receiving a vivid image. The reason for invoking a symbol is to go beyond the form and tap the abstract essence it represents.

5. **Personifying our inner wisdom.** Personification is a marvelous way to translate abstract patterns of wisdom into concrete images the subconscious mind can relate to. In using this approach to inner wisdom, however, it is important to always keep in mind that the personification we create is being guided and directed by our higher self, thereby leading us into a greater rapport with its wisdom. If we do not proceed with a strong dedication to truth, a personification can easily be taken over by our wishes and fantasies.

In personifying our inner wisdom, the most convenient image to use is that of a wise sage or teacher who can guide us and instruct us in the proper perspective regarding our object of inquiry. It is never necessary to see this image clearly; the point of this exercise is not to obtain clear visions, but to improve our understanding of life. Consequently, the emphasis should be placed on looking at life from the perspective of this wise teacher—the personification of our own higher wisdom. The actual dynamics of conversation are less important. Another useful personification is to think of our inner wisdom as a committee of experts seated at a round table. These experts are there to answer our questions concerning the object of our inquiry.

6. **Working with divine archetypes.** The archetypes are the patterns of wisdom and intelligence in the mind of God. They contain the insight, meaning, intelligence, and power from which genuine creative work draws its strength. To become a wise parent, therefore, it can be helpful to work directly

with the archetypes for parenting and growth. To become a wise citizen, it can be useful to work with the archetypes of responsibility, duty, and brotherhood. To become truly wise in any field of human endeavor, it is important to become familiar with the archetypes which govern it. This is not as difficult as it might seem at first. Taking the object of our inquiry, we reflect on the patterns of divine intelligence which govern it and the basic design by which it operates. As we ponder on these patterns, we invoke the appropriate archetypal force, resting in the belief that our invocation is being answered. We then communicate with this pure force of life. It may require a touch of imagination and a bit of experience to become comfortable with communicating with abstract patterns of intelligence, but if we persevere, we gradually begin to recognize the distinct qualities of the various archetypal forces of life. When first beginning, this process can be helped by using symbols to represent the various divine archetypes.

Once our use of one of these six methods of contacting the wisdom of the higher self is finished, it still remains to distill the wisdom we have touched into a definite intention to act. Each meditative exercise in working with the wisdom of the higher self should conclude by reviewing the insight gained, examining its larger implications, and then determining its practical application in our life.

COMMON SENSE

Until we have mastered these approaches to the wisdom of the higher self, there will always be a certain measure of doubt as to whether we are actually contacting our inner wisdom—or just the playacting department of the subconscious. This is a real concern, but it should never be allowed to become so intense that it actually interferes with the reception of guidance and intuition. We should always proceed with the quiet confidence that the higher self is just as interested in these meditative efforts as the personality is. It wants to help us be the right person and do the right thing. So our exercises will be overshadowed and supervised by the wisdom of the higher self. A measure of self-deception and fantasy may also creep in from time to time, but we must not be overly attentive to it. The more we work with these techniques, the more we will become familiar with what is wisdom, what is fantasy. In addition, our basic integrity and common sense will always prevent us from wandering too far astray.

Under no circumstances should we assume that we are duty bound to accept without reservation all input arising from these exercises. We all have an obligation to review advice and guidance, from whatever the source, before we act upon it. This good sense extends even to advice we believe to be coming from the higher self. If the insights we receive mesh with our values, principles, and sense of duty, it is reasonable to trust them. If they do not, we should be highly skeptical of them.

It is the failure to exercise this responsibility which leaves open the door to self-deception. By using simple common sense and good judgment, we can avoid the vast majority of problems which tend to arise—and far more quickly develop a useful rapport with the wisdom of the higher self.

THE TECHNIQUE
FOR INVOKING WISDOM

The technique for invoking the wisdom of the higher self can be summarized as follows:

1. We begin by entering a meditative state and contacting the higher self, as described in chapter five.

2. We define our need to know, giving focus to our invocation of wisdom.

3. We choose the appropriate method for making contact with the wisdom of the higher self, selecting from the various skills of Active Meditation. The choices include invoking the ideal solution, discerning purpose and principles, role playing, working with symbols, personification, and working with divine archetypes. Using whichever method we select, we then thoroughly investigate the topic we have in mind.

4. We conclude by reviewing the insights we have gained and building the intention to apply them to life, thereby touching the power to act wisely.

12

Applying Wisdom
To Solve Problems

OUR SPIRITUAL OBLIGATION

The differences among meditative traditions are perhaps never more obvious than in the ways they are designed to handle stress. Every human being must deal with problems, difficulties, and stressful conditions on a daily basis, whether he meditates or not. Because meditation connects us with the wisdom, peace, and greater insight of the higher self, it can be extremely effective in managing problem situations. But not all meditative approaches to problems and stress are equal.

Many of the passive systems of meditation, for example, endeavor to cope with stress by avoiding it. The meditative period is spent emptying the mind and emotions of all content, including stressful reactions. Since the emptiness is pleasant in comparison to the stress and worries of daily living, an illusion of managing stress is created. But once the meditative period is completed, and the meditator must confront his problems and anxieties anew, the stress returns. In fact, the meditator may well be more irritable than before.

These systems also frequently teach their devotees to become indifferent to the problems of the world. Instead of learning to solve problems, they withdraw from them and become absorbed entirely in the inner life. There is certainly nothing wrong with being absorbed in the inner life, but it should never be carried to the extreme of cutting off all interest in the outer life. Meditation is meant to be a means for bringing the life of the higher self into the life of the personality. As such, it does not make sense to use meditation to abandon the personality or to seek escape from its difficulties.

Active Meditation, therefore, puts its emphasis on reducing stress by *solving* our problems and difficulties—not by withdrawing from them. In this way, it applies the basic theme of the greater taking care of the lesser; instead of the personality seeking to become absorbed in the life of the higher self as a refuge from the problems of daily life, the personality invokes the wisdom and power of the higher self to correct the problems at hand. It involves heaven in the affairs of earth.

This, after all, is a fundamental goal of the Western tradition—not only to discover the presence of God, but to *practice* this presence as our primary spiritual obligation.

TURNING POINTS

Most people view problems as troublesome—something to avoid at all costs. And yet they are a natural phenomenon of life. The person who believes himself to be without problems is either asleep or self-deceived.

While no one would want to deliberately create problems for himself, it is nonetheless helpful to realize that many of our problems do serve worthwhile purposes. They motivate us to grow and become a better person. They give us experience in handling opposition and resistance with maturity. And in many cases, they are actually opportunities in disguise.

In fact, there is often a great deal of potential power in problems. A moment of crisis may be a turning point in our life, but if we manage it successfully the direction we turn will be for the better. At such times, our ability to gather resources, solicit the assistance of friends, and invoke the higher self may well be greater than at more "normal" times.

The key lies in how we respond to the problem.

If we habitually respond by seeking refuge in passive meditation, we will be completely unprepared to seize the opportunity of the turning point.

If we habitually respond by attacking the problem in the same mode which led to it in the first place, but more angrily and aggressively than before, the turning point will become so painful—or exhausting—that we cannot capitalize on it.

Yet if we habitually respond by seeking out the wise counsel and enlightened perspective of the higher self in Active Meditation, we will be able to see clearly the lessons being learned, the opportunities presented to us, and a reasonable solution to the problem.

This can be done by posing a series of questions the higher self can answer. These questions should examine why and how the problem has developed, what we have contributed to it, the lessons we can learn from it, the deeper issues behind the outer symptoms, and the most effective way to resolve it.

Some people are hesitant to ask specific questions of the higher self. They believe they should merely contact the wisdom of the higher self and let it guide them whither it will. After all, they reason, the personality knows so little and the higher self knows so much, why should the personality impose limits on the capacity of the higher self to guide us? This attitude, however, is sadly out of harmony with the way communication between the higher self and the personality occurs. It is the responsibility of the personality to initiate the request for assistance from the higher self—and to skillfully direct the guidance it receives. This is most successfully done by formulating penetrating questions which will invoke a response.

The meditative practice of waiting for the higher self to guide us, instead of taking the initiative to request specific answers, often results in serious self-deception. The meditator spends years nibbling at the edges of problems, thinking he is struggling bravely to cope with major issues, when in fact he is not working with the heart of the problems at all—just the symptoms.

The higher self is always striving to help the personality increase its responsibility—not decrease it. It will provide us with useful guidance and insight—but it still expects us to take this help and integrate it into our daily living. It expects us to make decisions and accept the consequences of them. It expects us to play an active role in working to resolve the problems we encounter. We should always know that we can turn to the higher self to strengthen our courage and determination, but it is up to us to confront the issues and challenges ourself. This is the way in which we become a competent agent of the wisdom, love, and power of the higher self.

There are three basic classifications of problems with which we must deal:

1. Personal problems.
2. Career problems.
3. Problems arising from creative activity.

The kind of questions to direct meditatively to the higher self will vary somewhat for each of these categories. Each will therefore be examined in greater detail by itself.

PERSONAL PROBLEMS

The single greatest difficulty in managing personal problems is that we are so intimately involved in them. As a result, it can be quite hard to achieve a meaningful level of detachment and view the situation with objectivity. All too often, we color the questions we ask with our wishes and expectations, so that the answers will please and satisfy us. But loaded questions always bring loaded answers.

Another factor to consider is that we are usually far more aware of the symptoms of the problem and our reactions to them—as well as our defenses against them—than we are of the genuine, underlying difficulty. A person who is lazy and parasitical, for example, is likely to find it hard to compete against others who are hardworking and skilled. But he will probably not recognize the true nature of his disadvantage. He will tend to think that society is discriminating against him unfairly and holding him down. If he admits his laziness at all, he will justify it as a rightful response to the treatment he has received. In this way, he obscures the basic problem—parasitism—and perpetuates a cycle of hostility and resentment.

The questions we pose in order to solve personal problems must therefore be designed so as to help us penetrate beyond our self-deception and arrive at the true problem we must confront. These are the basic questions to consider:

What are the patterns and trends which have led to this problem? In particular, we should examine what we have contributed to the problem—and how we have perhaps aggravated it. Many of our personal problems arise only because we have been negligent in attending to duties, commitments, assignments, and obligations. If we are being dunned by bill collectors, after all, the problem lies not in the obnoxious, persistent behavior of the bill collectors, but in our basic failure to pay what we owe. Just so, if we have a problem of loneliness, we ought to examine what efforts we have made lately to cultivate friends—and how we have treated the friends we already have. If we have been bitterly criticized by a colleague, we should consider the possibility that we have been critical or antagonistic toward him. At times, this investigation must become quite subtle. If we feel that our friends have been letting us down in a time of need, even though we have always been ready to help them, perhaps we need to consider the possibility that the "help" we have given them in the past has been rather self-serving and manipulative. Quite possibly it was not even perceived as help!

What is the psychological climate in which this problem arose? Many of our problems are subtly exacerbated by the context in which they are generated. A simple disagreement between two people may take on complex overtones if they happen to be members of the same family—especially if the family has strict traditions it expects individual members to respect. The same principle can affect other personal problems as well. Some of our problems, for example, are simply the problems of humanity in general, as is the case with the teenager who affects the superficiality and pettiness of popular role models. Others may be conditioned by psychic influences from mass consciousness—the fear of economic hard times, for example, or the chauvinism which usually accompanies nationalistic fervor. Examining the climate in which the problem arises can therefore provide us with many clues for managing it more intelligently. After all, if we try to treat a bigot by being a bigot, too, we will probably soon find that we are only increasing the intensity of the problem.

What is the real work to be done in solving this problem? It is easy to become absorbed in the minor issues and details of a problem and fail to recognize the larger issues involved. When this occurs, we usually end up pouring our time and energy into "correcting" aspects of the problem which are relatively unimportant. In such cases, we need to stand back and embrace the larger perspective, examining the real work to be done. The parent who is constantly at odds with his or her children may need to devote less attention to harping on the lack of respect of children for parents and more attention to learning the principles of good parenting. The person who has difficulty relating to strangers may need to become aware of the corrollary problem of not liking himself or anyone else all that much. As we make the effort to broaden our perspective on the real dimensions of our problems in these ways, we are able to see more clearly the changes to be made. Narrowness of attention can actually blind us to the roots of our difficulties.

What is the real question posed by this problem? The higher self sends us to earth in order to learn and serve, be helpful in the world, acquire greater skill and expertise, and honor our spiritual potential. If we, at the personality level, tend to view all work as an imposition, all conflict as harassment, all offers of cooperation as intrusions, and all criticism as an attack on our character, then it will be impossible to arrive at *any* enlightened solutions to the problems of our life. The higher self will be unable to help us reduce stress, because much of what we are defining as stress is an opportunity! It is therefore important to start viewing many of our problems in a new and different way, trying to determine their potential for success rather than their potential for failure.

As long as a problem is seen only as an obstacle, it may well be unsolvable. But if we begin to view it as an opportunity for growth, we can usually make it precisely that very quickly. To do this, we must ask ourself what we can learn from this problem—about ourself, human nature, the needs of others, how we can be helpful, and what new responsibilities we ought to accept. In this way, we begin approaching problems constructively instead of defensively.

What is the best possible solution? The one factor which prolongs and aggravates most problems is the unintelligent definition of what a "solution" to the problem will be. In most cases, the solution sought is no solution at all—just the desire to survive, avoid conflict, and wait for better times. As a result, we retreat into defensiveness—instead of seeing that we do have the option to take constructive steps to improve the situation. Sometimes, we even go a step beyond defensiveness and entertain a perverse desire for vengeance or punishment, thereby introducing elements which will intensify the problem, not resolve it.

It should be understood that some people do not actually want to solve their problems. They prefer to hide their weaknesses behind the outer appearance of great difficulty—they are addicted to the martyr complex they have carefully built up. These people, and those who seek revenge, would not consider the resolution of their problems as a moment of triumph, as it would rob them of their perverse delight in suffering or their justification for continued anger. As these tendencies can at times be very subtle, it is therefore quite important to examine our *motives* regarding our problems. Are we in any way secretly committed to sustaining this problem? Or have we carelessly set a goal which *de facto* makes the problem an open-ended one?

By taking the time meditatively to determine what the ideal solution to our problem will be, we orient our thoughts and attitudes toward resolving it, not prolonging it. We create a mental framework in which it becomes possible to see the constructive options and practical steps which lie before us. In doing this, however, we must take care not to limit our definition of "best possible solution" to what is best for us alone. Most personal problems involve other people. If we consider only what is best for us, we are severely limiting our choices and probably reducing our chances of discovering what truly is the best solution.

What new qualities, forces, and talents do we need to cultivate in order to resolve this difficulty? The object of meditating on our problems is not to convince us that everyone else is wrong and we are right. Indeed, nothing traps a person in his or her problems more than a sense of righteousness. The reason for meditating on difficulties is to devise enlightened ways of resolving them. This usually involves developing new qualities, forces, and talents which we can then apply to the situation at hand. Occasionally, it may also involve learning to stop acting in ways that irritate the problem. Often, the new skill to be learned is quite obvious—greater patience, renewed faith, or a stronger dose of courage. But sometimes it is more subtle, involving a greater intuitive capacity to appreciate the ways other people view these circumstances or the capacity to remain firm in our convictions without seeming dogmatic, obstinate, or pushy to others.

How best can we integrate these new qualities, forces, and talents into our self-expression? It is naive to think that new measures of patience or goodwill can simply be plastered on the outer surface of our character, thereby permanently hiding our old traits of rudeness, intolerance, and criticism. Plaster soon chips and wears thin, and this is also true of superficial changes in self-expression. To be effective, these new qualities, forces, and talents must be permanently worked into the foundation of our character. If our problem is rudeness and brusqueness, for example, it will be necessary not only to practice politeness and respect for others in the one situation which is most irritating to us, but in all of our dealings with others. In this way, the new skills become a permanent part of our character, not just a temporary convenience.

CAREER PROBLEMS

Many of the problems we encounter in the work place are merely extensions of personal problems, and need to be handled as such. Rudeness is rudeness, whether we happen to be with friends or at the office. But many problems from the work place are distinct from personal problems—especially if the work we do is part of a group enterprise. These are often problems which affect the whole business or activity, and must be solved with this in mind. They are not our personal problems alone. As a result, the kind of questions we direct at the higher self, in order to better understand and solve this problem, will be somewhat different. These are the basic questions to consider:

What mental framework are we using to define and solve this problem? Many experts in business management view problems with a very narrow mind set. Engineers, for example, tend to view *all* business problems in terms of nuts and bolts, machines, flow charts, and production—as though humans were machines or even behave like machines. Accountants tend to view the problems of the company as a whole in terms of what will make it easier for them to keep the books—or cut expenses—not in terms of what is best for customers, employees, or productivity. Such mental sets are extremely common—and many problems are created or aggravated by the fact that a person working in one mental set is unable to communicate effectively with someone using a different one. So it can be very helpful to determine the mental sets being used to define the problem. But it is also important to understand that *any* mental set can be limiting. It blinds the people who use it to the real issues at hand and the best methods for solving them. A person who views all aspects of a business as though it were a machine which can be fixed will be blind to the impact of his decisions on staff and customers. A person who sees the needs of a business only in terms of the bottom line of a financial report will never comprehend issues of purpose, quality, and style. A person concerned only with the public's impression of the work being done will tend to sacrifice long-term progress for a short-term impact. To truly solve the problems of business, therefore, we must be able to transcend the limitations the various mind sets of business impose upon us.

What is our actual responsibility in this situation? Many problems in the work place become aggravated because no one is willing to accept responsibility to initiate remedial action until specifically ordered to do so by a superior. Other problems are created when one person attempts to intrude in a situation where he or she has no responsibility—and no business. So it can be quite enlightening to examine the scope of responsibility we actually do have in any situation. This responsibility can be of two kinds. The first would be the specific duties spelled out by the job we hold. The second is the obligation we have to the welfare and growth of the entire enterprise we are a part of. It is this latter responsibility which is so often forgotten in the work place. Workers refuse to help their colleagues when it is clear they need assistance—and then later attempt to "help" when it is obviously not needed. They are often more interested in the mischief and embarrassment they can create than in the contribution they can make to the company or agency.

In what kind of environment has this problem developed? Long-standing morale problems, depressed market conditions, bad publicity about a product or service offered, or serious competition can affect our ability to work out a simple solution to problems. To try to remedy difficulties without considering these external factors can make it all but impossible to achieve success. And yet, these external factors are not always as troublesome as they sometimes first appear. Depressed market conditions, for example, often lead to a tightening of efficiency and internal discipline which continues to benefit the company long after the poor conditions pass away. And yet, to take advantage of these environmental conditions, we must first ascertain what they are.

What trends are inherent in this problem? Experience is a tremendous help in analyzing our problems. It enables us to understand the events and decisions from the past which may be affecting the problem we are facing today, and gives us a basis for projecting how this trend will continue, if left unchecked. We can examine, for instance, how this kind of problem has been resolved in the past—and whether or not that approach will work in the present. Sometimes, this examination of trends will indicate that no action is required; it is best to let the problem die of its own inertia. At other times, however, it will indicate that the trends which have led to this problem are far more serious than the problem itself has suggested, and swift action is necessary before conditions worsen. In this regard, it is useful to keep in mind that many trends are cyclical in nature and need to be treated accordingly.

What is the real problem to be solved? As with personal problems, it is important to separate the real difficulty from its symptoms. Sales may be declining, but the problem may not be in the sales force. Instead, it may involve bad management, faulty marketing strategy, or weak quality control. Assuming that the sales force is responsible for slumping sales may lead to more problems, not less. One of the best ways to separate the real issues from the symptoms is to consider how the problem at hand is affecting the whole enterprise and its capacity to fulfill its purpose. The reassignment of duties from one unit to another, for example, may strain relations between the personnel in these two units, and yet may be in the best interest of the company as a whole. The problem is therefore not the actual decision to reassign these duties—although the people affected may think so—but rather the petty bickering which is transpiring between these two units. By putting the problem in the context of the purpose of the enterprise as a whole, it is often relatively simple to see the larger dimensions involved— and the solution to implement.

Have we been asking the right question? Sometimes problems in the work place do not arise because of adverse conditions, but rather because we have made unrealistic assumptions or are working toward false goals. Many managers, for example, believe they can mold the people working for them into their own personal style. In the vast majority of cases, this is an unrealistic assumption; the employees will rebel against it. Yet the fault lies not in the employees, but in the false assumption made by the manager. If such a person were to ask the question, "Why are employees so disloyal in our modern society," he would be asking the wrong question. He should be asking instead, "What attitudes of mine have been causing my employees to rebel against me?"

What practical steps can be taken to solve this problem? The cardinal rule of working on problems of the work place is to tailor solutions to factors under our control. It serves no constructive purpose, after all, for a clerk to daydream about what he would do to correct a morale problem if he were the manager. But the same clerk does have the opportunity to decide how he can contribute to the improvement of morale, by being more cheerful, more supportive of the work of others, and more optimistic about the future of the company. As we examine the practical steps to be taken, therefore, we should consider what can be done within the sphere of authority we have—or how to obtain the power to implement these steps if we do not already have it. Other factors which will be involved in implementing the solution should also be considered—the time it will take, the cost, and the chances of success.

PROBLEMS ARISING FROM CREATIVE ACTIVITY

The third category of problems, those which arise from creative activity, differ from the first two in one major way— they are byproducts of our own innovative work. As such, they are usually not as troubling or threatening as the other two classifications of problems can be—but we still require skill and maturity to resolve them properly. Indeed, many times the problems arising from creative activity demand far more skill than any other type of problem.

Creative activity embraces a wide range of inspired self-expression, from establishing an enriched atmosphere for our family life to exploring innovative implications of a favorite hobby to researching the esoteric factors in the genesis of physical illness or a new breakthrough in science or technology. It includes the conventional fields of creativity—the arts, literature, drama, music, and dance—but is not limited solely to them. The problems which arise from these pursuits tend to involve the difficulty of developing creative ideas in the first place, the obstacles to be overcome in refining and perfecting these ideas, opposition from others who are jealous of our creativity or threatened by what we are producing, and the challenge of translating a good idea into a practical reality. The line of questions which best helps us resolve these problems also clearly reminds us of the value of invoking the greater to help in the affairs of the lesser. This must always be the underlying theme of creativity. These questions include:

What is the purpose of this creative activity? Answering this question correctly will be a great boon to our efforts to be inspired with good creative ideas. Many people, unfortunately, seek their inspiration from the greed, lust for attention, fantasies, pride, or illusions which move them to work creatively in the first place. None of these elements contains any creative inspiration, however; they can only stimulate us to copy what others have done before us. The real source of creative inspiration is archetypal life. To contact the archetypes, our primary motivation must be to serve the purposes of the creative ideas themselves—not our personal, petty desires. For a composer, this would be the purposes of the spirit of music; for a scientist, it would be the purposes of the spirit of scientific discovery; for a national leader, it would be the purposes of the national spirit. Meditation is an excellent time to become acquainted with the purpose and force of creative inspiration. Then, when we are ready to perform our creative activity, we will experience far fewer problems in receiving a high level of good inspiration.

What is the real need we are trying to serve? Many people who work creatively are aware of the purposes of their labors, but ignore the needs they will fill—the needs of the people who will benefit from the end result. This might be a parent who understands the principles of the art of parenting but does not adapt them to the individual children in his or her care. Or it could be an artist who becomes totally involved in a private communication with his muse and does not endeavor to use his art as a medium for conveying the inner realities of life to those who will view his paintings. Such shortsightedness limits the creative endeavor and diminishes the impact it will have. It becomes self-serving.

What effect do we seek to create? The one who would learn to work with causes must also become responsible for the effects he produces. A writer, for instance, must weigh not only the music and loveliness of the words he chooses, but also the meaning they convey. If they will confuse or distract the reader from an understanding of the basic themes being presented, they represent poor writing, no matter how clever they might be. Many people, unfortunately, are attracted to creative pursuits by the thrill they derive from producing something new from their own imagination. They have not yet developed a sense of responsibility to make sure that what they are creating will produce favorable effects. When this sense of responsibility is lacking, many problems can arise.

What resources of talent, time, raw materials, and opportunity are we able to draw on? An excellent inspiration does not become a creative masterpiece until it has been translated by the creator from the abstract into the concrete. Many would-be creative people are frustrated because they never manage to produce the great masterworks they claim to be capable of. Yet if they would examine their problem closely, they would see it is mostly the result of their own inability to coordinate talent, time, raw materials, and opportunity. The problem may simply be that they have not yet built up enough skills in their chosen field to work creatively. Or they may not be sufficiently disciplined to produce results. In any event, their frustration can only be reduced by examining the implications of this particular question.

What is the psychological climate in which we are seeking to be creative? There are several levels to examine in answering this particular question. The most important is our own psychological state. Elements of self-doubt, self-criticism, fear, resentment, and fatigue can sabotage creative endeavors. Yet if these elements are discovered, they can be removed in meditation by using appropriate mental housecleaning techniques *before* we launch into our creative endeavors. Another important influence on the psychological climate is generated by those around us. Friends or family members who are jealous of our work or antagonistic can disrupt the creative process at psychic levels. Various forces in mass consciousness can do the same—especially if our creative triumphs tend to put them in a bad light by comparison. The best way to manage these difficulties, if they should arise, is to increase our faith in our own skills and inspiration, and to renew our commitment to serving the purpose of our creative endeavors.

How best can we honor the creative forces we are working with? If creative endeavors are alive and vital, they will grow in scope, quality, and their value to humanity. The creative person should use the unique opportunity of meditation to review the effectiveness of his approach to creativity on a regular basis, always looking for ways to improve it. This would include examining our alignment with creative forces, the strength of our faith in the work we are doing, and the skills and talents we possess. It should also include periodic mental housecleaning, as well as reenergizing the ideals and posture we try to maintain during the creative process—dedication to excellence, a sense of responsibility, and responsiveness to the very best ideas and ideals within us.

SOLVING PROBLEMS

This question-and-answer approach to solving problems is not, of course, limited just to Active Meditation. It can be used by any intelligent person seeking to reflect on the meaning of the difficulties he or she faces. But it is especially powerful when used as a meditative exercise, because meditation is the natural communication between the greater and the lesser—between the higher self and the personality. At a meditative level, we are better able to see that our problems are multidimensional in structure and implication, just as we are a multidimensional being. Quite often, problems can only be solved to the fullest degree if we work on them subconsciously and unconsciously as well as consciously. This can only be done in meditation.

It is always important to keep in mind that when we ask questions at a meditative level, *we receive more than mere answers.* We receive an understanding of why these answers will resolve the problem—and we receive the power to implement the solution. It is this dynamic aspect of problem solving which distinguishes Active Meditation from ordinary thinking and reflection.

The meditative exercise for solving problems begins, as always, by establishing contact with the higher self, using the four-stage process of relaxation, detachment, concentration, and attunement described in chapter five. Once this contact has been reestablished, we should then take a few moments to dwell on the capacity of the greater to care for the lesser—the capacity of the higher self to help us understand and solve our problems. This can be done by meditating on the power behind various seed thoughts, such as "discovery of inner resources," "the perfect strength and wisdom of the higher self," and "the power of a creative approach to life."

Once we are properly responsive to the higher self, we can then proceed with the actual asking of questions. The first step is to define the problem, its antecedents, the climate in which we must deal with it, and the real problem behind the symptoms. Two of the skills of meditation can be most helpful in this regard:

- *Personification.* We can personify the capacity of the

higher self to resolve problems as an infinitely wise person with whom we can converse and receive answers to the questions we have in mind. Or, if we prefer, we can consult a committee of experts who can examine this problem from their various perspectives. In using this skill, however, we must be careful to keep our attention focused on solving the problem at hand, and not be swept away by a fantasy about the personification—or believe that the personification will solve our problem for us.

• *Role playing.* There are several ways this meditative skill can be used in defining the problem. If other people are involved, we can meditatively play their roles in the situation, thereby gaining insight into their motives, their attitudes, and what will be best for them. If we are being sabotaged by self-doubt, we can role play with the "inner critic" to better understand what is prompting this doubt—and then silence it. If we are working on a creative problem, we can imagine the ideal solution to our difficulty or challenge to be a spirit seeking to enter into life through an unborn embryo—the spirit of our own creative design. We, as the loving parent, communicate with this "unborn child" and see how we can help to bring it into life and nurture it to adulthood—full self-expression. It is also possible to use role playing to converse with a specific aspect of our subconscious which can help us solve this problem—a certain talent, an aspect of our personal pride, our capacity for patience and tolerance, or something else.

It may take several meditative sessions, on different occasions, to complete our definition of the problem and our understanding of the multidimensional forces contributing to it. But as this understanding grows, we should then move on to another set of questions—questions which will help us understand and implement the solution to our problem. There are again several meditative skills which can help us at this stage:

• *Working with the ideals of the higher self.* This skill is particularly useful in determining the best possible solution to our problem. If we find that our problem of loneliness is due in part to the selfish and manipulative way we treat our friends, for example, then the solution will lie in working to cultivate a number of the spiritual ideals of the higher self—a capacity to care about the interests and welfare of others, a healthy respect for the individuality of others, affection, kindness, and the willingness to share. We can give this exercise a practical focus by carefully rehearsing ways in which we can express these ideals to specific people we know.

• *Working with divine archetypes.* Divine archetypes contain the pattern for acting with enlightenment in every conceivable circumstance. The more we learn to interact with them, the more we master the skills of solving problems. If our problem involves unfair treatment, therefore, we can invoke the divine archetype of justice and see how it can most creatively be applied in this particular circumstance. If our problem involves an area of self-deception, we can invoke the divine archetype of truth to help us unravel this difficulty. As always, the beginner will find it easiest to gain access to these archetypal forces by using personifications such as the Muses or the Graces (as described in detail in the essays "The Act of Human Creation" and "Becoming Graceful" from *The Art of Living* series). But it is the force behind the personification which will help us solve the problem, not the image. It is also useful to keep in mind that these divine archetypes are *not* creations of our imagination. Our imagination may help create the way we visualize the archetype, but these forces are real and independent of us.

• *Working in a mental laboratory or studio.* Many of our problems deal with the important activities of our life, such as our work or creative endeavors. In such cases, it can sometimes be helpful to invent a mental laboratory or studio in which we can work on projects, research options, and carry on continuing conversations with personifications, subconscious roles, and so on. The nature of this workshop or studio would vary with the kind of work we do. An artist would create a mental studio with perfect lighting and experimental materials. The engineer would obviously prefer a formal laboratory with testing equipment and other devices. A chef would need a well-equipped mental kitchen in which he could experiment freely with different recipes and combinations, and refine new skills before trying them in physical life.

Once a solution is achieved—and again, this may require several meditative sessions—it is then important to conclude our work by focusing the power of the solution into our thoughts, feelings, and physical activities. This can be done by dwelling on a seed thought which represents the power of the solution we have discovered. The actual seed thought would of course vary with the kind of problem and its solution. In a personal problem, it might be "right human relations" or "self-sufficiency." In a problem of the work place, it might be "adaptability" or "thoroughness." In a problem arising from creative activity, it could be "resourcefulness."

In some cases, it may also be necessary to use the techniques of mental housecleaning, so the use of seed thoughts can be effective.

THE DIVINE CATECHISM

The more we take our problems into a meditative state, and invite the greater power of the higher self to help us solve them in wise and enlightened ways, the more we begin to understand the value of problems in our life. We are meant to ask questions about our problems and seek their answers; asking questions is an intelligent, healthy part of life. As we build skill in asking these questions, we gradually come to an interesting insight:

It is really the higher self which is asking us questions. Through our problems and challenges, we learn to give voice to these questions, and find their answers. This give-and-take of daily living is a divine catechism, through which the higher self teaches us the lessons of responsibility, creativity, and maturity.

Once we learn the answer to any one of the questions in the divine catechism, the problem associated with it ceases to be a problem. We know how to solve it.

THE TECHNIQUE
FOR SOLVING PROBLEMS

The technique for solving problems can be summarized as follows:

1. We begin by entering a meditative state and contacting the higher self, as described in chapter five.

2. We dwell on the capacity of the greater to assist the lesser in solving problems it faces. This can be done by contemplating various seed thoughts.

3. We ask questions which will help us define the problem, its antecedents, the psychological climate it is part of, and the real problem behind the symptoms. The meditative skills of personification and role playing can be used as appropriate.

4. We ask questions which will help us understand and implement the best possible solution to the problem. This will often involve working with the spiritual ideals of the higher self or divine archetypes. For certain kinds of problems, it may also be useful to create a mental laboratory or studio.

5. We focus the solution into our thoughts, feelings, and physical activities. Seed thoughts can again be used at this stage of the technique.

13

Creative
Self-Discovery

COLOR ME BRIGHT

When the birds of the world were first created, all were colored dull brown. They carried a tune nicely, but were not much to look at.

The drab complexions of the birds disturbed Lion, king of all animals. Calling before him a peacock, Lion commissioned him to paint the birds of the world bright colors. The peacock was flattered by this command, but stammered, "Your Highness, I know nothing of painting."

"Well, learn!" roared Lion.

So the peacock learned. He journeyed down to the riverbank and began dabbling in the muds and clays along the water's edge. He mixed yellow and blue and compared it with the moss on the bank. He learned to thin his colors with water for smoother application. He developed a secret way of adding luster to his colors, so they would shine.

Finally, after much experimentation, he had perfected a technique. Under the authority of Lion, he summoned the birds of the world one by one, to paint their feathers.

He started simply, coloring the raven black, the cardinal red. As he gained confidence, he became more creative, giving the flicker black speckles on a white breast, with bold yellow wings, and creating a delicate show of miniature brilliance for the hummingbirds. By the time the peacock began working on the tropical birds, he had matured into a master artist.

When his task was completed, the peacock returned to the king. "Sire," he said, "your request has been fulfilled. All the birds have been colored."

"I have seen your work," replied Lion, "and it is very good. But you overlooked one bird."

"Which?" inquired the peacock.

"Yourself," the king responded. And, indeed, the peacock looked as drab as ever.

"Not true, not true," the peacock protested. "I finished myself just this morning." And spreading open his tail feathers, he revealed a subtlety of iridescence, an elegance of design far surpassing his earlier efforts.

"Self-portraits," the bird observed as he promenaded before his liege, "usually tend to be the artist's best work."

A NEW IDENTITY

We do not come into the world just to reflect the light of the higher self and worship God, even though these practices *are* a step in the right direction for a person who has been trapped in the dull life of materialism. Nor do we come into the world merely to repair and restore our thoughts, feelings, and behavior, even though this work is a second step toward spiritual maturity. Like the peacock, we have been commissioned by our liege—the higher self—to perform creative service. We have been commanded to add color and light to everything in our character and life which is drab and dull.

Yet we do not know how. The higher self replies:

"Well, learn!"

And so we embark on a journey of creative self-discovery. Our goal on this journey is to learn how to embrace the fullness of the life of our higher self and translate it into our habits, attitudes, good works, and daily activities, enriching them and embodying them with meaning and purpose. This is a long journey, but each step along the way is significant and fulfilling. Actually, the journey is never ending. We succeed not by reaching a finite end of self-discovery, but rather by progressing steadily toward a more and more complete understanding of our individuality, our roots in brotherhood, our relationship with God, and the service we can perform. We succeed by integrating ourself with the intelligence, purpose, love, talents, and strength of the higher self—and the divine life it serves.

In a very real sense, this is a journey to a full realization of our human identity. We discover this identity not by looking around at all the other drab birds and trying to be as drab and as dull as they are, but by teaching ourself how to think, feel, and act as our higher self would have us do. In the words of an ancient saying, "We must love what God loves, know what God knows, and do what God would seek to do with and through us." Gradually, we transform the focus and capacity of our consciousness. We become an artist of life, not just an observer; a builder of life, not just a survivor; a contributor to life, not just a consumer; a healer of life, not just one who seeks for something better.

In human life, of course, we are commissioned to do more than merely paint our "feathers" lovely colors. We are given the task of developing a full range of self-expression through the personality—physically, emotionally, and mentally. Then, as this full complement of skills, qualities, habits, and characteristics is developed, we are meant to take them, one by one, and attune them to the power and purpose of the higher self, so that each of them reveals the glory of its divine origin through its expression on earth. To put it symbolically, we gather to ourself the many components of our personality, lift them up to heaven, and give them a new name—a sacred name. In this way, we create a new identity for ourself—an identity which reveals the love, wisdom, and power of the higher self through all we do. This work occurs within the recesses of our own heart and mind, unnoticed by the world, but it is the greatest masterpiece of all, our own self-portrait.

The spiritual ideals of life are all active and alive at the inner dimensions of the higher self. We do not have to create them. But they can only become active and alive within the outer dimensions of the personality as we become a creative agent, infusing them into our character and "naming" them as vital parts of *our* individuality, identity, and self-expression.

To do this, however, we must become creative. We must learn to translate the beauty, harmony, and glory of the inner realms of life into tangible forms of expression on earth. We must learn to "breathe" the energies and forces of divine life into the forms we create, so that they endure and inspire. We must learn to interact with the divine archetypes of the higher self, the patterns for all creation, and use them as blueprints for our activity on earth.

This work of creativity is the culminating triumph of Active Meditation—the heart and fiber of the Western tradition of spiritual growth. It is the dynamism of creativity which activates the full potential of our mind, nurtures the higher expressions of compassion and love, vivifies our inner genius, and motivates us to harness our self-expression for spiritual service. Without creativity, life is a colorless monotony of unchanging dullness. With it, new life constantly enters our mind and heart, enriching our spiritual stature and accomplishments. We enter into a more abundant life and fulfill the promise of human individuality.

We complete the work begun when the higher self first decided to enter into earth life and develop the personality.

A HEALTHY BALANCE

Creativity is an important theme in human life, both individually and collectively. Everywhere we look, we can find the evidence of the use of creativity by humanity to meet its needs, expand its self-expression, and discover its unique identity among the many kingdoms of life. In order to meet the needs of better housing, food, clothing, and health, we have taught ourselves to be innovative in science, technology, agriculture, and medicine. In probing the nature of our self-expression, we have taught ourselves to be creative in the arts, literature, drama, music, and dance. In order to define and enrich our unique identity, we have taught ourselves to explore the realms of religion, philosophy, psychology, and the esoteric sciences.

All of this activity has enriched the experience of society and the individual, both at inner and outer levels. Any intelligent observer of life, however, can also see that the development of creativity in humanity has not been a straight line to paradise. Wherever there is creativity, resistance to change can also be found. And so, even though enormous progress has been made in developing the creative spirit of humanity, much remains to be done. Many obstacles and difficulties yet remain to be overcome.

Actually, resistance to change is a necessary part of the phenomenon of creativity. The traditions and habits of society can sometimes be antagonistic to our drive to be innovative, by preserving the status quo, but they also serve to preserve and protect the accomplishments we have already made. Without this force of preservation, we might well become entirely experimental in orientation, and be unable to stabilize our innovative works. For a society to be alive, therefore, it must be creative. But for a society to be stable, it must also have a rich accumulation of tradition and custom. Ideally, the two forces work together in healthy balance, exploring new applications of the creative spirit while maintaining and protecting the good works already achieved.

The same pattern applies to the individual as well as society. It is the force of creativity which helps the individual grow and become more fully aware of his purpose and potential, but creativity must also be blended with a rich awareness of tradition, experience, and habit. If not, we are likely to be confused, indecisive, disorganized, and perhaps even hysterical or psychotic. To maintain health and balance as an individual, we need a blend of both creativity and the capacity to protect and preserve what we have achieved. Out of the interaction of these two forces, a true sense of our identity as an individual can slowly emerge.

Another way of stating this basic premise is to say that our identity is derived both from the life of spirit and the life of the personality. The person who is grounded entirely in the life of the personality has not yet discovered his true identity—but neither is the person who has abandoned the personality in the hopes of becoming absorbed in the bliss of spirit. The higher self has created the personality for a good reason. If we are to uncover the mystery of our life, we had therefore better learn to view the personality *as a part of the spiritual experience.* We had better learn to view the personality creatively.

This is simply a matter of common sense.

A CREATIVE AGENT

The work of successful meditation should therefore include exercises designed to balance the creative and the conserving elements within our character, and nurture a creative view of self-discovery. Such exercises should help us to:

1. Stir up our creative resources and talents.

2. Integrate them with our habits, traditions, and established views of life, thereby stabilizing our creative talents.

3. Participate in the work of "lifting up" the personality into the wholeness inherent in the higher self, thereby transforming the quality and significance of our life.

As we use meditative skills in this way, we gradually discover, through first-hand experience, what it means to become a creative agent of divine forces. We strip this subject of all of its mystical and mythical mushiness, and see it in the clear light of common sense. We are designed to serve as a steward and builder of the divine plan for humanity. Before this is possible, we must purify the personality and purge it of unwholesome elements. We must likewise reorient our priorities in living so that we consider the needs of the higher self first, and the needs of the personality second.

In specific, there are several basic themes we should explore in meditation, as we endeavor to discover our creative potential and true identity:

- The proper function of the personality in physical life.
- Our opportunities for service to the higher self and the rest of humanity.
- Our opportunities for developing character strengths and abilities so that we may serve more wisely.
- Our responsibility to the higher self, to others, to our work, and to society.
- The enlightened response to imperfection in the world.
- The enlightened response to public opinion and the customs and pressures of mass consciousness.
- The role we can play in civilization and culture.

Each of these themes is a rich topic for our own meditative self-discovery.

THE PROPER FUNCTION OF THE PERSONALITY

There are two basic forces which can control the functioning of the personality. The first is the innate life of the personality itself. The second is the design of the higher self for the enlightened self-expression of the personality.

The vast majority of people are controlled by the innate life of the personality—the fears, desires, craving for sensation, and instincts of the physical body, emotions, and mind. This innate life is conditioned by subtle manifestations of the law of attraction working at a level not yet appreciated by modern psychology, by childhood experiences involving parents and peers, by the groups we associate with, by mass consciousness, and by various unconscious and astrological forces. From an esoteric perspective, there is little difference between two people controlled by the innate life of the personality, even though the two people in question might well consider themselves profoundly different. A person under the influence of this innate life has little individuality and almost no sense of identity; he or she is just a slave to instinct, sensation, and social conditioning.

Only those people who detach from the instincts and sensations of the innate life and become responsive to the higher self are able to be guided, at the personality level, by the design of the higher self for enlightened self-expression. This design is nothing less than an inspired blueprint for ideal thought, feeling, and behavior in every aspect of personal life. It is the true source of individuality and identity.

The personality can only function properly when it is controlled and guided by the design of the higher self. It is therefore of great importance to discriminate between this creative design and the innate life of the personality. It is also quite helpful to understand exactly how the design of the higher self activates and guides the functioning of the personality.

The design of the higher self for the self-expression of the personality is a fifth-dimensional idea. This means that the design embodies the power required to implement it. At the level of the fifth dimension (the abstract mind), ideas include not only intelligence but also the full power to reproduce the idea at concrete levels. Therefore, as we become aware of and responsive to this design, meditatively, we also tap a far greater measure of personal power than if we are in tune only with the innate life of the personality. The power of the innate life is really nothing more than the power to *sense* and *react*. The power of the design of the higher self for the personality is the power to *act*, to *create*, to *build*, and to *heal*.

In no way does this mean that as soon as we tap the design of the higher self for the personality, miracles begin to happen and we can sit back and let the higher self take over and run our life without any effort on our part. Nothing could be further from the truth. In order for the personality to tap into this design of the higher self, it must become a creative partner of the higher self, fully involved in being the channel through which the higher self works and operates.

In many ways, the design of the higher self for the functioning of the personality is so different from the prevalent norm for behavior that it may seem strange at first. Indeed, many people struggle for quite awhile before they learn to view life from the perspective of the higher self. The reason why is simple. The average person, and society itself, is so imbued with rampant selfishness, hedonism, competitiveness, greed, and materialism that almost all of our values and goals must be laundered and reconsidered before we can begin to understand the ideals and purposes that motivate the higher self.

OUR OPPORTUNITIES TO SERVE

If we intend to serve the higher self, we cannot allow ourself to accept society's *opinion* as to what constitutes service. That is the path to self-deception. Instead, we must strive to understand what the higher self views as progress and service.

Much of what we term "service" to humanity and society today is tinged with large measures of self-pity, guilt, the desire for attention, and even greed. The person who unthinkingly accepts these premises will be serving only the illusions of society, not the purposes of the higher self. It is therefore important to become fully aware of the criteria of the higher self for service.

The higher self defines service as any act which contributes to and helps advance the evolutionary plan of God for humanity and the planet. It has little if any interest in providing for the pleasure, comfort, or freedom from conflict of the personality. This does not rule out a comfortable life, family, career, or rest and relaxation for the personality—but in a society which is obsessed with guaranteeing work, income, housing, and the creature comforts of life for everyone, whether or not he has earned them, it is important to understand the higher self's perspective on service and progress.

OUR OPPORTUNITIES TO GROW

Not everything that the personality would prize as a step toward maturity or success is necessarily viewed as growth by the higher self. Indeed, society has accepted a number of "ideals" for personal self-expression which are either useless or a hindrance to the life of the higher self:

- The ability to manipulate the opinions of others.
- A competitive spirit that will sacrifice anything to win.
- A capacity to suppress guilt and shame.
- Fanaticism.
- A preoccupation with being charming or glamorous.
- Personal toughness.

At the same time, society commonly regards a number of spiritual virtues as signs of weakness—sensitivity, a capacity for kindness, a sense of ethics, the willingness to share and cooperate, and tolerance. If a person sets his goals for growth by the standards of society, therefore, he is greatly distorting the meaning and purpose of growth. He is more likely to grow into greater immaturity than maturity. For this reason, it is important for the true aspirant to use the time of meditation to become aware of how the higher self views the process of growth—and set his or her priorities accordingly.

OUR RESPONSIBILITIES

The higher self is responsive to the divine plan and the laws of universal life. It expects the personality to likewise be responsive to those activities and factors in human society which advance the divine plan and embody the laws of universal life. In daily living, this means recognizing our responsibilities to family, work, nation, and society, and acting to fulfill them as wisely and actively as possible.

It is unfortunate that various religious and philosophical systems have distorted the value of responsibility, encouraging their devotees to turn over their individual responsibilities to God. This is done in order to make it easier to focus one's full efforts on becoming absorbed in the transcendent nature of God, but the inevitable consequence is a weakening of the enlightened sense of responsibility. The devotees of these systems become more passive toward life, not more active. As a result, they become less of a constructive force for good in the world.

It can therefore be quite helpful to examine meditatively the perspective of the higher self toward our responsibilities to life, and determine what it means to nurture growth and the enlightenment of family, friends, nation, and society.

THE ENLIGHTENED RESPONSE TO IMPERFECTION

Everyone who would serve the life of the higher self must eventually come to terms with the imperfections of society. We do not live in "the best of all possible worlds," and it can be a rude awakening when an idealistic person discovers this obvious fact. Some people respond to this discovery by abandoning their ideals and becoming cynical. The more popular response is to become angry and resentful. Our modern society has developed a whole panoply of justifications for "the constructive use of anger" and the "creative use of rage." The enlightened person, however, knows that these are nothing but infantile responses to infantile problems.

The higher self is totally free of anger, fear, jealousy, ignorance, and possessiveness. It responds to imperfection by seeking to heal it. If we are seeking to improve our rapport with the higher self, we should strive to do the same—and understand that the clever manipulation of fear, hostility, anger, or jealousy will never be supported by the higher self, no matter how noble our ultimate goal might be.

This is not to say that the feelings of anger, fear, or jealousy will never arise in people who enjoy good working relationships with their higher self. But when they do, they will be recognized as reactions arising from the unredeemed aspects of the personality—or mass consciousness. The enlightened person will endeavor to control these impulses and heal the patterns which produced them.

The great strength of the higher self lies in its capacity to be cheerful, optimistic, forgiving, and affectionate, *even in the face of imperfection, opposition, or resistance.* The enlightened personality learns to call on these inner strengths in dealing with the problems and frustrations of living.

After all, none of us came to earth for the purpose of protesting, complaining, or being obnoxious. We came in order to help heal the problems of society and create a better life on earth.

THE ENLIGHTENED RESPONSE
TO MASS CONSCIOUSNESS

One of the most subtle challenges confronting the meditator is learning to distinguish among impulses arising from his own subconscious, impulses arising from mass consciousness, and the legitimate guidance of the higher self. The distinction between impulses from the subconscious and the guidance of the higher self can be mastered by using the techniques of mental housecleaning and healing the emotions, but the difference between impulses from mass consciousness and the higher self is not so readily discerned. The pressure to conform can be enormous. Quite often, the voice of mass consciousness speaks with far greater authoritativeness than the quiet whisper of the higher self. And the common practice of religious and spiritual leaders to demand obedience from their devotees complicates the problem even more. Once we become accustomed to conforming to a group mind, it becomes quite difficult to distinguish between the authority of mass consciousness and the authority of the higher self.

And yet, if we are going to discover our true identity, and become a creative force in the world, we must learn to make this distinction and become responsive only to the guidance and motivation of the higher self. We must learn to recognize the subtle urges and pressures which come to us psychically from mass consciousness and respond to them with the spirit and power of self-determination.

THE ROLE WE CAN PLAY IN CIVILIZATION

As we explore these fundamental themes meditatively, and become more aware of the true nature of our human identity, we begin to understand that we have an important role to play in the unfoldment of society and civilization. Like the individual, society as a whole is evolving and progressing. There are many imperfections in society, just as there are many imperfections within most of us individually—pettiness, selfishness, avarice, fear, and laziness. Society does not understand the nature of its identity or inner potential any more than most individuals do. It often fails to see the benefits of changes and innovative trends until long after they have been established. And yet, looking at society from the perspective of the higher self, we begin to see where vitality and creativity are alive and active, and how we can help. We begin to understand how the higher self seeks to help the development of society—and our role in being a catalyst for constructive change.

This prepares us for an active life of service.

CREATIVE SELF-DISCOVERY

By contemplating these issues and themes in a meditative state, we set the stage for the personality to be lifted up, briefly, into the light and wisdom of the higher self. During these times, there may be flashes of spiritual intuition and an experiencing of the actual qualities of the wisdom, love, and will of the higher self. There will also be an understanding of how the higher self views some aspect of our life, identity, or efforts to be creative. At first, these moments of direct contact with the higher self may be few and far between. Our efforts to understand who we are and what we can do in life may well be focused on sorting out the various beliefs we already hold on these topics. But with time and repeated practice, we will slowly establish beyond all doubt the genuine perspective and attitude of the higher self toward life. At this point, our understanding of the higher self will be something more than *just another opinion*—it will be a dynamic basis for our creative involvement in living.

The recommended meditative exercise for exploring these themes of self-discovery begins, as customary, by establishing contact with the higher self, as described in chapter five. The higher self is the fount of our wisdom, love, and strength, and it must always be the central focus of our meditative efforts.

Once this meditative contact is reestablished, the next step is to refine the quality of this contact a bit more than is usually required. This can be done by practicing devotion to the ideals of the higher self. We review several of the key spiritual ideals of the higher self and let our adoration and love for the value of these ideals build in magnitude. In this way, we rise above the "ideals" of the personality, which are often self-serving and colored by mass consciousness and social prejudice.

To this devotion we can then add a steady dedication to the life and purpose of the higher self, thereby connecting our mind and personal will with the wisdom and will-to-life of the higher self. The act of dedication focuses our intention to work with the wisdom and will of the higher self in our own life and in the contributions we make to society. As such, it is something more than devotion or mere positive thinking. It is a commitment to understand and to act in accordance with the authority of the higher self.

At this point, we begin the actual activity of creative self-discovery, investigating one of the themes described earlier or a related topic. There are several meditative skills we can use to help us in this process:

• *Working with spiritual ideals.* In reviewing an area of responsibility, an aspect of our thought or feeling, our role in some activity of life, or the approach we should take to a certain facet of growth, we can invoke a clear understanding of the spiritual ideals which ought to guide us by asking the higher self directly, "What is your attitude and perspective regarding this issue?" If our devotion is strong and our intention is clear, then we are bound to experience some measure of the actual force of its perspective and understanding of this aspect of our life. Usually, the response will be more of the nature of a direct experience of the quality of the ideal, rather than images we see or words we hear mentally.

• *Personification.* In contemplating the nature of our true identity, it can be helpful to personify this true identity as a benevolent saint who has chosen to return to earth and live in our personality and serve humanity. As we view our life, opportunities, problems, and challenges through the perspective of this benevolent saint, we begin to grasp elements of our true identity and the quality of consciousness of the higher self.

• *Role playing.* In working to better understand the contribution we can make to society, we can play the role of an assistant to a great spiritual leader, who assigns us a task to complete. This task is something which can be completed within the parameters of our life experience, but will challenge our ingenuity and resourcefulness. We may well have to develop new qualities and expressions of love, patience, or wisdom to be successful. But as we complete the task, we will be making a contribution to society.

• *Working with divine archetypes.* In reviewing our enlightened response to imperfection or the proper function of the personality in any aspect of life, it can be quite helpful to work with the appropriate archetype which governs this facet of human expression. Guided by the archetype, we can more readily see what is lacking and how best it can be corrected.

• *Seed thoughts.* Much insight into the nature of our identity and creative potential can be derived by meditating on seed thoughts such as "self-realization," "the life of service," "opportunities to serve," "the enlightenment of the personal-" ity," or "the greater takes care of the lesser."

Once this reflection on our identity and creative potential is completed, it is then important to conclude the meditation by *honoring* the insights and power gained. This portion of the technique is designed to increase and activate a strong sense of personal honor, so that we will be more motivated to take the good we have gained and put it to work in our life. Personal honor focuses a steady intention to aspire to the best within us at all times—and never do less than our best. It holds open a steady line of force between the higher self and the personality, so that the creative view we have attained can be sustained during our nonmeditative activities.

Personal honor can be cultivated by the skillful use of the symbol of a transparent, golden jewel carved in the perfect image of our likeness. We should visualize this jewel as representing the pure life, will, wisdom, and love of the higher self, and imagine it superimposed over the heart. As we work with this jewel, we should come to view it as our most precious possession—a possession of great value and beauty. Because it is such a marvelous treasure, it commands our deepest respect and honor. Indeed, serving it and helping it become more brilliant and filled with life becomes a question of personal honor for us.

Throughout the use of this technique for creative self-discovery, it is important to keep in mind that the higher self truly is interested in helping us cultivate this more enlightened perspective on life. At the same time, there is a part of our personality which is capable of distracting us from our goal and confusing these new insights with doubt and skepticism. Our duty is to keep our devotion and dedication clearly focused on a more enlightened understanding of the role we play in life. As distractions and confusion arise, we should refer back to the techniques for mental housecleaning and use them as appropriate.

THE TECHNIQUE
FOR CREATIVE SELF-DISCOVERY

The technique for creative self-discovery can be summarized as follows:

1. We begin by entering a meditative state and contacting the higher self, as described in chapter five.

2. We build devotion to the ideals of the higher self.

3. To this devotion, we add dedication to the life and purpose of the higher self.

4. We investigate the nature of our creative potential and the way the higher self views our work, our responsibilities, and the contributions we can make to life. In pursuing this understanding, there are several meditative skills which can be helpful: spiritual ideals, personification, role playing, divine archetypes, and seed thoughts.

5. We conclude by honoring the insights and new perspectives gained—making it a matter of personal honor to incorporate this life of the higher self into our daily self-expression. This activity can be helped through the use of the symbol of a golden jewel.

14

Grounding The Life
Of The Higher Self

GROUNDING

Each human being is designed to be a single, integrated self. We are not meant to have one self which meditates and one self which is busy and active in daily life. For the sake of clarity, we speak of the parent within and the child within, the higher self and the personality—but the goal of Active Meditation is to integrate these different parts, not increase the distinction between them. The self which meditates should therefore be seen as the same as the self which is active and busy in life. This is just a matter of good sense.

And yet, strangely enough, few meditative systems see the one who meditates as the same as the one who is involved in active self-expression. Most glorify the meditating self and discredit the active, involved self, and thereby keep them separate. In many cases, they seem disinterested in relating the work and themes of meditation into the fabric of daily life; instead, they try to draw the individual entirely out of the active world and into an ashram, monastery, or other hermitage, where he can devote his full attention to the meditating self. As a result, the insights gained in meditation are not integrated into the individual's potential for self-expression and activity.

The seven techniques of Active Meditation which have been presented are not designed to be used in an ashram or a monastery. They could be, but they are designed primarily to be used by the individual who is active in daily life and is seeking to integrate the life of the higher self into the busy, productive, and fulfilling life of the personality. They are deliberately pragmatic in approach. As such, it is not enough just to learn to use these techniques at a meditative level. We must also complete the process, and learn to translate the wisdom, love, and insights gained into our daily self-expression. This stage is known as the process of *grounding* the qualities, skills, and principles of the higher self in the life of the personality. It brings heaven to earth and lays the foundation for eventually building the city of God in the physical world.

One of the great problems among meditators has always been the tendency to become "airy-fairy"—to turn their back on the earth and float up to the clouds. They become impractical, dreamy, and sometimes disoriented. Yet there is no need for this to happen in the practice of meditation. If we understand the value of human self-expression, and its role in spiritual growth, there will be no difficulty in keeping our consciousness grounded in daily life, even as we become a citizen of heaven.

OUR SPIRITUAL DUTY

In watching a movie or play, it is easy to forget that the characters being portrayed are not living, human beings—they are merely fictional characters who are brought to life for a few brief moments by skillful actors. But they are brought to life so cleverly and charmingly that we overlook the actor behind the makeup, until the curtain call or the end of the movie. Then we realize that the actor has a life of his own which is quite different from the character he has portrayed. When the actor removes his makeup and costumes, he is once again himself.

There are always stories of actors who confuse the roles they play with their own identity—who do not know who they are once they remove the mask. But these are never truly gifted actors. The best actor is always the individual who knows himself, his values, and his principles so well that he can enrich the character he is portraying—he can make an intelligent statement about life while assuming a fictional identity. In other words, he does not just *play* a role—he expresses himself through the role!

We, too, play roles—as citizen, parent, spouse, friend,

worker, consumer, and provider. But like the truly gifted actor, we are not meant just to play these parts. We are designed to enrich the roles we play, and make an intelligent statement about life through everything we do. We are meant to express ourself—our higher self!

Unfortunately, not everyone is able to remove the makeup and the costumes and still be able to act in life. They are too involved with the roles they play—imitating television and movie heroes or friends and associates they admire. Imitating the behavior of others, however, is not a genuine form of self-expression. It is the kind of approach to life we would expect from a pre-adolescent, who is ga-ga over the very latest pop star—not from an adult.

Others have moved beyond the imitating stage, but they are still immersed in the roles they play. They are "true to their feelings," which means they let their emotions dictate how they will react to the events of life. Yet feelings are all they have to give to life. They are unable to make a meaningful or creative statement about the inner dimensions and values of life. They do not recognize the actor behind the role any more than the person who merely imitates.

True self-expression is something more than imitating others and being honest with our feelings. It involves two factors:

1. Knowing who we are when we have taken off all the makeup and costumes of the roles we play—knowing our true self.

2. Expressing the values, principles, and talents of this true self—the higher self—in everything we do. The ancient statement, "To thine own self be true," captures the essence of this—if it is thought of as an injunction to be true to the higher self, not a justification for selfish behavior.

This kind of self-expression is what heals and enriches the personality and gives the greater within us a chance to contribute to life. It enables the light within us to shine forth in and through everything we do.

In the West, true self-expression is not just a goal, *it is a duty!* It is our obligation to spiritualize civilization and enrich the physical plane. The one who seeks to grow spiritually must therefore strive for self-expression, or he will not be in harmony with the basic direction of the spiritual life. The collective work of spiritualizing civilization can only be achieved as *individuals* strive to bring new light and love into their daily labors.

Meditation is an excellent opportunity for discovering who we are and the spiritual design of our character. It can bring us many fascinating and important insights into our place in the universe. But meditation is designed to do more than just expand our self-awareness. It must create an outlet for the expression of the higher self as well. In this way, the personality and the higher self can have the opportunity to work together, as a partnership. This partnership is the true secret of individuality.

THE HIGHER SELF'S COMMITMENT

The value of enlightened self-expression is enormous, both for the personality and for the higher self.

In the personality, self-expression stirs up the life force, giving focus to our good ideas, plans, and intentions and breaking up congested areas of consciousness.

It is surprising how frequently congestion is a problem among spiritual aspirants. A fact which is poorly appreciated in the West is that the personality as a whole breathes, just as the physical body breathes. The breath of the personality is the figurative inhalation of inspiration, power, and compassion from the higher self. But the inhalation must be followed by

334

exhalation, not only in the physical body but also in the personality. If it is not, then congestion will ensue.

And so, if we have breathed in inspiration, power, and compassion from the higher self, we must complete the cycle, by expressing wisdom, strength, and goodwill in our acts and good works. If we fail to do so, the personality may gradually become restless, depressed, irritable, and frustrated. Its self-image may deteriorate. Consciousness has been bottled up, just as though we were holding our physical breath. At the physical level, the breath can only be held a short while before the lungs will forcibly expel it. But at the psychological level, the congestion can be much more severe, leading to long-term problems.

It should be noted that people with congestive psychological problems may be quite busy in daily activities. It is not the volume of activity which measures self-expression, but rather the degree to which we express our inner nature and qualities. To honor wisdom, we must engage in intelligent activities. To honor love, we must treat others with goodwill, affection, compassion, and tolerance. To honor the purpose of the higher self, we must seek to serve the divine plan. As we do, we learn to breathe psychologically—and our capacity to breathe in larger measures of the power, talent, love, and wisdom of the higher self increases. This is the dynamic effect of enlightened self-expression.

For the higher self, the value of self-expression is the doorway it provides for influencing life on the physical plane directly. As the personality becomes more and more responsive to expressing the purpose and qualities of the higher self in daily life, the plans and intentions of the higher self are able to be brought to fruition on the physical plane. The higher self takes a vital interest in the life of the personality; it invests portions of its own wisdom, talent, love, power, and plans in creating the personality. As the personality finds outlets for these facets of the life of the higher self, it fulfills the commitment the higher self has made to participate in the plan for humanity and civilization.

Truly, only the person who has cultivated an enlightened self-expression is able to understand fully what it means to participate in the life of humanity—to help one another and work collectively toward the goals of the higher self.

A MULTIDIMENSIONAL PHENOMENON

Some people, of course, believe that enlightened self-expression will develop spontaneously as we expand our self-awareness, but this is mostly just a pleasant self-deception. One does not become a skilled and talented writer simply by contacting a good creative idea—the ability to translate that idea into clear prose is also required. No idea can teach anyone to be a good writer; the lessons of clear writing are learned through self-discipline, practice, and the training of the mind. Nor does one become a skilled composer merely by clairaudiently hearing a lovely melody on the inner planes. The ability to translate the "music of the spheres" into a composition which can be played by other musicians, and appeal to the tastes of those who listen to it, is also required.

Self-expression is a multidimensional phenomenon—a creative phenomenon, if understood properly. For a quality or talent of the higher self to achieve self-expression, it must pass first through the concrete mind, then through the emotions, and finally be embodied in physical activity. If these three vehicles are not properly coordinated, or are untrained, or are bogged down either in antagonistic feelings or thoughts, the whole process of self-expression will be aborted, no matter how much white light we may be able to bask in while meditating. It is naive to dismiss the work of self-expression as an automatic process which does not need our intelligent involvement. Only people who know nothing at all about self-expression would ever believe it!

The grounding of the work we do in meditation, through our enlightened self-expression, is of utmost importance to the practice of Active Meditation. It is not something which can be casually dismissed as an afterthought. There are certain specific steps to be taken:

1. During meditations.
2. At the end of meditations.
3. During our nonmeditative activities.

These steps will help us coordinate our self-expression, harmonize it with the insights we gain while meditating, and make it a more complete and enlightened statement of the message of the higher self.

AT MEDITATIVE LEVELS

During meditations, the work of translating the ideals and wisdom of the higher self into an enlightened self-expression primarily involves removing obstacles which might sabotage this enlightened self-expression, strengthening our intention to act, and generating an ideal psychological atmosphere in which we can honor the insights we have gained. This work should be integrated into our use of each of the seven techniques for personal growth already given.

The work of removing obstacles which might sabotage our enlightened self-expression will obviously employ many of the principles of effective mental housecleaning. We should be especially interested in locating and removing elements of self-doubt, ambivalence, fear of criticism or loss, and hesitation. Often, we will not know exactly what the nature of an obstacle to self-expression is, but this lack of knowledge need not deter us. We can use our meditations to call up the "dissenting voice" of our subconscious and give it the opportunity to speak to us. We may find, for example, that we are in danger of being sabotaged by a deep-seated fear of criticism. If left unchecked, this fear of criticism could easily inhibit our self-expression. But having become aware of it, we can bargain with it and suggest that it work with us to build and rehearse better ways of acting—so we will be less likely to make mistakes and draw criticism. In this way, a potentially negative force, which otherwise would only nag at our efforts to be productive, can be harnessed to help us.

In addition to removing obstacles, the period of meditation is also ideal for strengthening our intention to act—in changing a habit, in approaching our work with creativity, in implementing a new plan, in treating others with greater kindness, or in any other new program of self-expression. Once we have decided how we intend to act, we dwell on the purpose of acting in this way, taking care always to think of this purpose as inclusively as possible. If our intention is to treat others more kindly, for example, we define the purpose of acting in this way not just in terms of improving our relationships or feeling better personally, but even more importantly in terms of fulfilling the design of humanity to establish "peace on earth, goodwill toward all men and women." For as we enrich our self-expression with kindness and goodwill, we help not only ourself but the whole of humanity. By registering this "greater purpose" behind our acts, we are able to tap a powerful source of motivation, strengthening our will to act.

The power of this purpose can then be translated into the actual energies of self-expression by meditating on appropriate seed thoughts, such as: "the greater expresses itself through the lesser," "the courage to act," "purpose determines my self-expression," and "the complete fulfillment of purpose."

A third step which can be taken during meditation is to

generate a cheerful and optimistic psychological climate in which to act and mentally rehearse expressing it—especially in circumstances of resistance, temptation, or discouragement. In this way, we "coat" our plans and intentions with a positive attitude and the power of optimism; we stir up the emotions to cooperate in the effort before us, rather than sabotage or resist it. To be effective, this activity of rehearsing an enthusiastic and cheerful approach should be done thoroughly and completely. It is not a procedure to rush through; at least several minutes should be spent building and maintaining it.

In general, every aspect of our self-expression can be strengthened by making it a regular meditative habit to cultivate a warm and quietly enthusiastic respect for ourself, our talents and ideas, and our intended work. If we lack adequate self-respect, it can be very difficult to sustain *any* constructive activity, no matter how much we recognize its value. It is important to keep in mind, however, that the first reaction to the effort to build a healthier self-respect is sometimes the exact opposite of what we intend. It is possible to stir up ancient feelings of inferiority, self-rejection, and self-denial which could easily overwhelm our enlightened efforts, unless we see this reaction for what it is and manage it intelligently, by using the proper techniques for mental housecleaning and strengthening our self-image.

Three points must be kept in mind as we work meditatively to generate a cheerful attitude toward our self-expression and a healthy respect for what we do:

1. We are not just "feeling good" about what we are doing; we are striving to translate the joy and goodwill of the higher self into our attitudes and moods. Good feelings alone do not necessarily guarantee contact with the higher self; most of the time, they are just expressions of the innate life of the emotions. The work of grounding is designed to *charge* our self-expression with the qualities and powers of the higher self.

The fact that these qualities and forces are in part grounded through the emotions—our attitudes and moods—does not mean that we are dealing either with "nice feelings" or mere wishes. We are harnessing the emotions to become an effective vehicle of the love and joy of the higher self.

2. Many people find it difficult to remain cheerful and optimistic in the face of the problems and imperfections of their lives. This difficulty can be avoided, however, by making sure that our state of mind responds to our spiritual ideals, not the difficulties we face. This is a subtle but crucial difference which in effect moves the epicenter of our moods and feelings from the actual conditions of outer life to the ideals of the inner life. The premise of any good meditative system, after all, is that the subtle, invisible forces of spirit are the real substance of life—not our problems and deficiencies. Spiritual powers can be invoked and used to heal and redeem the imperfect. But for this to occur, our moods and attitudes must magnify the ideal conditions of spirit—not the actual conditions of form.

3. We must do more than just affectionately dream about lovely plans and lofty ideas; *we must fully intend to involve ourself in bringing them to fruition physically!* This involves much more than just looking at an imaginary mental picture of the desired result. We must assume "ownership" of the work or activity before us, and consider our responsibilities to it.

CONTEMPLATION

The very end of a meditation is an important time in the activity of grounding. True meditation is a state in which we deliberately detach ourself from the physical world and our emotional reactions, in order to work at inner levels of consciousness. If we are working at a true meditative level, we will be dealing with abstract qualities, ideals, and energies. *If we do not use the end of a meditation to reconnect ourself with the concrete dimensions of life, much of what we have gained will simply be left at the higher level, in its original abstract form.* Our meditation will have been a pleasant interlude in our daily activity—but not a constructive force for good in our individual life.

Most systems of meditation, unfortunately, ignore the value of this step in the meditative process. As a result, the transcendent levels the meditator touches do not become grounded in self-expression. The inner life is enriched, but the outer life remains impoverished. At times, in fact, the capacity to act in the outer life may even be weakened, thereby defeating the true goal of meditation—to establish a better rapport between the higher self and the personality.

The work of grounding the abstract qualities of the higher self in the concrete thoughts, feelings, and plans of the personality at the end of a meditation is known as *contemplation*. In many systems of meditation, the word "contemplation" is used to refer to the adoration of the glories of the transcendent nature of God or the inner virtues of spirit. There can be great value to such practices, but contemplation also has its practical side. The word itself derives from a Latin phrase meaning "laying the foundation of a temple." Contemplation is therefore a two-stage process, which *begins* with meditating on a sacred subject or ideal, but *concludes* with laying out plans and specific intentions for putting that sacred subject or ideal to work in daily life, "building the temple."

In other words, we end the meditation by quietly reflecting on the implications and meaning of the insights we have just gained, relating them to the needs and opportunities of our daily self-expression. There are several questions which can be considered during this period of contemplation:

• What new and deeper realizations have we gained about our spiritual nature and powers?

- How does this new understanding strengthen us in the pursuit of our daily activities?

- How does this meditative experience alter our view and attitudes concerning ourself, our work, our past, and our problems?

- Has this strengthened our intention to act in life—to take charge of improving the quality of our life and becoming a more responsible agent of the higher self?

- What new expectations do we have about ourself and our self-expression?

By reviewing questions of this nature in a contemplative mood at the end of meditation, we gradually saturate our subconscious with a vivid awareness of our inner life. This, in turn, helps build the *expectation* subconsciously that the higher self is able and ready to help the personality throughout the day, whenever there is a need for such assistance. We begin to understand that we *always* have access to the greater life and power of the higher self, not just in meditations but at all times throughout the course of our daily activities.

As part of this contemplation, it is also important to mentally rehearse the ways we expect to apply, in daily life, the key insights we have gained and the changes we have made in meditation. If we have been working to treat family members with greater kindness and forgiveness, for example, we should rehearse specific instances in which we can express these qualities actively. Or, if we have been working to establish a new set of values, we should rehearse specific ways we can honor these values. In this way, we ground the abstract intention and enthusiasm to act in finite instances of self-expression. We relate the gains of meditation to the opportunities of our outer life.

The period of contemplation at the end of a meditation is likewise an excellent occasion to charge the personality with a special blessing for its self-expression. This can be done by dwelling on a mantra such as:

The life of my spirit pours through me, strengthening my courage to honor my ideals and my duty to serve in all that I do and say. May goodwill be the keynote of my self-expression.

As we contemplate this mantra, we hold the thought that the higher self is flooding us with its power, compassion, wisdom, and courage. This simple technique can both refresh and reenergize the personality, so that it is better prepared for the activities ahead. It also widens the channel between the inner and the outer life.

IN OUR DAILY ACTIVITIES

The most important sphere for the work of grounding the insights and forces we tap during meditation is, of course, our ordinary state of consciousness. It does no good to behold lovely visions and insights during meditation, and then forget all about them as we pursue our work and obligations during the remainder of the day. And yet, as obvious as this principle is, it is amazing how many people overlook it.

As usual, we must be ruled by common sense. The single most important action we can take during our daily activities to ground the life of the higher self is to *put into practice* our goals and ideals. In other words, if we are working in meditation to heal a certain area of emotional expression, we should strive to express the ideal emotion in our actual dealings with others. It is senseless to fill ourself with goodwill and compassion during a meditation and then continue to treat others selfishly, unkindly, and harshly. Or, if we are striving to enrich our self-esteem, we must try to hold an enlightened opinion of ourself and the work we do throughout each day.

As the cliché puts it, nothing succeeds like success. Nothing will help the work of meditation more than supporting it with small achievements toward our goals every day. And yet, it is amazing how frequently students of psychological conditioning and spiritual growth fail to implement this basic principle. The momentum of habits, feelings, attitudes, and beliefs does not arise out of nowhere; it is generated by a specific pattern of actual expression. The most effective way of redirecting psychological momentum is therefore to change the pattern of expression.

Nevertheless, even though nothing succeeds like success, we must be practical. Fifteen minutes of success followed by two hours of failure or frustration is not at all helpful. We must know when to quit. In the early stages of working to change a habit or improve our emotions, it is important to look for small achievements which indicate progress toward our goal, rather than a miraculous overnight cure produced by a marathon of redemptive work. Small but regular efforts to treat others kindly, to be confident and optimistic about our future, to achieve greater self-discipline, or to develop intuitive insight will produce far better results than a frenzied, all-out assault on our weaknesses and deficiencies.

In this regard, it is important always to work with a healthy respect for the subconscious. It is in the subconscious that we build up the patterns of self-expression, good or bad. The subconscious is therefore the primary site for the grounding of meditative work in our self-expression. Some people, however, arbitrarily assume that they can dispense with the subconscious by declaring it null and void during their meditations. They believe that an enlightened person is able to bypass the subconscious and work directly with spirit, but it does not happen this way. As long as we are incarnate, we have a subconscious; it is an inseparable part of human nature.

Others go to the opposite extreme, assuming that the subconscious is some kind of enemy to be feared. This is just as absurd. The subconscious is the product of our experiences. If our experiences embody and reflect the wisdom, love, and talent of the higher self, the subconscious will be healthy and our self-expression will be enlightened. If, by contrast, we allow our experiences to be of random quality, the quality of our subconscious may be quite low, its structure disorganized, and its function chaotic.

The work of putting into practice the life of the higher self can be supported in a number of other ways as well:

Recalling the mood, perspective, and strength of our meditative state. As often as possible during the day, we should pause and recall the detachment and poise we have achieved during our meditations. By bringing this memory back into mind, we refresh our thinking and feeling with some of the actual qualities we have tapped during meditation. This recollection of meditative experiences is not as difficult as some people try to make it. These people usually have no trouble at all, for example, recalling an unpleasant experience which fills them with anger. All they need to do is put the same principle to work in a healthy way, and use the memory of their meditations to fill them with compassion, wisdom, and detachment, thereby displacing elements of fear, doubt, or worry which may be cluttering up our consciousness.

It should never be forgotten that detachment is not meant to be reserved exclusively for the state of meditation. It can be very helpful in maintaining an enlightened perspective as we go about our daily work in the midst of difficulties and imperfection. Its purpose is not to defend us against this negativity, but to help us preserve our identification with the higher self.

It is also useful to cultivate the habit of pausing briefly throughout the day to be thankful that we have the capacity to rise above negativity.

Reviewing recent behavior and accomplishments. Near the end of each day, we should set aside a period of time to review the successes and struggles of the personality in grounding the values and ideals of the higher self in its self-expression.

If desired, this can be combined with the practice of keeping a journal or written record of the progress we are making.

The major purpose of this review is to give formal recognition to the successes and achievements we have made during the day. Few people are oriented toward giving themselves credit for the good they do; they have overdosed on false concepts of humility and self-rejection. But giving ourself credit for the gains we make is a fundamentally healthy practice. It reinforces the efforts of the higher self to help us transform our behavior and attitudes.

In addition, this period of review serves to identify more clearly the behavior patterns and traits which either help or hinder our efforts to implement the plans and intentions of the higher self. We are therefore able to make adjustments and revisions in our approach to self-expression as the need arises— before the problem has become serious. And there are always small adjustments to be made, because we are part of a living plan. We are designed to grow a small amount every day, in both self-awareness and self-expression.

Reviewing our actual behavior and attitudes, day by day, is also an excellent way to protect ourself from self-deception. It is much easier to spot inconsistencies and excuses for falling short of the mark if we confront them when they are still fresh in our mind, than if we let the experiences of one day slide unexamined into the next. For exactly the same reason, a daily review can also bring in many new insights and understandings. We are much more likely to grasp the symbolic significance of events if we review them on a daily basis.

In this regard, it is helpful to keep in mind that the wisdom of the higher self can be active throughout the whole day; it is not restricted to periods of meditation. Any time we seek to comprehend the meaning and pattern of experiences, we will tap this great source of insight to some degree.

Acting in life as if we were enlightened. Many people limit themselves by approaching their tasks and responsibilities with the assumption that they will not succeed. They are filled with fear, doubt, and resentment. The more intelligent way to act in life, however, is to behave *as though* we were free of these deficiencies and able to act with the courage, confidence, and goodwill of the higher self. By acting in this way, we put the emphasis on succeeding, not the obstacles in our way.

This is *not* a recommendation to fantasize that we are free of all distress. Rather, it is an aspect of intelligent detachment. It helps us realize that we do have the capacity to act with enlightenment in our life—and we do not have to wait until we are a saint to begin honoring this potential.

Acting with the conviction that our efforts are supported by the work we have already done, in meditation. One of the key principles of Active Meditation is the use of mental rehearsals during meditation to anticipate ideal behavior in daily life. If we have conducted these mental rehearsals, then in fact we will be well prepared to act successfully and wisely in the actual circumstances of life. As a result, we should proceed with our duties and the challenges of daily living with the confidence that much of what we are trying to accomplish has already been done, in part, at inner levels. We are now completing the work, bringing the rehearsals of the inner dimensions into reality in the outer dimensions. In a very real sense, being able to act in this way helps us learn the elementary lessons of fourth-dimensional thinking.

A NEW MEANING

When meditation is grounded in our daily self-expression in these ways, a curious phenomenon develops. The levels of awareness and power we tap during our meditative periods gradually become the ordinary levels of awareness and power we use in the daily circumstances of life. As this occurs, of course, the levels of awareness and power we tap in meditation become progressively more sublime.

This is the true state of transcendence. We have done something more than just escape the physical plane and discover spirit. We have learned to ground spirit in the physical plane, thereby lifting up that which is of the earth and giving it a new identity, a new meaning, and a new purpose.

Herman Sets
The Record Straight

Always ready to take our own advice, we decided it was time to review how the book was progressing. "Do you suppose we're giving people too much to digest?" Bob wondered.

"I don't know," Carl replied, "but I am beginning to appreciate why some people are attracted to passive meditation. There's less for them to learn."

We both chuckled at that idea. Herman did, too. Soon, our angelic friend was standing before us again.

"We didn't know you were eavesdropping," Carl remarked.

"Oh, I'm always eavesdropping," Herman replied. "It's just like you put it in your last chapter—the higher self is not something you contact only in meditation. It's there to help you whenever you are doing something it would be interested in. Whenever you are working on the book, I'm hovering around nearby, helping out."

"Why don't you materialize more frequently?" Bob asked.

"Too much trouble," Herman answered. "Not just for me, either. It would be too much trouble for you, too."

"What do you mean?" Carl asked.

"How much of the book have you actually written while I was materialized?" Herman inquired.

"None, I guess."

"Exactly," Herman continued, self-satisfied—as much as an angel might be. "You get more done if I'm in the background most of the time. The higher self works that way, too."

"Well, why have you appeared now?" Bob asked.

"You were wondering if you were giving people too much to digest," Herman answered. "I thought I would drop in and set the record straight."

"Very good."

"The higher self frequently gives the personality more than the personality would like to digest. It stimulates the personality to grow, to stretch itself beyond its current limits, even though the personality would rather stay just the way it is. Don't worry about demanding too much from the reader. If he wants to learn to meditate, he'd better get used to it. Meditation should always be a challenge. It should never put the meditator to sleep.

"The one thing I am concerned about is that your readers not get the impression that meditation is a bunch of formulas. You don't suppose you've broken down your techniques too much, do you? They are beginning to sound almost like dance steps—lead with the right foot, slide with the left, and try to avoid stepping on your partner's toes."

We all laughed. "Well, there are some who would say that meditation is the only dance there is," Bob observed. "I don't think either one of us wants our readers to take these techniques as rigid formulas. They are meant to be guides, not formulas. If they become too restrictive, they should be adapted to the individual's needs."

"After all, we *are* calling it 'Active Meditation,'" Carl added. "If a person took a technique and never grew with it, that wouldn't be very active, would it? It would just be more passiveness in the guise of activity."

"Well, make sure that idea comes across to the reader," Herman suggested. "The Western mind is so in love with formulas that many people don't realize there are higher levels of thinking. They want to be able to memorize a recipe and use it without variation. As you both well know, meditation doesn't work that way."

"Still, there are certain basics which are so fundamental to the meditative process that they must be mastered," Bob said, "and I wouldn't want any reader to miss this point. We've both seen far too many people meditate a while and then think they are *beyond* meditation. And they haven't even mastered the basics."

"That's an important point," Carl agreed. "While it is

certainly true that a meditator could get stuck in any of these techniques if he used them as formulas, it is also true that the potential of these techniques will never be exhausted—if they are used as doorways to the higher self. It would seem to me that the key lies in how the techniques are used—not in the techniques themselves."

"I guess I didn't have to set the record straight," chuckled Herman. "You just did it for yourselves."

"It's always nice to have you drop in, anyway," Bob remarked drolly.

"Oh, it's my pleasure," Herman retorted. "But when are you going to come and visit me?"

"There's nothing like a smart aleck angel," Carl observed.

Herman laughed, then faded and was on his way.

15

The Evolution
Of Consciousness

STIMULATING GROWTH

It is always pathetic to hear the story of a person who begins a long and promising journey, but never arrives at his destination. We have all known of young, bright people who embark on an ambitious course of study at college, yet drop out after a year and waste the opportunity. Or of a man and a woman who marry with great happiness and expectations, only to separate in bitterness a year or two later.

Unfortunately, this also occurs in personal growth. A person hears about the marvels of meditation, learns how to do it, but then never follows through. He has started the journey, but does not complete it. And so he misses out on the rich potential he had hoped to tap.

Meditation, like everything else, has its dropouts, but the cause of the tragedy is usually different than in broken marriages or collegiate failure. Sometimes, the tyranny of old habits is still too strong, and resistance to change is greater than the commitment to enrich life. Soon, the person is finding elaborate excuses for not meditating regularly—for not facing the issues before him. In other cases, the meditator has been too zealously schooled in the passive approach to meditating. Instead of taking charge and putting meditation to work, he waits for the higher powers to make themselves known and take control of his life. Very quickly, the meditative experience stagnates and loses its appeal.

For some people, the problem lies in misunderstanding the nature and purpose of meditation. They think of it only as a technique for relaxing and reducing stress. As a result, they are soon bored by the "meditative" experience and abandon it.

There are also people who do use meditation actively and successfully for a while, achieving a number of important breakthroughs and improvements in their lives. Yet at a certain point, these people seem to assume that the gains they have made represent the full meditative experience. And so they stop—and the growth they have been making stops, too. Such people are very much like the couple who decided to vacation at the seashore. And so they started driving toward the coast, and drove several hours, but then stopped at a motel. Because the motel had a pool, they decided they had reached their goal, and went no further.

Active Meditation is not a start-and-stop proposition. It is meant to be a progressive experience which brings us almost unlimited possibilities for enriching our self-expression and serving humanity—as we continue to use it. *Active Meditation is designed to stimulate growth.* This is not an accidental by-product of meditating—it is the central purpose of meditation. The mere fact that people will tend to have other motives for using meditation does not alter this basic condition.

Meditation flourishes in a climate of growth. Where the willingness to grow is lacking, meditation will quickly stagnate. The creed of Active Meditation is to live life with a maximum of wisdom, love, dignity, beauty, courage, and skill. If we are able to keep this principle in mind, then the true purpose of meditation will always be self-evident. We will never be tempted to abandon it—or our responsibilites, relationships, and creative opportunities, for that matter—because we will always be looking forward to the next improvement in consciousness and maturity.

Yet for real growth to occur, our commitment to growing must be something more than just a lovely philosophy. It must be an active feature of our self-expression, embracing *all* areas of consciousness.

Our sense of purpose should become more refined.

Our command of spiritual will should deepen.

Our range of awareness should expand to include not only a wider domain of ideas but also a greater capacity to understand and apply them.

The maturity of our mind and its ability to regulate our behavior should increase.

Our expression of affection, devotion, compassion, goodwill, and tolerance should be enriched.

Our skills in managing the problems and challenges of life should improve.

The productivity of our physical efforts should increase.

Our capacity to make a contribution to civilization should become greater.

If this kind of change and enrichment is not being pursued, then our meditations must not be fulfilling the purpose they are designed to serve. The very life and meaning of meditation are missing.

A CHANGING EQUATION

To appreciate the full potential of Active Meditation, therefore, we must plan our use of meditative techniques in terms of the growth we can achieve. In doing this, it is important to understand that the genuine growth of consciousness and character is not a mechanical process. It does not proceed in the same way as assembling a machine or constructing a building would. *We are a living system.* If we make a significant change in any aspect of our thoughts or attitudes, it will evoke growth in every other aspect of our personality and character as well. A richer experience of the benevolent force of the higher self, for instance, will eventually change every aspect of our self-expression—our attitudes about ourself, our past, our work, our relationships, and the future. This, in turn, will provoke changes in our values, our self-esteem, and perhaps some of our goals. We may even undergo a certain amount of conflict, as old bigotry is challenged by the "new wave" of benevolence. Assumptions we were perfectly comfortable with in the past now make us uneasy, unsure. So they must be examined, reevaluated, and healed. In no way are the changes of Active Meditation overnight miracles; the potential for enrichment is vast, but the enrichment builds step by step, over a long period of time.

The new life of the higher self cannot be added to the personality as though it were a postage stamp, to be licked and affixed to its proper position. Each new addition to consciousness must be blended into the basic structure of our character. This, in turn, rearranges the structure itself, and every thought, habit, attitude, and memory must be reexamined and reevaluated. To put the proposition in mathematical terms, the whole equation is changed and must be refigured.

Once we acquire the knack of making these modifications, the process is not nearly as difficult as it may seem at first. It primarily involves being able to deal with our values, character, thoughts, habits, and feelings *as a single whole.* The spiritual life is replete with platitudes about wholeness, holistic healing, oneness, synthesis, and one-pointedness. This is merely a practical opportunity to translate the platitudes into an actual skill.

Nevertheless, some people will prefer to ignore this adaptive and integrative process of growth. To some extent, they will be able to get away with it for awhile, but it will leave their mental household in disorder. They will soon become prey to ambivalence, doubt, and conflict—the symptoms which betray a lack of wholeness.

We can only deceive ourself so long. Ultimately, we must come to grips with the basic reality of growth—that the conflict of opposing attitudes, habits, and psychological forces must be resolved before major degrees of new life can enter. The failure to acknowledge inconsistencies in our character and work to resolve them is probably the greatest stumbling block to growth.

THE CYCLES OF GROWTH

The dynamic changes which will occur in consciousness as we work with the techniques of Active Meditation will involve two major fields of activity: the integration of the higher self with the personality and the integration of our present state of waking consciousness with our past states of thought, feeling, and intention.

Most people who meditate look primarily for signs they are growing in the first field of activity, the integration of the higher self with the personality, and naturally so. But it is important not to overlook the significance of integrating the growth we are making with our past states of thought, feeling, and intention as well. The conscious experiences we have while meditating are not necessarily reliable indicators of genuine growth. We must never assume, for example, that fifteen minutes of bliss will immediately and completely saturate our entire subconscious storehouse of memories and associations. In actual fact, it may not touch them at all, *unless we consciously direct the bliss we are experiencing into our memory patterns.*

Unfortunately, few meditators spend much time working on cycle after cycle of integrating the state of consciousness they are able to attain in the present into their memories, habits, and attitudes from the past. They apparently believe the past is past—and irrelevant. But this is not true. Our earlier states of consciousness are the foundation on which our present state of awareness is constructed. For genuine growth to occur, therefore, we must work to integrate the *whole* of our character with the higher self, not just the most obvious parts of it. This will involve cleansing and renewing many issues and habits from the past—including the far distant past.

We should always keep in mind that the marvelous insights, glorious feelings of compassion, and sense of oneness with God that we experience in meditation may only be oases of partial enlightenment within a desert of unredeemed imperfection. They are a sign we are moving in the right direction—but never an excuse for ignoring the problems which remain. We should also understand that growth is not a journey which always proceeds in a straight line, as though we were on a rocket traveling from Earth to Jupiter. It is more a cycle which repeats itself over and over again. The cycle goes both forward into the future and backward into the past, thereby enabling us to achieve full integration. There are five phases to this cycle of growth:

1. The invocation of new life from the higher self.

2. The registration and comprehension of this new life.

3. The revision of self-image, attitudes, and values, incorporating this new life and our expanded comprehension.

4. A consolidation of the progress we have made, leading to an awareness of the implications inherent in this facet of growth.

5. A return to phase one and a repetition of the entire cycle.

To properly understand this cycle, we must realize that phase one always follows after the completion of an earlier cycle. In other words, new life from spirit does not pour into the personality just as the result of idle curiosity or a simplistic use of meditation. It enters into the life of the personality as the result of the effort to honor the impulse to grow *already active within us.* If we are seeking genuine solutions and improvements in our daily life—not merely escape from discomfort—and are ready to work to implement these improvements, then there will be a genuine influx of whatever spiritual qualities we need.

The second phase of the cycle is the activity of conscious attunement to this new life. If we do not become aware of new insights, they cannot help us. If we do not actually feel and radiate new compassion and tolerance, we cannot heal our resentments or bitterness. If we do not sense new courage and confidence, we cannot act with greater initiative in daily life. This is just a matter of common sense. It is true in spite of the fact that so many naive people fervently believe that it is not necessary—that all we have to do is make our needs known to the benevolent omniscience of God, and He will take care of them for us. The spiritual adult sees through this preposterous notion, and takes the responsibility to register and comprehend the meaning of this new life in the context of his own needs. There are a number of key areas to consider in this regard:

- How does this new life affect our self-image?

- How does this new life strengthen our relationship with the higher self? How will this stronger bond of partnership influence our meditations and self-expression from now on?

- How does this new life modify our attitudes and perspectives toward our work and responsibilities? Will this change our behavior in any way in the future?

- How does this new life enlighten our attitudes and perspectives about past conflicts and difficulties? Have areas of repressed self-deception been uncovered? Are we able to use this new life to heal problems from the past?

- How does this new life affect our ideals? Have they been refined or strengthened? Are we more aware of their importance and relevance to our life? Can we make them more central to our waking thought and action hereafter?

- How does this new life add to our sense of purpose and motivation?

- What have we discovered about our basic temperament? Are we now more aware of our strengths and limitations? Are we better able to control our self-expression and use it with enlightenment?

- What have we discovered about the inner side of life—universal order, divine archetypes, the universal presence of goodwill, or the innate brotherhood of humanity? How does this enrich our daily activities?

The third phase of the cycle takes the new insights and understanding which has been registered by answering these questions and seeks, deliberately and consciously, to integrate them into our memories and associations—the structure of our character. While this phase of growth may not seem as exciting or glamorous as the discovery of new insights and cosmic forces, it is nonetheless essential to the evolution of consciousness—as essential as eating and breathing is to the health of the physical body. We have not really grown much in goodwill until we are able to focus the goodwill we experience in meditation and use it to cultivate tolerance and forgiveness toward our enemies from the past, people we have condemned, and situations which have threatened us. Just feeling good about life and others is *not* enough. By the same token, we have not really grown much in wisdom until we are able to review painful episodes from the past and see the lessons we have learned from them, the strength we have cultivated by enduring these situations, and the contributions these events have made to our overall destiny and duty.

The meditative skill of blessing is especially valuable in integrating the new life of the higher self into memories and associations from the past, as it is designed to give focus to our deepest benevolent impulses about life. At one time or another, however, all seven techniques of personal growth in Active Meditation will be used in pursuing this phase.

The fourth phase of the cycle of growth consolidates the progress we have made during the earlier stages of the cycle. The work of consolidation consists partly of recognizing that certain goals of growth have largely been reached, and can now be left behind, and partly of understanding the larger dimensions and implications within which this growth has been occurring. Over long periods of time, it is indeed quite possible to resolve major problems and difficulties, both from the past and the present. The more we work with effective meditative techniques and principles, the more the life of the personality becomes redeemed, purified, and aligned with the higher self. So it is quite reasonable, at times, to look back and realize that certain problems have now been managed fully, and we can turn our attention to new issues of growth. Nevertheless, in most cases we should expect the new issues to be related to the issues we have resolved. The lessons we are learning now are almost always preparation for greater lessons yet to come. Consolidation is the mysterious stage in growth where old trends and chapters come to a close, but reappear in a new set of challenges. It is therefore an excellent time to refocus our commitment and dedication to growth, and to realize that growth occurs not only in consciousness but also in achievement.

Once the phase of consolidation is completed, the fifth phase of the cycle is activated—which takes us back to phase one and the cycle begins again. This may seem a discouraging prospect to the beginning meditator, but it really is not. After all, it is the nature of cycles to repeat themselves, over and over again. But each new repetition of the cycle brings fresh wisdom, renewed vigor, greater compassion, and a higher level of achievement.

Actually, there is a great deal of wisdom in the cyclic nature of growth. The wisdom, love, and strength of the higher self are not finite quantities. They cannot come pouring into the awareness of the personality as though we were dipping a ladle into a vat of hot wax and pouring the wax into a candle mold. They must be added gradually, layer after layer, as though the candle was being dipped first into one color of wax, then another, and then still another, until many cycles of dipping had occurred and the candle was complete. The personality can only grow effectively if it registers and learns to express the new life it has acquired, before going on to a new cycle and the greater stimulation it will bring.

It is unfortunate that many people believe that once they have "worked through" a problem they are done with it for all time. Usually, it is only the first cycle of the problem which has ended, and it will likely reappear in a new and more challenging form in the not-too-distant future. When it does reappear, however, they are often quite crestfallen, because the problem they thought they had solved for all time has now come back to haunt them. If these people better understood the cyclic nature of growth, however, they would better understand the dynamics of what has happened. Progress in the evolution of consciousness paves the way to further progress. Growth is never meant to cease—not even with the death of the physical body.

THE NEED FOR FLEXIBILITY

It must be understood that these cycles of growth rarely unfold with the precision the five phases suggest. The preserving-conserving nature of the personality will tend to send false signals that everything is well and no further improvement is necessary. The lazy elements within our character will balk at the notion of integrating new life into old memories and associations. Blind spots will find clever ways of hiding from detection. Rationalizations and selfishness will have an odd way of reproducing themselves. All of these factors tend to cause the smooth development of growth to falter.

Yet if we pursue the major themes of our personal growth, we will begin to comprehend the general outlines of the lessons the higher self has planned for this particular incarnation. These lessons will be different for us than for our friends, but they will be based on a great deal of wisdom and careful planning—planning which the higher self initiated long before this incarnation began.

In this context, then, it will be easier to see the approach we should take in using the techniques of Active Meditation. Because growth in consciousness is a dynamic process, changing as our rapport with the higher self changes, we can expect our use of meditation to be a changing process as well. At first, we may concentrate on enriching our emotions or improving our self-image. Once a certain amount of progress has been made in these areas, we will start to focus more on the use of the techniques for mental housecleaning, solving problems, and contacting the wisdom of the higher self. Yet a while later, we may find ourself returning to the technique for healing the emotions and using it in an entirely different way than at first.

There is no set formula for how to use the techniques of Active Meditation, and we should steadfastly resist the temptation to establish one. Each person must decide for himself the areas of growth needing the greatest support and concentrate on them, always remaining flexible so that his priorities can be shifted and adapted as growth occurs and new opportunities to grow develop. Indeed, the techniques themselves can be adapted and modified as circumstances require, so long as they remain true to the basic principles upon which they are founded.

This need for flexibility and growth is often overlooked by systems of meditation and spiritual growth. A technique for relaxation or stress control will be taught, for example, but once the meditator becomes proficient in it, he is not encouraged to go beyond it and work at higher levels of growth. He is instructed instead to continue to use that one technique over and over again, until he is so thoroughly at ease—emotionally, mentally, and spiritually, as well as physically—that he is unable to do anything at all! Such rigidity all but defeats the spirit of growth. Or, the meditator will be taught a concept which helps him grow beyond his limited ideas and beliefs. In time, though, the bold new concept itself becomes old and limiting. Yet the meditator has invested so much energy and effort in working with this concept that he is unable to grow beyond it. He becomes stuck in the concept for the rest of his life.

It is very easy to become a victim of the momentum of a technique or a system. But it need not occur, if we keep in mind that meditation is not an end unto itself. It is merely a method for establishing better contact between the higher self and the personality. It will therefore grow as we grow. We should look for this growth in our practice of meditation and welcome it, just as we look for growth in consciousness, and embrace it.

16

Meditating
To Help Others

RADIATING LIGHT

The same principles of Active Meditation which are so effective in stimulating personal growth can also be used to help other people and society. The influence of the light, love, and strength of the higher self is not limited just to our own consciousness. By holding a certain ideal or quality of the higher self in mind while meditating, we can radiate its light to specific individuals or to segments of society, for healing, purification, inspiration, or blessing. The good that can be done in this way is enormous. In fact, there are many who believe that the work of blessing and healing the world is the *primary* value of meditation. It is certainly true that this is one of the major ways in which we learn to think and act as the higher self thinks and acts. Consequently, this use of meditation is highly recommended.

Many beginners, however, confuse the use of meditation to help others with prayer. This confusion is quite understandable, as both prayer and meditation can be used to help others—and in fact can be used together. But there are a few differences which ought to be kept in mind:

• **Prayer** is the invocation of a transpersonal, divine blessing. Anyone with good intentions and faith in universal divine forces can pray effectively, because a prayer to help others or society is a request for a divine agency to intercede on behalf of a needy individual or group.

• **Meditation** is the radiation of a transpersonal, divine blessing. The meditator contacts the higher self, and through the higher self, the force of the blessing or healing to be given. A significant portion of this divine force is brought into the aura or consciousness of the meditator, and then radiated to the person or group who is being helped. While anyone can pray and invoke a blessing, if a person who has not worked to cleanse and purify his thoughts and emotions tries to meditate on helping others, the results may be disastrous. Instead of radiating light, love, and the power of spirit, he may well end up radiating his own selfishness, bigotry, wishes, fears, and resentments. Fortunately, the risk of this occurring with sincere and mature people of goodwill is small, because the potential for good usually outweighs the potential to harm. Still, it is important to understand that the integrity and quality of our bodies of thought and feeling *are* involved in the activity of radiating light and healing energies. There is a greater responsibility in using meditation to help others than there is in praying for others.

THE DUTY TO HELP

There are many worthwhile reasons for spending some of our time in meditation helping others. Probably the most important is that the higher self itself is actively involved in healing the problems of humanity and promoting the evolution of consciousness in the human race. Since we are striving to value what the higher self values and act as the higher self acts, learning to help others is a natural way to honor the wisdom and love of the higher self.

Some additional reasons for helping others through meditative activity include:

• It is part of our duty as a human being to help society grow and develop. The value of society and civilization to us individually is immeasurable. It has helped clothe us, feed us, protect us, educate us, and inspire us; it has given us a context in which to discover our individuality, find meaning in life, and grow as a human being. In turn, we have an obligation to help society.

• There comes a time in our evolution when it becomes appropriate to help support the efforts of those individuals who have helped us—the teachers, leaders, and guides of the human race who have nursed us in our efforts to grow. This obligation cannot be fulfilled by helping them directly, since they are the leaders, and we the followers. Rather, it is fulfilled by lending support to their work. These people are usually a part of the Hierarchy—a vast organization of enlightened people who are the custodians of the divine plan for the evolution of humanity and civilization. The Hierarchy as a group operates on the subtle dimensions of life, rather than the physical plane; as such, its methods of helping humanity are primarily meditative ones. As we learn to use meditation to help heal and inspire society, we give the work of the Hierarchy support. We may also become a channel through which the members of the Hierarchy can work more directly.

• Humanity has a tremendous need for greater wisdom, love, and enlightened direction. If we can radiate even a small portion of these treasures of spirit into the mind and emotions of humanity, we perform a useful service.

• Using meditation to help others opens up a new opportunity for self-expression. Many people have an urgent need to increase their enlightened self-expression in life, thereby grounding intentions, ideas, and goodwill. Serving humanity and helping others is an excellent way of enriching self-expression.

• As we work in these ways, we realize more profoundly that we are, in a very real sense, a citizen of the universe. We experience the true meaning and power of brotherhood—that collectively we are the body of light which is the Christ, and individually the different parts of it. The work of helping others activates some of the most significant and powerful aspects of our individuality as a human being. It likewise helps us develop an awareness of the Aquarian spirit.

• The use of meditation to help others also gradually builds a rapport, physically and telepathically, with other people who are working with similar purpose and intent. This can greatly enrich the impact of the light and love which is radiated—and helps us find new friends and acquaintances who share similar interests and activities.

PREPARING TO HELP

Because the meditative effort to help others puts us right in the midst of the work being done, radiating the love, light, and power of the higher realms of consciousness to others, it is important to make sure we are well prepared to handle these energies intelligently, *before we begin.* We must be able to remain relatively pure in intention, understanding, and attitude while we are meditating.

More than anything else, we need to be sure that our intention is to offer genuine help, not just sympathy or good wishes. Many people, however, have no real understanding of what genuine help is. If a friend is sick, they pray for the friend to feel better. Yet if the friend is sick primarily because he worries too much at work, they would be better advised to pray for their friend's enlightenment. Or, if a friend is suffering abuse at the hands of another person, they try to visualize their friend being delivered from this situation—or his antagonist being brought to justice. But being rescued miraculously might abort a learning process which both people need—and it may well be that the friend needs to confront justice as much as his antagonist. We must understand that there is great danger in projecting our *personal* judgments about a situation while we are trying to help meditatively. We are usually not in a position to judge.

The same is true in helping society and groups in society. Some people, for example, meditate quite diligently to help the Russian Jews escape persecution. On the surface, this seems like a noble activity, but it is still *the projection of a personal preference upon a circumstance we cannot judge.* The enlightened way to help, by contrast, would be to invoke the forces of goodwill and divine justice for *both victim and persecutor alike.* By proceeding in this way, we are not making personal judgments—we are leaving judgment to universal law. We are merely offering help, not just to a specific group, but to the society as a whole.

An important part of preparing to help others meditatively, therefore, is to detach ourself from our personal wants and wishes. This automatically tends to cleanse our consciousness of factors and influences which would pollute or distort the light and love we seek to radiate. An effective way of making this detachment is to offer our assistance to the higher spiritual intelligences who guide the destiny of the group, nation, or institution of society we are seeking to help—or to the higher self, if it is an individual. If we seek to work with these intelligences as an agent of universal goodwill, then we can be sure the quality of light we radiate will be benevolent and pure.

HELPING OTHERS

When working on our own problems, we have a certain latitude and flexibility which cannot be a part of working to help others. The reason for this should be obvious. If we make a mistake in working to redirect our emotions or improve a habit, we alone are affected by the consequences. Yet if we make a mistake while working to help others, or society, the consequences will involve more than ourself alone. We must therefore always work with a deep and reverent appreciation for the individual destiny of other people and the purpose and collective destiny of nations and groups in society. We must always honor the principle of free will and work impersonally.

Our goal should be to help create a climate of healing and enlightenment in which the person or group can heal or enlighten itself, rather than arbitrarily impose an answer that we personally would like to see come to pass. In other words, we should limit ourself to reinforcing the spiritual will and plan for the people or group involved, not directly intervening in their problems. In this regard, the guidelines for helping others meditatively are a good deal different than helping others physically. Since the recipient of our help may not be consciously aware of the help we are offering, we must be more cautious and circumspect. We must focus our efforts on radiating the energies of goodwill, wisdom, courage, divine order, or healing vitality—not specific plans and ideas as to how these energies should change conditions once they arrive.

As a general rule, the act of radiating light and love proceeds much more effectively if we *broadcast* the energy to a large group of people instead of a single individual. A light bulb illumines the whole room with light, not just a single point on one wall. This does not mean that we should never work to help individuals, however. It means that we can best help individuals by simultaneously working to help others with similar problems. If we have a friend, for example, who is suffering from despondency, and we want to radiate healing energies to him, the help we can offer will be much more powerful if we work to help *everyone* in our community who is suffering from despondency and pessimism.

The specific procedure to use in radiating light and love to others will vary with the kind of help we are seeking to give. The following format is offered as a starting point for beginners—and a reference point for those who already have experience in helping others meditatively:

1. We begin by determining the scope of the help we seek to offer, and the individuals or groups we seek to assist.

2. Next, we ascertain the quality of light and love we need

to radiate. Genuine help can be given meditatively *only* if we have determined the nature of the enlightened qualities which are missing or deficient in the individual or group we are trying to help. The real problem in an angry person is not his anger, but rather his lack of compassion. We would therefore send him compassion. The real problem in society is not war or the threat of a nuclear holocaust, but rather the selfishness, ignorance, intolerance, malice, greed, jealousy, prejudice, laziness, and nationalism which lead to competition and strife. These difficulties clearly betray a lack of goodwill, tolerance, wisdom, and understanding of the Hierarchical plan for humanity. We should therefore send society the light of goodwill, tolerance, wisdom, and the will to fulfill its fundamental design. If we are going to radiate light, we must be willing to work on these terms.

3. We establish meditative contact with the higher self, as described in chapter five.

4. Through our contact with our own higher self, we make contact with the higher self of the person we are seeking to help or the spiritual forces which nurture and protect the segment of society we are seeking to help, asking for guidance in offering this help. These forces should be invoked in a spirit of devotion and with the confidence that there truly are forces and intelligences in the universe which guide the destiny and evolution of society and its institutions. There probably will be no conscious indication that this contact has been made, yet if we make it with reverence, conviction, and the intention to help, we can be sure our invocation will be answered.

5. Using the creative imagination, we visualize the light of the quality we are invoking being gathered around us. We give our full attention to the light of this quality. Once we are attuned to it effectively, we then visualize sending it forth to the person, group, or aspect of society we are seeking to help. There are many variations which are possible at this stage of

the work. If we are sending help to a large group of people, for example, we can visualize the spiritual light we are sending entering the minds and hearts of the individuals in the group, enriching the lesser portion of light in each of them and adding to their goodwill and wisdom.

In using the creative imagination in these ways, however, it is important to remember that visualization is just a skill for directing spiritual forces; the image we create is *not* the force itself. It is just a convenient vehicle. Our primary attention should therefore be centered on holding steady in our consciousness the quality of the light we are sending. Anyone, even the higher animals, is able to visualize images, but only enlightened and skillful meditators are able to use visualization as a channel for healing qualities and divine energies.

It is likewise important to keep in mind the value of remaining impersonal as we radiate light to others. As long as we remain detached and impersonal, we will be able to serve as an effective agent for these forces. But if we lose our detachment, we open the gateway for the influx of our personal fears and desires, thereby weakening the contact with the higher energies and polluting our effort. Achieving this detachment is a great challenge to the meditator, as it requires that we work without personal concern for the outcome of our efforts. But it is a necessary part of helping others effectively, for it enables us to work with the actual forces of spirit—and be protected as well from the unpleasant aspects of the problem we are seeking to heal.

6. We hold our attention, as well as the intention to help in this radiation of light and love, for as long as appropriate. This can be anywhere from a few minutes to fifteen or twenty minutes. Rarely would it be desirable to spend more time than this, however, unless we are highly experienced in the art of meditation and know that we will not suffer undue strain from the effort.

7. The session can be brought to an end by detaching from the focus of attention we have been holding, taking care to remain impersonal toward the work we have done. Our work has been to launch universal energies to help others. Now that we have done so, it is best to turn our attention to other matters and not be consumed by a personal curiosity as to the impact we have had.

THE GREAT INVOCATION

The effort to help others can be made even more effective if we use a universal invocation to help focus our attention and energies. This would obviously not apply to meditative work to assist specific individuals, but it can be enormously powerful as a way to radiate goodwill, wisdom, and spiritual will to the whole of humanity.

One of the best invocations to use in this manner is the Great Invocation, which was first published in the writings of Alice A. Bailey during the 1940's. It has been widely used by spiritual aspirants since that time, and its merit has been fully proven. It summons the wisdom, love, and will of God, directing these qualities into the mind and heart and will of mankind, and then evokes our participation in the fulfillment of the divine plan for humanity and civilization. The full text of the Great Invocation is:

From the point of Light within the Mind of God
Let light stream forth into the minds of men.
Let Light descend on Earth.

From the point of Love within the Heart of God
Let love stream forth into the hearts of men.
May Christ return to Earth.

From the center where the Will of God is known
Let purpose guide the little wills of men—
The purpose which the Masters know and serve.

From the center which we call the race of men
Let the Plan of Love and Light work out.
And may it seal the door where evil dwells.

Let Light and Love and Power restore the Plan on Earth.

After entering the meditative state, each stanza in the Great Invocation can be stated, mentally, or aloud, with the certain conviction that there is a reservoir of light, love, and divine will which is set aside for all men and women to call upon, for the purpose of blessing humanity and stimulating its evolution. This light and love and power will help redeem humanity from the darkness and selfishness which grips the bulk of our race.

It is a good idea to pause for a short while at the end of each stanza to allow the quality of the particular force it has invoked to stream out—to the minds, the hearts, and the little wills of men and women everywhere. After using the Great Invocation a few times, the meditator will soon find the right and proper pace for using this invocation most effectively.

Daily use of the Great Invocation is an excellent way to enrich the quality of our meditations and enhance our efforts to contribute to the redemption of humanity.

17

Group Meditations

THE GROUP FORMAT

Meditation is primarily an individual endeavor—the process of establishing, nurturing, and expanding contact between the higher self and the personality. Most of the activity of meditation is therefore pursued in the privacy of our own mind and heart. Nevertheless, there are times when meditation can also be effectively pursued in a *group* format. A number of people with similar intent meditate together, using the same techniques and skills. The result is a collective effort which can be far more powerful than the sum of the benefits of each individual working by himself.

There can be a number of reasons why individuals would meditate together as a group:

• To learn the principles and techniques of meditation. In this case, the group would consist of students who are being instructed in the skills and philosophy of meditation. The teacher would lead the students through each meditation, thereby giving structure and direction to the process, until the students were familiar with this meditative format. The value of this kind of group meditation is that the teacher, if he is competent, is able to facilitate contact with the higher forces of life for the students. By holding his mind steady in the divine energy of compassion, for example, the teacher can help his students experience the quality of compassion more powerfully than if they were meditating on their own. He may also be able to discern when problems arise, and make suggestions for correcting them.

• To help the members of the group enrich their spiritual life. The act of setting a formal time, place, and topic for a group meditation helps to establish a meditative discipline for the people who will be participating in it. This can be quite beneficial for those individuals who have not yet cultivated a daily habit of working with meditation. Usually, it is best if these sessions can be led by someone who is well versed in meditative skills. Any of the seven techniques for personal growth can be used.

• To help invoke the spiritual purpose behind a certain group activity. This use of group meditation can be an especially powerful opportunity for people who work together in a medical clinic, office, school, church, or similar endeavor. At the beginning of each work day, or on any occasion when the members may congregate, the group begins with a meditation to invoke purpose, wisdom, and direction for the work they will be doing.

• To radiate light and love to enlighten humanity. This is beyond doubt the most creative use of the group format for meditation, as it draws together a number of people who have dedicated themselves to contributing to the good of humanity. There are groups of this nature scattered throughout the world, and the contributions they make to the evolution of mankind and civilization are substantial.

It should be understood that it is not necessary for the members of a group to congregate *physically* in the same place in order to have a group meditation—except in the case of a group which is learning to meditate. The real work of any meditation, individual or group, transpires at nonphysical levels—the physical body is not involved, except to help ground and focus the results.

It is therefore quite plausible for a group to meet meditatively, on the inner dimensions of life, even though their physical bodies may be in many different locations. This is a true "meeting of the minds," in which the meditators are brought together by their common intention, philosophy, dedication, and mental activity. The link is a telepathic one, rather than physical. But the results can be just as powerful as if the meditators were together physically—and indeed, in many cases, they are even more powerful.

A COMMON BOND

Not every collection of physical people necessarily constitutes a group that can meditate effectively together. There has to be a compatibility among group members which strengthens the mutual effort. The fundamental characteristics of a group which is able to meditate together would be:

1. The group is united by a common bond of purpose and a mutual effort to work with the life of spirit.

2. The members share an enlightened philosophy which orients them toward serving humanity.

3. The members are all used to contacting the higher self in similar ways, using similar techniques. These techniques may be either devotional or mental in focus, but the approach used by the group should be uniform. It is not possible to establish unity if one member can only meditate in the presence of a guru, another must rely on a mantra, and a third is straining to center himself in the love petals of the egoic lotus.

4. The group has a common goal and works in unison to achieve it. This goal could be learning the basic principles of meditation, improving the quality of the lives of the members of the group, enriching the work atmosphere the members share, or healing problems in humanity. But the goal should be clearly understood by all members of the group, and each individual should keep his attention focused on it. The usefulness of the light and love a group can contact is quickly dissipated if the members start going in divergent directions with it.

Even when all of these factors are present, it must be understood that group unity can be a fragile bond, easily disrupted. Something as apparently harmless as social chitchat and gossiping among group members before the work of meditation begins—or even after it concludes—can greatly weaken the effort to invoke divine energies and radiate them into the world. Over a period of time, it can subtly undermine the purpose and dedication of the group. Members show up at the appointed time and place more interested in learning what has happened to their friends than in performing the group service.

More severe disruptions can occur when a member of a group is so intensely selfish, bigoted, hostile, or emotional that he clashes with the attitudes and level of refinement of the other members. If possible, such people should be excluded from the group from the very beginning. But if these characteristics become evident only after the group has already been formed, it may be necessary to ask the individual to drop out. Common sense should always be the rule. It is a tragic mistake to sacrifice the effectiveness of a whole group merely to indulge the immaturity of a single member.

In general, the scope of a group should not be too broad, either in philosophical orientation or in level of consciousness. The weakest members of a group will always have a dampening effect upon the group as a whole, and will place undue strain and limitation on the more evolved and sincere members. The purpose of group meditation is to bring in more energy than is possible working individually. As this greater measure of energy is brought in, it will tend to overstimulate the deficiencies of the weakest members. The result can be just as unfair to the weak members, who are not ready to deal with such problems, as to the strong ones, whose efforts are diminished. It is best to avoid such dilemmas by striving to form a group which is basically compatible.

INDIVIDUALITY

It is never an enlightened act to give up our individuality in order to be part of a group, whether the group is pursuing a physical or a meditative activity. In groups which meditate together, it is especially important to understand that unity is not achieved by sacrificing either our sense of individuality or our personal responsibility. It is achieved as a group of *individuals* work together to fulfill a common purpose and reach a common goal, using similar methods and techniques. Even though the group meditates together, each member is still expected to contact his own higher self and draw the qualities and energies to be used in the group work through the channel of his own individuality. It is not desirable simply to plug into the group mind and draw these forces and qualities from it. Nevertheless, it often happens.

An effective group will therefore cherish the ideal of individuality and encourage its members to strengthen their sense of identity as individuals. The stronger the individual members of a group are, the stronger the group unity can be. This will be viewed as a bold statement by many, but it is just common sense. A group in which the individual members are expected to pay obeisance to a central leader or guru is not a group at all—just an extension of the leader. A group in which the individual members reinforce the weaknesses and pettiness of one another is not a group either—just a collection of neurotic people.

It would be best for such "groups" to make no effort to meditate together at all. Neither meaningful growth nor effective service can occur in such climates.

MEDITATING IN A GROUP

Before any group effort to meditate together is launched, it is important for the group to determine and define the purpose it is serving—the *real* purpose, not the professed purpose. If the group is gathering to learn to meditate, the purpose will be defined by the teacher. But in groups which come together for the betterment of humanity, each group member should contribute to this process of determining purpose. It is always our intention which determines the ultimate outcome of our labors, either physically or meditatively. Doing the right thing for the wrong purpose is therefore the wrong thing! If the purpose of the group is clearly understood, however, it will serve as a reliable guide for everything which follows. In this regard, it is useful for the group to periodically review the purpose it seeks to serve, and determine if the group has strayed from it or become lax in its habits. It is all too easy for a group which begins with a noble purpose to be sidetracked by some narrow religious or social issue—or, even worse, become the personal fiefdom of a strong personality, who uses the group as an opportunity to enrich either his reputation or his bank account—or both.

Just as each group must assume the responsibility of determining the purpose it will seek to fulfill, it must also develop a meditative format which will be appropriate for the kind of activity it is engaged in. There is no magic formula which will guarantee group success. Still, it is possible to sketch out a rough outline of how a group meditation might proceed:

1. The first step, as in individual meditations, is to make contact with the higher self. *Each member should make this contact on his own.* This is done simply by setting aside a minute or two at the beginning of the meditation for each individual to contact his own higher self. Once this contact is made, and the group is beginning to invoke a specific divine quality or force, the telepathic rapport the group needs in order to function as a unit will be established automatically, by virtue of the fact that the individual members are all focusing their attention on the same aspect of the inner life. It is therefore not necessary to try to develop a telepathic rapport at the personality level—and in fact it can be quite dangerous. If the group members try to attune to the inner levels *as a group,* they will probably tune in only to the group mind—their collective and

personalized thoughts and feelings about the group—instead of a valid level of spiritual life.

The group should therefore resist dismissing the need for proper attunement. Such practices as resting for a moment while "thinking about God," visualizing a common symbol, or repeating a favorite phrase are not adequate substitutes for the attunement of each individual to his or her higher self. In order to be ready to work effectively in meditation—as an individual or a group—we must take the time to detach from the concerns of the personality, focus our devotion, concentrate on an enlightened intention, and attune to the love, wisdom, and power of the higher self.

The goal of meditation is always to strengthen contact between the higher self and the personality, and this is just as true in group format as individually. It is through the higher self that we can most easily establish telepathic rapport with the other members of the group—as well as inner plane ashrams, invisible teachers, divine archetypes, and other spiritual agencies. It is important to emphasize this point, because many groups quickly get swept away in the glamour that they can bypass the soul while working in group format. Undoubtedly they can—but they are no longer meditating!

2. Once the individual members of the group have made contact with the higher self, the work of the group turns to invoking the needed spiritual forces and qualities. This will naturally vary with the intent of the group. If the group is meditating to improve the skills of the individual members, the spiritual forces invoked will be determined by the technique they choose to practice. If the group is working to radiate light and love to humanity, it will invoke whatever quality the members have agreed to focus on in this session.

In either case, however, we must dispense with the common religious notion that God already knows what we need and we do not have to bother specifying or requesting anything. This absurd notion, reinforced by generations of bully-ing by religious leaders, throws the whole meditative science of invocation and evocation out the window in one ignorant swoop. Even though the higher self does know our needs more clearly than we do, the personality nevertheless has an obliga-tion to invoke divine forces to help it in its work. They do not arrive automatically.

This phase of invoking spiritual force can be reinforced quite effectively by the use of liturgical formulas or phrases, spoken either mentally or aloud, as in the following examples:

"May God's love and peace be with us and those we seek to help."

"May the power of the Hierarchical plan for humanity transform the imperfections of life into the spiritual ideal."

"May the love and wisdom of God turn the minds and hearts of all people toward tolerance and goodwill."

"May God's love and the agents of His healing vitality be with us today as we seek to help those in need."

Whatever phrase or formula is used, it should be inven-tive, active, positive, and brief.

3. Having invoked spiritual force, the attention of the group should shift to *registering* this force—if the purpose of the group meditation is to help the members individually—or to *radiating* the light to others—if the purpose of the group meditation is to help others. In a group which is meditating to help themselves, each member should focus the force which has been contacted in such a way that it enriches some aspect of his character. In a group which is meditating to help others, the members should proceed with a clear intention to honor the forces which have been contacted with a maximum of integrity and thoroughness, neither adding to nor subtracting from the actual force and substance that has been invoked. Their personal effort is in giving these forces an outlet into the planes of human thought and activity—not in modifying them.

Throughout, each person should work with a clear understanding of the results the meditation is designed to produce. This need not be complex; it can be as simple as "the enlightenment of humanity" or "the progressive transformation of human attitudes toward cooperation and goodwill." In addition to this clear understanding, we should also work with a firm conviction and faith that we *are* participating in something quite powerful. This is especially important if the purpose of the group meditation is to help others or enlighten humanity.

The creative imagination can be used to visualize the impact of the spiritual forces we have invoked—for example, by imagining beams of light radiating from the inner dimensions of the group to the people or aspect of society we are helping.

The actual time spent working with these energies will vary, but should run from five to fifteen minutes.

4. If the group is planning to work together regularly, it is useful to develop a format that will heighten the repetitive and cumulative effect of meditating.

OUR PART

When the group format is used for the work of helping others, it is important for each participant to remain impersonal in attitude, working as the higher self would work—with patience, benevolence, wisdom, dignity, reverence, and the will-to-good. Working impersonally does not mean acting in a wooden, robot-like way, however. It means rising above our personal interests, prejudices, and likes and dislikes, so we may work with divine qualities *at their level*, not ours.

Some people would have us believe that working impersonally means we do not make a difference—that God does all the work, not us. This is absolutely not true, and we should

391

never be swayed by such sophistry. Indeed, to be successful in using meditation to help others, we must be able to hold the conviction that *we do make a difference!* We make a difference because meditation is an active process in which we prepare our mind and emotions, take responsibility for a certain piece of work, and then follow through to completion. It is quite possible that we may never perfectly grasp, at the personality level, the fullness of the power we invoke, but as long as we approach our work with respect and reverence for the wisdom and benevolence of the energies we are invoking, our efforts to be an agent of light will be effective.

The need for an impersonal attitude extends even after the meditation is completed. Once the group has finished radiating the light to others, it is best for the members of the group to "forget" all about it until the work is taken up again. There is danger that too much curiosity, desire, fear, or speculation about how the light is working may actually call some of the light back again. In this regard, metaphysicians and New Thought students have been correctly trained "to leave the problem in the light," once they are finished praying. If we are to ground the light, we must send it to its target and then leave it to do whatever work it can in the minds and hearts of those who need it. If we figuratively "run after the light" to see how it is doing, we are apt to disrupt a delicate process—as well as open a psychic door for unpleasant energies to flow back to us.

Having done our part, we let the light do its.

SERVING THE PLAN

The contribution which can be made by using meditative techniques in a group format is tremendous. If our religious institutions would stop being so preoccupied with dogma, theology, and building the "materialistic church," and grasp the potential and the power of group meditations, many of them could once again become a constructive force for good in humanity. Unfortunately, few religions recognize the value of actually working with spirit. As a result, most of the groups which participate in the grand activity of radiating the light and cooperating with the Hierarchy operate outside of formal religion.

Until the time when the usefulness of meditation and the duty of each human being to help spiritualize civilization is recognized by the churches, group meditation will have to remain apart from religion. Yet the opportunity is there, wherever a group of like-minded and dedicated individuals comes together, and wonders:

"How can we serve the plan of God?"

Our Silent Partner Speaks

We were feeling a bit self-indulgent. Bob was leaning back in his chair, sipping coffee and munching on a cookie. "Well, that really tells it like it is—everything you need to know about meditation. Now all we have to do is make a few comments about aids and problems of meditation, and we'll be done."

Carl looked up from the steadily-growing pile of manuscript. "I agree. The ideas are really coming together nicely. All it is going to need is a little tightening up here and some editing there."

"Is that so?" boomed a voice from nowhere in particular.

It was our silent partner, breaking his silence once again. He seemed to have an uncanny knack for always showing up just in time to catch us putting our editorial foot into our editorial mouth. It was Herman's special charm.

"Well, we didn't mean that literally, of course," Carl mumbled. "One book can't contain *everything* the reader needs to know about meditation. But we are trying to make it as definitive as possible." He paused for awhile and then added, "And I think we are doing a fairly good job of it."

"Probably," Herman admitted, a sly smile flitting across his face. "It will do, I guess. For someone who is used to reading books in the fifth dimension, as I am, the claim of anyone on earth to have written down everything you need to know about *any* subject is more than a little pretentious. I know the two of you were just kidding, and did not actually believe it, but there are people who make such claims quite seriously. They claim to be the guardian of the Whole Truth on some subject, infallible messengers from God. That kind of claim has caused a lot of mischief on earth."

"Well, we would never claim to be in possession of the whole truth," said Bob.

"No," Carl added, "just inspired by an angel." All three of us laughed.

"Inspired may not be the proper word," Herman replied.

"Chided and pushed, perhaps—maybe even scolded."

By now, we knew exactly what he meant.

"That's why I showed up again. I want to caution you about the remaining chapters you are going to write. You sometimes write with a touch of dogmatism—even *contempt*, I daresay—for meditative practices which were common and useful as recently as, oh, five thousand years ago. In fact, I can vividly remember—well, never mind. You just ought to think about the fact that the golden words you are setting down in this book will one day be out-of-date, too. They will sound backward and harmful in a thousand years or so—maybe even less."

"Maybe even before the book is published," Carl joked.

"No," Herman observed. "I don't think humanity is evolving *that* rapidly."

We had gotten Herman's message, however. "I suppose any strong statement will sound arrogant or dogmatic to some people," Bob said, shifting in his chair to look more directly at Herman. "You can't set out to reform hideously outdated practices without making bold statements that will jar people into recognizing how outdated the old traditions have become. That's exactly what we want this book to do, after all—inspire people to start thinking more for themselves. We don't want them to *believe* our ideas any more than anyone else's. We want them to take our common sense observations and experiment with them, so that meditation can help them as it has helped us. If they experiment with these ideas, they will soon enough prove their validity—through their own experiences and growth. That's how we did it—and that's how the reader can do it, too."

"All right, all right!" Herman was smiling as though he had just swallowed the Cheshire cat—a chocolate one, of course, or whatever angels enjoy for a treat. "But do you see the impact a little criticism can have?"

Bob looked at the floor. Carl looked at Bob.

Faint laughter was heard. As it receded into silence, Bob spoke. "I see his point. But I have a point, too. Intelligent people deserve something more than mushy statements which never address the fundamental issues of meditation and enlightenment. If we have to risk sounding dogmatic and critical in order to explain these ideas intelligently, then so be it."

"I have no argument with that," Carl agreed. "But I think we can accommodate common sense, wisdom, and good manners all at the same time."

"Well, see that you do," boomed the invisible voice from above our heads. But there was more merriment in his tone than disapproval.

18

Aids To Meditation

HELPFUL PRACTICES

Pen and paper are valuable aids to a writer. An electric typewriter is an even better one. But the act of writing has little to do with either scribbling on paper or typing on a typewriter. The *act* of writing occurs as the author translates ideas, observations, and insights into words which express his perspective and understanding. The tools he uses to register these words so that others may read them are important, but far from central.

The same can be said about meditation. There are many helpful aids the meditator can use to enhance the meditative experience, from the choice of a proper environment to instruction from a competent teacher, but the act of meditating has little to do with whether or not these adjuncts are being used. The *act* of meditating occurs as the personality contacts the higher self and then translates the spiritual qualities and forces of the higher self into practical expression in daily life. The aids which might be used to enrich the meditative experience can be important—but they are far from central.

Nevertheless, many sincere people have fallen into the bad habit of overemphasizing the use of aids to meditation, at the expense of the actual meditative experience itself. They become involved in the *forms* of meditation, forgetting that genuine meditation is an experience in consciousness. For them, it would be better to use no aids at all, until they have learned to regard meditation entirely as an event in consciousness. Otherwise, they will continue to be like the man who was served a magnificent meal on a paper plate, only to throw away the food and nibble on the plate.

Our need for practices and rituals which enrich the meditative experience will vary as we progress in our use of Active Meditation. In the early stages, for example, the use of flowers and music may be quite important, especially if we have come

403

from a background of spiritual experience in which these elements are emphasized. But the more we experience meditation as an event in consciousness, the less significant many of these adjuncts will seem. Still, all of them do have their value, when properly understood and used.

As always, common sense should rule. If a particular practice is helpful to us, we should continue using it. But if we have become trapped in a certain practice, and our meditations are sterile, we had better reexamine the usefulness of this ritual, and perhaps discard it. Under no circumstances should we make the mistake of substituting ritualistic practices for the actual work of meditation. It is very easy to become so absorbed in worrying about posture, breathing, and the direction we are facing that we forget all about making contact with the higher self and integrating its love, wisdom, and power into our character and self-expression. But when this occurs, we are no longer meditating.

There are four basic categories of aids to meditation—choosing the proper time to meditate, preparing the surroundings in which we meditate, preparing the body for meditation, and preparing consciousness for meditation. Not every practice listed in each category will be useful to any one meditator. But many of them will be. The key, as always, is to experiment with the practices which seem most likely to benefit the actual work of meditation.

THE PROPER TIME TO MEDITATE

In many systems of spiritual growth the correct timing of meditations is highly valued. And, indeed, an enlightened use of timing can be a valuable aid to effective meditation. There are several factors to consider in this regard:

Regularity. Since Active Meditation is designed to complement a full and busy involvement in daily life, most people find it best to establish a routine of meditating at approximately the same time every day. There are no fixed rules as to when or how often this should be, however; it is primarily a matter of personal choice and convenience. One possible program is to meditate twenty to thirty minutes in the morning, before the activity of the day begins, and again in the evening. Each person needs to work out his or her own schedule.

The advantage of building up a regular routine is that the subconscious begins to expect and look forward to meditating at the specified time. It becomes as much a part of our daily life as brushing our teeth or eating lunch. This is a desirable condition to cultivate, as it gradually helps the subconscious become more and more receptive to the higher self.

Meditating at special times. Some people make a major point of meditating at sunrise, noon, and sunset each day, at the time of the new and full moons each month, and at the summer and winter solstices. This is not just a personal idiosyncrasy, but rather an effort to take advantage of the solar and spiritual "tides" which sweep through our environment, physically and psychospiritually. It is a practice which is rooted in ancient tradition.

The ancients made far more use of astronomical timing and the position of the sun than we do today. These were not superstitious heathens, but enlightened people who studied the impact of solar and zodiacal forces on human consciousness and applied the knowledge they gained to improving the quality of their contact with the higher self. They held that each of the heavenly bodies is multidimensional in nature, just as man is—that the physical sun veils a more central, spiritual sun which is the Logos or higher self of the solar system. This spiritual sun is the source of all spiritual forces and qualities within the system, and the physical sun is an important facet of its self-expression. As such, it makes excellent sense to attune our

405

individual spiritual exercises to the timing of the physical sun. Sunrise is an excellent time to awaken to new opportunities for attunement to the higher self, because the solar radiations are flowing toward us. At noon, the solar tides shift, and the radiations begin to recede. Sunset marks the nocturnal eclipse of the physical sun. It is therefore a little easier to invoke and receive inspiration, guidance, and divine powers in the time before noon, and a little easier to dispel unwanted forces and ground spiritual forces in the time after noon.

The same principles also extend to the time of the new and full moon and the summer and winter solstices. The moon affects our spiritual environment in much the same way it controls the physical tides. The spiritual forces conditioning the environment of the earth are magnified at the time of the full moon and at their lowest strength at the time of the new moon. In addition, the Hierarchy, the huge organization which guides the development of humanity from the inner planes, uses the time of the full moon to radiate more light to earth and communicate with those who are serving as its agents. For those who do not yet have a strong bond with the higher self and have not made much progress in purifying the personality, the time of the full moon is primarily a time of heightened irritability and difficulty. But for the experienced meditator, who uses the principles of Active Meditation effectively, the time of the full moon is an excellent time to contact the light of the higher self and radiate it to the world. Many meditation groups take advantage of this period to contact the Hierarchy and serve as its agent in blessing the whole human race.

The new moon also provides favorable opportunities for meditative work, but of a different nature. It is a propitious time to reevaluate and refine our values and goals, redirect the momentum of our self-expression, and focus on mental housecleaning.

The summer and winter solstices represent turning points

in the solar year, and therefore make excellent times to meditate on long-term plans for service and self-expression. It is interesting to note, in this regard, that Christmas coincides roughly with the winter solstice, which marks the return of the sun after six months of progressively shorter days and longer nights. It is a time of renewal and reaffirmation of our faith in the spiritual power of life, somewhat similar to the time of the new moon, but on a larger scale.

It is useful to recognize that our psychospiritual environment does change to a degree throughout each day, each month, and the whole year. The change is slight, but significant. And so it is reasonable to make the most out of whatever slight advantage these changes bring us. At the same time, however, it is important to remember that our primary relationship in meditation is between the personality and the higher self—and the position of the sun or the moon does little to alter this basic rapport. We should therefore be able to meditate successfully at any time of the day or night—to receive guidance and power, do mental housecleaning, or radiate light to others. If we become too dependent upon the movement of the sun or the moon, we are no longer meditating—just worshipping nature forces.

It should also be kept in mind that much of the enhancement of meditative work at these times derives from the faith and expectations of the one who is meditating, as well as his cultural conditioning.

Meditating on religious holidays. A large outpouring of aspiration and love for God always helps facilitate our efforts to contact the spiritual realms of life. Religious holidays and special observances can be very powerful times, releasing an extra measure of spiritual force not only for the faithful but for all sincere aspirants, regardless of their religious ties. As such, the major festivals of *all* of the major world religions provide excellent opportunities for meditating, either for personal

407

growth or for world service. The only warning in this regard is that some religious festivals in certain religions focus excessively on the suffering of humanity, thereby evoking more collective self-pity than any light of God. This does not provide a healthy climate for meditating.

THE PLACE OF MEDITATION

We should be able to meditate anywhere, not only in theory but in actuality. The presence of God is to be found everywhere, not just in a specially designated meditation room. Far too many people become so dependent on meditating only in a protected and highly refined environment that they end up almost like a hothouse plant—unable to exist outside its own special home. When this occurs, there is reason to believe that they are not actually meditating at all. The higher self should not be limited by any condition of the physical plane.

Nevertheless, it is certainly true that some places are more conducive to effective meditation than others. There are also a number of practical steps which can be taken to prepare a room for a higher quality of contact with the higher self. The proper choice and preparation of the surroundings in which we meditate can therefore be an important aid to the entire process. These are the factors to consider:

Meditating in nature. Some people put great stock in taking advantage of the "good vibes" of being outdoors and away from man-made structures. If our home or workplace tends to be saturated with human pettiness, sickness, or jealousy, getting away from it occasionally and meditating outdoors can be a useful practice. The forces of nature, especially the higher forms of the vegetable kingdom, create a favorable presence which fosters human health, both physically and psychologically. Being outdoors in the sunlight also brings us the added benefit of the sun's vitality and subtle radiations. These solar forces can contribute to the purification and enrichment of our consciousness.

Nevertheless, there are some disadvantages to meditating outdoors, too. The most obvious is that nature can be very distracting. Sunburn, insects, and even the chirping of birds can interfere with our concentration. On the subtle level, the distractions can be even more serious. It is possible to become too grounded in the etheric forces of the physical planet or overwhelmed by the pleasing but powerful astral forces of nature. A person who is adept at detaching from physical sensation will have no problem in becoming too grounded in the natural magnetic flows of etheric force from the earth. But others will actually have far better meditations if they are inside a man-made building which interrupts the natural etheric force field. As for the strong astral forces of nature, these vary in intensity and quality from location to location, but can be a significant distraction to people who are rather emotionally oriented in consciousness.

It should also be understood that some people are attracted to meditating outdoors not because they love nature so much but because they dislike people. In these people, meditating outdoors on a regular basis will subtly reinforce their already bad habit of intolerance and contempt for their fellow human beings. Such misanthropes need to stay at home and spend their time cultivating goodwill toward mankind and a sense of brotherhood—not escaping to the woods.

The only real test of the benefits of meditating outdoors is to try it in a number of locales and compare the results with indoor meditations. In making this determination, however, it is important to remember that feeling good while we are meditating is not a meaningful reflection of the value of the meditation. We may *enjoy* meditating in nature more than indoors, because the quiet gurgling of a pleasant stream or the chirping of birds helps relax us, but this does not mean that we actually accomplish more in these outdoor meditations than in our indoor ones. These pleasant sensations may actually serve to distract us from our real goal—improving contact with the higher self.

Magnetic sites. Some locations on the planet are more highly charged with magnetic energy than others. Ancient people were often far more appreciative of this fact than modern mystics and occultists. Talented individuals, gifted with extra sensitivity, would be consulted before a temple or church was built so that the best possible site of high magnetism could be selected. This is one reason, for example, why many temples and churches in Europe and the Middle East have been built on top of the ruins of the holy buildings of earlier civilizations. These "high points" often occur along the ridges and tops of hills or at the intersections of valleys and small streams. There can be value in meditating at these particular locations, as they recharge the vitality of the etheric body and enhance the condition of the emotional body. They facilitate contact with the higher forces.

Along with the high points of the earth, there are also sites which are notably low in magnetism. The subtle forces of life tend to "sink" in these particular spots, and they are unwholesome places to live, let alone meditate. Even insensitive people will notice an odd fatigue and irritability after spending an hour or two in one of these places; highly sensitive individuals may become mildly ill with headaches, nausea, or vague muscle weakness, even though they may not know why they feel this way. These symptoms can certainly develop for many reasons unassociated with the condition of our physical surroundings, but as we grow in inner sensitivity, it is important to take these factors into account.

Meditation rooms. There can be a powerful advantage in meditating in a room which has been specifically prepared or reserved for spiritual work. This could be a religious chapel or sanctuary, or a special room set aside at home for meditating.

A chapel which has been consecrated for holy activities can be ideal for most meditative work. Unfortunately, not all chapels and sanctuaries are uniform in their consecration. Excessive division, greed, or bigotry among the members of the congregation may impair the holiness of the building. In some instances, we would be better off trying to meditate in a bus station.

It is not always possible to set aside a room solely for meditation in the average home. But the effect can be simulated to some degree by setting aside a specific corner of a room—or a designated chair. By meditating regularly in the same place, we tend to dispel antagonistic forces which would interfere with our meditative work and collect favorable forces. Obviously, this is a cumulative effect which builds over a period of time.

The greatest factors which condition the atmosphere of the place in which we meditate are the customary thoughts and feelings of the people who use this place on a regular basis, including ourself. In the case of our home, this would be our family. In the case of an office, it would be those we work with. Walls and furniture have a remarkable capacity to absorb the feelings and desires of human beings. Even the building as a whole can be affected in this way, which can be a factor for those who live in apartment buildings and condominiums. Once saturated with intensely negative qualities, a physical structure can be very hard to cleanse and purify. It would therefore not be advisable to meditate in a chair which had belonged to a bitter and resentful aunt, in a room once occupied by a hyperactive child, or in an area where many strident arguments have occurred. In some cases, it is better to buy new furniture than to surround ourself with polluted relics of the past.

Prayers of consecration. A good way to prepare a room for meditation is to bless it and consecrate the activities which are about to transpire to the expression of divine light and love. The prayer itself can be a simple request to divine forces to help us conduct our meditations in peace and confidence. The sincerity of our aspiration and dedication is more important than the actual words of the prayer. If desired, the prayer can be accompanied by the use of the creative imagination to visualize a brightly colored light pouring through the room, flooding it with divine presence and washing away discordant forces.

Candles. Artificial lighting, regardless of color, has little impact on the quality of a meditation. Light from devotional candles, however, can be quite useful in creating a proper atmosphere for meditation. Naturally, it is not the flame of the candle itself which contributes to the quality of the meditation, but rather the prayerful attitude of devotion with which we light it—and the divine forces we invoke. This makes the subtle essence of the candle burn more brightly on the etheric and astral planes, radiating light and burning away adverse forces in the vicinity. The use of devotional candles in Catholic and Orthodox churches is based on the same principle.

It would make no sense to meditate on the candle flame itself, however. We are seeking to make contact with the higher self, not a wick. Staring at a candle is not even an aid to concentration, let alone meditation. It is just an aid to deadness.

Incense. The use of incense, especially if it has been blessed, is also an effective way to dispel adverse forces and flood a room with qualities that are harmonious to effective meditation. The aromatic resins of the barks and oils of certain plants are magnetically harmonious with the higher qualities of thought and emotion. The use of sandalwood, frankincense, myrrh, and patchouli, as well as other incense of their type, can provide these benefits. Some of the modern, fruit-scented incenses, however, do not. A nice feeling about the scent of an incense is not sufficient reason to use it as an aid to meditation. Its benefit in helping to create a better climate for the growth of consciousness is the sole factor to be considered.

The act of blessing the incense before lighting it can be done by holding the incense and praying over it in the same manner as blessing the room. In this case, however, it is definitely helpful to use the creative imagination to visualize the substance of our blessing and the qualities we are invoking being absorbed into the incense. The key to making this visualization effective is to hold our mind and attitude steady in an ideal quality of thought and feeling. This should be done for approximately one minute.

Flowers. The fragrance of fresh flowers will attract favorable qualities from the subtle planes, just as the fragrance of incense does. In addition, the flowers will either contain or attract elemental forces which are also in magnetic harmony with the higher qualities of the emotions.

Music. Inspired music can be used, either before or during a meditation, to generate a soothing and uplifting effect upon consciousness. The music must be chosen with discrimination, however, so as to produce a response in the subtle bodies of thought and feeling of reverence, joy, patience, aspiration, peace, or goodwill. The refined pieces of classical music are usually the best in this regard. All too much of our modern popular music (rock and roll and jazz) has a debasing and destructive impact on consciousness, not a helpful one. It is far better to choose a soothing selection from Debussy, Mozart, or a similar composer.

A picture or statue of a holy person. A picture or statue of a holy person can enhance the psychological rapport between the meditator and the qualities he admires in the consciousness of the holy person. In a sense, it serves as a psychic placebo, and as such, can be helpful to people with a strong devotional nature. It enables the meditator to make contact with the higher qualities of the holy person he so strongly reveres.

The holy person may be the founder of a religion, a saint or martyr, an angel, or the head of a group the meditator has an allegiance to. It must be understood, however, that not everyone who claims to be a saint or a spiritual leader is one. Many modern "gurus" are not, in fact, highly evolved people— and do not merit the devotion they elicit from their followers. A few even have corrupt consciousnesses. To keep a picture or statue of such an individual in the room where we meditate would have the unfortunate effect of linking our consciousness with the impure consciousness of the teacher or guru.

In some circumstances, the picture or statue a meditator places in his room and makes the object of his devotion and reverence will become a symbol which invokes the actual forces surrounding this holy person. The substance of the symbol becomes impregnated in time with these forces. The picture or statue will then serve as a talisman of the divine quality it represents, and will have a favorable effect on the consciousness of the meditator.

Religious symbols. The major symbols of a religion, when placed in the room where we meditate, can have the same benefit as a picture or statue of a holy person. In addition, they can remind us of certain archetypal forces which can help us focus divine qualities and ideals. It can be most productive to meditate on the forces which major religious symbols represent.

Relics. If genuine, a religious relic can radiate a tremendous amount of spiritual force which is very useful in building up a positive state of energized qualities in the room where we meditate. Because relics are already impregnated with a powerful spiritual force, they have something more than a placebo effect. They radiate their strength and blessing into the room whether or not anyone is there to appreciate it.

We should always keep in mind that all of these aids to preparing a room for meditation can become hindrances if we use them fanatically or carelessly—and will be rendered useless if we treat them with indifference or disbelief. We should use them always to help establish a favorable climate for meditation—not as a substitute for meditation itself. Naturally, the personal factor is important in which of these aids to choose. Some people will be terribly distracted by music or incense, while others will find it can be beneficial. As always, common sense should be the rule.

PREPARING THE BODY FOR MEDITATION

The body is not really used in meditation, except to register in the brain the events which are occurring in consciousness. It is not the body which is active in Active Meditation; it is the mind and the higher self. As such, the best way to prepare the body for a meditation is to make it comfortable and forget it. If we are able to think while walking, sitting, lying down, or curled up on a lounge chair, it is also possible to meditate in these positions. The entire practice of preparing the physical body for Active Meditation can therefore be reduced to the simple procedures of making it comfortable and relaxing it, withdrawing our attention from it, and focusing our concentration inward.

Nevertheless, because most traditions of meditation put an inordinate amount of attention on what to do with the physical body, it is necessary to comment on some of these practices in this section on aids to meditation. It must be kept in mind that all of these practices are relatively unimportant—or useless— but have become important to some people due to spiritual tradition and social pressure.

Our interest in injecting common sense into what we do with the physical body is by no means a spiteful one. There is grave danger that if we give too much attention to the body when we are supposed to be meditating, we may in fact produce a "body consciousness" which is largely earthbound. This is exactly *the opposite* of what meditation is designed to do.

It is always wise to keep in mind that if God can flood the whole universe with His life, love, and wisdom, then surely these divine forces can penetrate into our consciousness no matter what position the physical body happens to be in.

There are several factors about preparing the physical body for meditation which deserve comment:

The direction to face. The best direction to face while meditating is always *inward,* toward our highest self! Nevertheless, there are always a few "authorities" who will insist that we should face the rising sun to take in spiritual energies and toward the west or north to ground or send away energies. Others will suggest different formulas. There is a relevant relationship between the major directions and the alchemical elements: east with air and mental forces, south with fire and the fiery will, west with water and the emotions, north with earth and grounding energies, and upward with the akasha and the realm of divine archetypes. The problem is that all of these qualities must be contacted in the fourth and fifth dimensions, where the concept of direction is rather different than on the physical plane. The direction the physical body is facing is virtually irrelevant.

Posture. Any posture which facilitates alertness, comfort, and convenience will suffice. It is ridiculous wasting time to learn to sit in a lotus position unless we already know how to do it—and most people in the West do not. The same can be said for the fanatical efforts made by some to keep the spine erect. Whatever minor benefit which might come from keeping a straight spine during meditation can be more than lost by the amount of attention we would have to give to keeping the body erect. This is merely a question of common sense. For those who are *convinced* that the spine must be straight and erect, it would be best to sit in a chair with a tall straight back and then forget about the body. Nevertheless, this is a limiting belief that ought to be outgrown.

Lying down can be a comfortable position, but many people associate lying down with falling asleep. It is therefore not especially recommended for meditation.

The rationale behind the straight, erect spine is the fact that the various levels of subtle energy which circulate in the area of the spine work slightly better if they are able to flow in parallel with the subtle forces of matter which emanate from the center of the earth upward. In the Western tradition of Active Meditation, however, the emphasis is placed on the quality of consciousness and its expression, not on the movement of subtle matter. This is of secondary importance and will usually take care of itself. In other words, it needs little direct attention.

Some people insist that the correct posture for meditation must include keeping the knees or ankles together and closing the hands into a fist—or forming circles with the thumbs and forefingers. The idea is that these positions "close" the energy systems of our bodies so as to concentrate the forces of the higher self within the sphere of our attention. On the other hand, if the intent is to send energies outward, these people claim that the best position is to have the legs slightly apart and the palms open and outward. The actual value of these positions is very slight, although it can be useful to hold the hands palm outward while radiating spiritual energies or giving a blessing. Once again, common sense must rule. The reception and radiation of spiritual energies are processes that are controlled primarily by the use of the will and the mental focus of our thought and attitude. If we are able to use the spiritual will, the position of the body hardly matters. If not, no positioning of the body will compensate for the lack!

Indeed, the concept of posture should always be seen as a

symbol for the inner posture we need to attain, not the posture of the physical body. The true posture of meditation is one in which the *mind* is held erect—in moral rectitude, integrity, poise, confidence, the dignity of an enlightened self-image, and the strength of the higher self. It is this posture the meditator should practice—not the posture of the physical form.

Yoga asanas. The postures of hatha yoga are best reserved for fanatics who delight in difficult disciplines and masochism. The serious meditator will find it easier to make an effective contact with the higher self if he is not burdened with attempting these asanas.

Originally, the asanas were exercises of the mind, designed to place the meditator in rapport with his spiritual self. Long ago, however, they degenerated into a set of physical movements. At best, they are useless to the meditator, and at worst, they can be a terrible hindrance. The advocates of hatha yoga, of course, will tell a different story, maintaining that these same asanas will stimulate specific energy flows throughout the physical body. They will, which is precisely why they have nothing to do with meditation. Meditation is an act in consciousness—not in the physical body. Yoga postures do not improve the quality of a meditation any more than they will help us comprehend a novel.

Yoga enthusiasts will undoubtedly protest these statements vociferously, claiming that they obtain a powerful alteration of consciousness when engaged in their postures. But common sense tells us that even simple physical strain and exhaustion can also alter consciousness—yet we do not believe them to be spiritual techniques. They may even claim the yoga asanas help ground the "high level" energies contacted in meditation. In the West, however, the proper way to ground the energies of meditation is to get busy and contribute something useful and constructive to the spiritualization of the world and the development of civilization.

Ritual dance. The value of ritual dance to meditation is roughly the same as the value of yoga asanas. Ritual dances had their origin in ancient times, when religious groups would use them as part of religious celebrations—as a *symbolic* personification of how divine forces interact with the physical plane and humanity. These dances were used very effectively by both the Hindus and the ancient Egyptians. In more primitive cultures, however, this genre of dance was often debased, stripped of its symbolic meaning, and used as a way of promoting an exhausted state of consciousness nearing delirium. The use of drugs and intoxicants often accompanied the dancing, in order to produce trance states and astral clairvoyance.

Those who have resurrected ritual dance for the New Age, unfortunately, tend to use it more in the primitive than the symbolic context. Indeed, it is usually promoted by "teachers" who have little to offer in effective and genuine contact with the higher self, yet want to keep their students entertained. It is especially attractive to people who desire strong emotional experiences and mindless astral goo in a group setting.

Whether the use of these dances is enlightened or not, however, it should not be construed as a meditative experience—or even a prelude to a meditative experience. If people want to dance, it is their business, but they should not delude themselves into believing it to be a spiritual exercise which leads to enlightenment.

PREPARING CONSCIOUSNESS FOR MEDITATION

An effective aid for preparing consciousness for meditation will serve a number of purposes. It will:

1. Take our attention off of mundane concerns and issues.

2. Mobilize our alertness and responsiveness to the higher self.

3. Prepare our immediate psychospiritual environment—the subtle or psychic equivalent of preparing the room where we are meditating.

4. Put us on the wavelength of spiritual qualities.

5. Help us invoke the qualities and life of the higher self.

If a practice can help us achieve any of these five goals, or a combination of them, it is useful. If not, it should be avoided, no matter how much religious sentiment or tradition may be attached to it.

There are a number of practices which are helpful in preparing consciousness for meditation. They include:

Affirmations, prayers, and invocations. These can have great value in preparing us for effective meditation, but their benefit will depend somewhat on how skillfully we use them. Affirmations can trap us in a concrete intellectual state—or even a state of wishful thinking which blocks off genuine transcendent qualities. The unskilled use of invocations can focus us too much on our problems or needs. Some prayers may keep us stuck in a devotional state. And for some people, prayers are merely words which do not reflect or embody the quality of thought they need.

Under no circumstance should the use of prayer or affirmations be substituted for the meditative work of making contact with the higher self. This cannot be achieved through prayer or invocation alone, no matter how sincere we are. Prayers and affirmations have important benefits of their own, used either in a meditation or nonmeditatively, but if we use them as a substitute for meditative contact, we simply are not meditating. The correct use of prayers, invocations, and affirmations *as an aid to meditation* is to focus attention on the qualities we seek, dispel undesired forces, and cleanse our consciousness prior to contacting the higher self.

Breathing exercises. The breath has long been a symbol for the inflow and outflow of spiritual energies. In a number of meditative systems, an elaborate science of breath has been developed. As long as it is understood that the real "breathing" of the meditative state occurs in the subtle bodies, certain breathing exercises can be a useful aid to the preparation of consciousness for meditation. But it is very easy to trivialize a breathing exercise. We live in a culture which encourages the lazy of mind and heart to look for shortcuts to enlightenment. Since everyone already knows how to breathe, the possibility that breathing exercises might help enlighten us has great appeal! Unfortunately, this appeal has been enhanced by unscrupulous teachers who promote breathing exercises as the *most important factor* in health, purification, and illumination. Yet if this were true, the whole of humanity and most of the animal kingdom should have achieved perfect health, purity, and enlightenment long ago.

One of the values of breathing exercises is that they can be a way to concentrate our attention on something simple while disconnecting from mundane, outer-directed thoughts. The act of exhalation is tied automatically to the physiological relaxation of the muscles in the chest and diaphragm. If we mentally "tune in" to these natural processes, we can associate other levels of relaxation with the physical act of breathing as well.

At a more complex level, the act of breathing can become a symbol for transferring energies of consciousness, as though it were a "pump" which could discharge excess tension or anxiety with each exhalation or breathe in tranquillity, affection, and peace with each inhalation. The same procedure can be used to discharge any negative feeling or congested condition in consciousness or breathe in a higher quality of energy. The weakness of this technique is that it does *nothing* to transform the habits or reactive patterns which caused these problems in the first place. It merely transfers energy. As a result, it can be useful as a "quick fix" in consciousness, but has no long-term impact or benefit.

One of the problems of using breathing exercises in meditation, therefore, is that it can generate the illusion that we are doing something quite significant to manage stress and dissolve problems, while we are actually doing nothing at all. If we fully understand that we are only achieving a temporary relief from a problem, and will have to use other methods to solve the real difficulty permanently, then breathing exercises can be a useful aid to meditation. Otherwise, we should avoid them.

Another problem is that not all breathing exercises are really a part of meditation. Linking the breathing process with the skillful use of the will can be very productive in revitalizing the etheric body and circulating etheric energies. But a meditative level of consciousness is not required to do this. It can be done in a state of mind similar to that used for positive thinking and self-hypnosis. Yet many people firmly believe that the use of any breathing exercise constitutes meditation. They forget that the purpose of meditation is to increase rapport between the personality and the higher self—not to hyperventilate.

The type of breathing which *does* lead to a genuine transformation and enrichment of consciousness is not associated with the physical breath at all. It is the inhalation of the life of the soul into the subtle bodies; it occurs not in the lungs or the respiratory tract but rather at a point in the aura near the top of the head. This inner breathing becomes possible consciously only after the meditator has established direct contact with the higher self and is able to ground its life in outer expression. At that point, the subtle bodies begin breathing automatically in this fashion.

Prolonged use of breathing exercises, especially those involving deep breathing, can actually produce a number of unfortunate effects, despite the claims of the many advocates of pranayama (the Hindu term for breathing exercises). These unfortunate effects include:

1. The meditator may become parasitic. The meditator

has learned, by default, to draw energy from the astral plane, through the solar plexus, rather than from the higher self. As a result, when he is in the vicinity of other people—at home, in a group meditation, or at a retreat—he soon begins drawing his energies from the astral bodies of those around him. This is parasitism—an activity which is directly contrary to the practices of Active Meditation and spiritual growth.

2. The meditator may develop the hyperventilation syndrome. A dramatic loss of carbon dioxide in the system will alter the chemical composition of the blood, inducing light-headedness, dizziness, numbness in the fingers and nose, and a paradoxical sensation of shortness of breath, as well as heightened anxiety. Slyly encouraging hyperventilation is a favorite technique of phony teachers of meditation because it produces an odd and, for almost everyone, totally unfamiliar state of consciousness very quickly—even in dogs, cats, and horses. Yet it is nothing but a state of chemical intoxication caused by the rapid alkalinization of the blood. It has *no* place in the practices of a serious student of self-development, meditation, or enlightenment. The victims of this practice belong in a clinic—and those who teach it belong in limbo!

3. The meditator becomes progressively more bored. Even though some people mistake boredom for actual meditation, it is not.

In Active Meditation, the use of the breath as an aid to meditation is usually limited to focusing briefly on the symbolic value of our *normal* rate of breathing, for the transfer of energies at inner levels. It is not necessary to quicken the rate of breathing or deepen the intensity of the breath to do this— nor is it viewed as healthy.

Mantras. The use of mantras or short phrases of words in meditation is a practice which is many thousands of years old. During this time, mantras have proven their value as an aid to meditation. They are especially helpful when used to enter the meditative state—calming the emotions and mundane thoughts while redirecting the mind inward.

A mantra can be anything from a single syllable to a complete phrase. Many of the ancient Buddhists deliberately chose a "nonsense sound" which had no meaning at all. But it can be even more effective to choose a mantra which is in keeping with the theme of preparing for meditation, such as "I am at peace." The mantra is sounded mentally.

Mantras can also be used quite effectively in combination with seed thoughts, as described in chapter six. A mantra such as "God is love" can help attune us to the abstract force of archetypal love. By then adapting this mantra to a more active form, "God loves me," we can use it to focus archetypal love into our emotions, healing them. Yet a third variation, "The love of God pours through my love, filling me with compassion and forgiveness for others," could be used to focus the quality of love into our self-expression.

The use of the mantra "OM" must be considered in a class by itself. When sounded from the highest level we can reach meditatively, the OM tends to unleash a blast of spiritual light and power which cleanses our subtle bodies and dissipates inharmonious qualities from our psychospiritual environment.

The problem with sounding the OM, or any other mantra, is that far too many people have come to believe that sounding mantras *is* meditation. They therefore spend the whole of their time in meditation doing nothing but repeating a single syllable. There is no question that it is always easier to sound the OM a few times than it is to energize a state of devotion, aspiration, conviction, or dedication, but only the latter practice can integrate the personality with the higher self and cleanse the aura and consciousness.

The absurd and deadly degree to which mantras have been championed in recent years must surely qualify them as one of the top rackets of the millenium. Thousands of people have paid millions of dollars to obtain a secret Sanskrit mantra, supposedly designed for their use alone but actually drawn from a list of only sixteen words and assigned entirely on the basis of sex and age. They were instructed to repeat this mantra twice daily as their entire meditative practice. The result has been perniciously damaging to many good people, harming the associative mechanism of the mind and inducing an intense state of passivity toward life. In people who have continued practicing this "technique" for a number of years, it has even led to the disconnection of the mental body and soul from the rest of the system, producing an odd form of schizophrenia not usually recognized for what it is—an extremely damaged state of consciousness which has about as much to do with enlightenment as a skull fracture!

The lesson to be learned from this misuse of mantras is an important one for all of us. Anything which is good for us can become harmful if used improperly or to excess. There is never any real danger in any meditative practice—if it is used with common sense. But common sense seems to be a difficult quality for some people to acquire.

Alignment to a teacher, group, or ashram. Learning the skills of meditation from a teacher can be helpful for two basic reasons: the teacher can help us make inner connections with spirit we cannot learn from a book, and can provide us with an opportunity to become aligned with the inner spiritual dimensions he serves. If these inner spiritual dimensions are more powerful and enlightened than our ordinary state of consciousness, thinking briefly about the teacher at the start of a meditation can help us reestablish a meditative contact with the higher self. This is done by recalling the memory of an earlier contact with the teacher, visualizing his image, or contemplating a symbol representing the quality of his consciousness. The same process can be used to attune to a spiritual group or ashram we may belong to.

The value of this practice depends on the relationship we have with our teacher or the group, plus the importance we place on making this kind of alignment. When done properly, it can be quite helpful in establishing a telepathic or psychic contact with the psychospiritual atmosphere which surrounds the teacher or group. If this psychospiritual atmosphere is an enlightened one, the results can be most helpful, as it increases the strength and power with which we can act meditatively.

Nevertheless, there can be dangers in this practice:

1. It may cause us to become too dependent on the power of the teacher or the group. It is valuable to recognize the wisdom and acknowledge the support of a teacher or group, but this alignment should never negate our own individuality and capacity to contact the higher self. In the West, we have an obligation to seek out our own spirit and cultivate our own spiritual strengths and self-sufficiency.

2. We may end up aligning with an astral image of the teacher or the group mind. As a result, we tune in to what we like and admire about the teacher or the collective personality of the group—not necessarily the qualities and forces which will help us improve our contact with spirit. These qualities and forces are found more at the mental level than emotionally.

3. Not all teachers are enlightened beings. Some are wolves in sheep's clothing. Indeed, a number of teachers and the groups surrounding them work very carefully to cultivate psychological control over the people who take their courses or participate in their activities. Consciously aligning with such people or groups at the start of a meditation can heighten this bond. If the meditator then decides to leave the group at some later time, he can find it extremely difficult to do so, being pursued and harassed at a psychic level—and perhaps even the physical—for some time.

The ideal in the Western tradition of Active Meditation is to use the assistance and support of a teacher and group as needed, but to maintain our own sense of individuality and responsibility for the growth and service we pursue. This includes the obligation to contribute our own strengths and talents to the work of the group as well as drawing on it when we have the need.

The use of color. The mental image of specific colors can be used in a number of ways to enhance our meditative work:

1. To increase the health and vitality of the subtle bodies, especially the etheric and astral vehicles.

2. To dispel negativity and unpleasant forces which may have gathered in these bodies.

3. To help in radiating healing forces to others.

In using color, however, we must understand that the colors themselves do not contain any force or quality. They are symbols for the spiritual forces we seek to invoke and direct. In other words, the mental act of bathing in a colored mist will not necessarily do any good, unless we are simultaneously contemplating a healing or spiritual quality and directing it at a specific deficiency or need.

To work intelligently with color, therefore, we must have a knowledge of what we need and the quality or force which will help us meet this need. We must also know the symbolic value of the colors we use. Not all green light has a healing effect. Nor does all blue light lead to serenity.

As for visualizing a color, it is never necessary to go to excess, as some meditators do. It is not even necessary to visualize the color vividly. In fact, an intense visualization of a color can be a distraction, if we become more interested in the intensity of the color than in the quality and force it represents.

Reading. One of the best aids for preparing consciousness for meditation is something which never occurs in meditation, but apart from it. This is the practice of reading widely in books which will stimulate a deeper understanding of our psychospiritual nature, the associative mechanism of the mind, and the life of spirit. Reading a book written by an enlightened person helps attune our mind and thoughts to the archetypal ideas and forces which inspired him in his writing, thereby strengthening our mind and capacity to interact with these forces. It can also give us valuable information not otherwise available.

In connection with meditation, for example, it can be most useful to read books which describe our invisible anatomy and the esoteric aspects of psychology. Throughout this book, we have endeavored to approach all esoteric and occult subjects in ordinary language, to demonstrate their eminently practical and sensible application to life. Nonetheless, it can be quite useful to explore these subjects in greater detail. Some of the areas to read about would be:

• Our inner anatomy—the nature of our subtle bodies and the force centers or chakras which operate within them. The three subtle bodies of the personality are the etheric (the subtle portion of the physical body), the astral (the emotions), and the mental body. In each of these bodies, there are seven major chakras or force centers, overlying the base of the spine and the major endocrine organs—the adrenals gonads, pancreas, thymus, thyroid, pituitary, and pineal.

• The basic nature of man—his existence as personality, soul, and spirit.

• The seven levels of energy—the logoic, monadic, atmic, buddhic, mental, astral, and physical planes—and their relationship to the evolution of consciousness.

In addition, it can be quite useful to read fiction which stimulates the imagination and attunes us to the inner realities of life. One of the great problems the meditator must contend with is the fact that the subconscious is not used to dealing with the inner dimensions of life and may view them as dark and strange, even though they are not. By reading the excellent science fiction and fantasy which is available today, however, the subconscious becomes more accustomed to working multi-dimensionally and symbolically. In addition, this kind of reading stimulates the associative mechanism of the mind and sometimes even exposes us to archetypal qualities.

Building faith in God. The enlightened use of faith prepares the emotions to be receptive and responsive to the divine forces of the higher self which we contact in meditation. By resting our faith in the God within us, the higher self, we lift our attitudes and thoughts to a transpersonal level which makes it much easier for meditation to proceed. At the same time, however, it should be understood that even faith can be overdone—especially if it is used to the *exclusion* of other meditative activities. Having faith in the power of the higher self to heal us will not actually heal us, unless we simultaneously get busy and correct the problems which caused us to become ill in the first place. We must never let the use of faith in meditation cause our efforts to deteriorate into a mindless, emotional state of devotional goo.

THE THREE BEST AIDS

The greatest aids to meditation, of course, are a strong and unqualified devotion to our higher self, an unwavering dedication to cooperate with the higher self as an intelligent partner, and common sense. There are other labels we could attach to these three factors—trust, respect, reverence, and wisdom—but these other labels only help explain what devotion, dedication, and common sense mean. They do not change them.

Indeed, these three "aids" to effective meditation are changeless. When all the mantras, rules, observances, and breathing exercises have been forgotten, these three basic attitudes will remain. The intelligent meditator, therefore, begins by cultivating *them*.

19

Problems
In Meditation

UNDERSTANDING PROBLEMS

In every aspect of life, from growing up to pursuing a career, we encounter problems. Meditation is no exception. There will be triumphs, but there will also be disappointments. There will be moments of breakthrough, but also moments of frustration. It would be unreasonable to expect that the work of contacting the higher self will proceed without any difficulty or hardship. At the same time, however, it would also be unreasonable to believe it will be one problem after another.

What is reasonable is to have a good understanding of the kinds of problems which are likely to arise in meditation—and either avoid them or be prepared to meet them wisely. In this regard, there are two types of problems to discuss:

1. The problems which will arise in the use of the techniques of Active Meditation.

2. The problems which will arise in the use of other meditative techniques.

The techniques which are used in Active Meditation have been carefully designed to suit the temperament of the Western individual, his active involvement in daily life, and the goals of spiritual growth in the West. As a result, unless the techniques are used improperly or distorted, the problems arising from the use of Active Meditation are not likely to be major. They are most likely to center around the unwillingness of the subconscious of the meditator to cooperate with the process of self-discovery.

The more serious problems tend to arise when the Western individual begins using techniques which were not designed for the Western consciousness—or practices which were helpful five thousand years ago but are now out of date. It is tempting just to ignore these problems, as they will not arise in the use of Active Meditation. But we owe it to ourself to have a thorough understanding of the kind of problems which are likely to arise, even if not in our own practices. It gives us a much more complete understanding of the psychological dynamics of meditation—and their physiological impact.

There are six fundamental causes for the problems which arise in meditation. These are:

• Resistance of the personality to change. Old habits have a way of clinging to life. Carefully rationalized failures resist exposure to the truth. Pockets of resentment will try to sabotage the development of insight and forgiveness. Highly refined elements of selfishness and vanity will challenge our efforts to be more generous and detached. In order to grow, we must be prepared to meet these forces of resistance and gradually transform them into the power to cooperate with the higher life. We must see resistance as the natural friction between our ideals and our actual level of thought and feeling. If we can cultivate this perspective, then the resistance of the personality need not be as distressing as it often is.

• Using an improper form of meditation. The skillful craftsman knows his tools. The same rule applies to meditation. If we use a meditative system which will only help us relax, when we are expecting to make contact with the higher self, we may well end up confused and disappointed. More seriously, if we use a simplistic meditative technique too long, we may end up damaging the mechanisms of the subtle bodies.

• Meditating for the wrong reasons—for example, to escape the unpleasantness of the world by seeking out an inner world of fantasy or tranquillity.

• Rushing toward enlightenment. People who are accustomed to pursuing their goals in life with great zeal will often try to apply this same zeal to the work of meditation. But growth has its own pace. While it can be accelerated to a very large degree by actively pursuing it, there is a limit to how much we can speed it up. When zeal becomes impatience, a great deal of conflict and anxiety can be generated. The mature meditator will find the pace of growth which is suited to the needs of the higher self, not the expectations of the personality.

• Excessive use of meditation. Just as our muscles can become tired from walking or running too far, so also the "muscles" of our emotions and mind can become fatigued from excessive use. Active Meditation connects us with forces and energies which are a good deal more potent than the level of thought and feeling we use in everyday life. It is therefore quite possible to become fatigued mentally and emotionally. Problems of this nature can be avoided by not straining beyond our natural limits, and corrected, if necessary, simply by resting.

• Distractions and problems which have nothing to do with meditation. The problems and influences we carry with us day by day, affecting our mood, self-confidence, and alertness, will also affect our meditations. This is just a matter of common sense. If we begin a meditation in a grumpy, sour mood, this attitude will adversely affect the quality of the meditation. Meditating every day does not mean that we will magically become immune to the problems and difficulties we have traditionally carried with us. We must therefore be ready to adapt and modify our meditative routines to dispel and correct these problems as they arise.

Understanding these basic *causes* of problems in meditation, it is now possible to examine the *symptoms* of the problems which are likely to arise, one by one, and what can be done to correct them.

FALLING ASLEEP

Falling asleep during a meditation is a very common problem, especially for people who are just beginning to meditate— or people who are taking up a new and more powerful type of meditation than they have used before. It can also occur in people who have become bored with the meditative techniques they are using, or are encountering resistance to their personal growth. The remedy to the problem will therefore depend upon why we are falling asleep. There are a number of possibilities.

1. We are tired and fatigued before we start meditating. The remedy is to take a nap before meditating. If we are consistently tired when we meditate, the remedy lies in finding a time of day to meditate when we will be better rested. It can also be helpful sometimes to change the position in which we meditate. If we fall asleep while meditating lying down, we should try sitting up.

2. We start the meditation alert, but fall asleep while relaxing the body. The remedy is to instruct the subconscious that the mind and higher self are to remain alert even while the physical body relaxes. This instruction can be given just prior to beginning to relax. It can also be helpful to dwell on the idea that meditation is a worthwhile activity which is meaningful to us. We therefore want to give it our full attention and interest.

3. We start the meditation alert, but fall asleep while contacting higher levels of energy. The stimulation of the more powerful energies is causing us to lose consciousness briefly. The remedy is to instruct the subconscious that it does not have to try to absorb excessive amounts of energy—just the right amount to lift us up to the most ideal level of consciousness.

4. We go too deep into meditation and lose consciousness. The remedy is to shorten the period of meditation and lighten the level at which we operate. Many people believe that the deeper the level, the better the meditation. But this is not necessarily true. We can experience a very effective contact with the higher self at relatively light levels of meditation. The person who is always falling asleep because he is going too deep, by contrast, is not accomplishing very much. He needs to change his habits.

5. Our meditation is dull and boring. If we approach our meditations passively, waiting for something to happen, we may fall asleep simply because we are bored. The remedy is to become more active—taking charge of our meditations so that they stir up meaningful activity.

6. None of the above. Sometimes there is *no* obvious reason for falling asleep during a meditation. In these cases, the problem usually arises because the subconscious is protecting itself from exposure and change. Our resistance is so strong that we fall asleep, as though we were drugged by inertia. There are other ways that resistance can sabotage a meditation, of course—for example, playing up to our fantasies of wish fulfillment—but falling asleep is one of the ways this happens. The remedy is to reassure the subconscious that we are not out to destroy it; we are only interested in making some minor improvements which will improve the efficiency of the subconscious. By appealing to the deeper levels of common sense within us, it is often possible to neutralize this resistance and resume having effective meditations.

We will be most prone to this problem of being drugged into a state of sleepiness by our resistance if we happen to be either an angry or a critical person. Anger and criticism estrange us not only from other people, but also from the nurturing parent within our own subconscious. The remedy in this case obviously lies in becoming more compassionate and benevolent—toward others and toward ourself.

If none of these remedies keeps us from falling asleep, there is one more remedy which is guaranteed to work—meditating with our eyes open. It is always better to meditate with the eyes closed, but keeping them open is certainly a better option than always falling asleep. This is not as difficult as it might seem at first. Anyone who can sustain a quiet and lofty level of thought with his eyes open can also meditate with his eyes open.

POOR CONCENTRATION

Difficulty in concentrating is another problem common to the meditative state, especially for beginners. We sit down to contact the higher self, and soon find our mind wandering in almost every direction *except* the higher self. We are bombarded by thoughts, impressions, images, and feelings, and do not know how to sort them out. In most cases, the problem is a lack of self-discipline. In ordinary states of consciousness, we are accustomed to dealing with a large number of sensory impressions at the same time. Distractions do not trouble us that much—they are assimilated with the rest of the impressions. But in meditation, attention is being focused on a specific technique or line of thought. When other impressions arise, they can easily catch our attention and distract us from what we intended to do.

As always, the key to improving concentration lies in using our common sense. Above all, we must resist the usual nonsense about having to "still the mind" in order to meditate successfully. Nothing could be more disastrous to concentration. By making a negative state the goal, we almost guarantee that memories and distractions will rush in to fill the void. Instead, we need to remember that the purpose of meditation is to increase our contact with the higher self. This is most easily accomplished by dwelling on themes which are harmonious to the love, wisdom, and strength of the higher self. The best way to increase concentration, therefore, is to focus attention on these themes. If the mind is given something to do, it will usually have little trouble concentrating.

This is just a matter of common sense. Anyone who is able to become fully absorbed in a good novel, a movie, or an interesting conversation should have no problem concentrating during meditation. It is just a question of making sure that we work on themes and projects which are interesting to us!

Still, distractions do arise and must be managed. It will therefore be helpful to evaluate the different types of distraction and their remedies:

1. External distractions. If we are attempting to meditate in the same room where people are talking, the radio is playing, or there are other disturbing noises, it will be extremely difficult to concentrate. The obvious solution is to meditate in a location which is relatively free of distracting noises.

2. A boring technique. Quite often, it is the meditative technique itself which is the principal distraction. It is so boring that there is no incentive to continue focusing on it. Staring at an empty plate is not going to hold our attention for long if we have the opportunity to go over to a lavish smorgasbord and help ourself.

3. Our attitude. The ideal attitude for meditating is a mood of quiet optimism and confidence that something worthwhile but very subtle is happening. We want to learn more about it, so we pay attention—at every dimension of our awareness. Unfortunately, many people do not spend enough time cultivating this ideal attitude. Instead, they get themselves all worked up, as though the Pope were coming for a visit. Or, they strain and strain to see a vision or make contact with the higher self, as though aggressiveness or pushiness will improve the intensity of the meditation. Usually, it just interferes with the subtle levels of the experience. Still others approach meditation fearfully, as though they were about to plunge into the unknown, where a wrathful god will come to judge and punish them. Such distracting attitudes can easily destroy our capacity to concentrate.

When attitude is the major distraction, it is important to treat the subconscious to a series of pleasant and constructive meditative experiences, so it will be eager to cooperate in the future. Some people need to approach their early meditations as an experiment in exploring the higher reaches of their humanity. They should deliberately cultivate an attitude of looking for the highest, the best, the loveliest, and the most mature elements of their consciousness—as though they were visiting a wonderful art museum. There will be time enough later on, once they have acquired a decent level of concentration, to look in the overflowing wastebaskets, inspect the cobwebs in the corner, and clean up the mud on the floor. For the moment, they should avoid these aspects of the subconscious, and look instead at the real beauty which is in their higher nature.

4. The fanatical pursuit of "total concentration." Over the centuries, the meaning of concentration has been blurred. Instead of representing a relaxed, enjoyable focus of attention on an interesting technique or subject, it has come to represent a perfect and unwavering fixation on a single point, totally oblivious to all intruding sensations. As a result, many decent people have become intimidated by the idea of concentration, as though the merest whiff of a stray thought while meditating indicates that they do not have good concentration. This is a totally unrealistic view. The remedy is to adopt a more moderate definition—something which would be roughly parallel to the kind of concentration we use while talking to a good friend in a crowded restaurant. There are many other people talking all around us, but we are not distracted by them, because we are so interested in our conversation. In the same way, we should become so interested in what the higher self has to say to us that we just do not pay attention to the distractions which arise.

5. The fanatical pursuit of all impressions. At the other end of the spectrum are those people who have trained themselves to pursue every stray thought, memory, or flash of mental vision which "spontaneously" appears to them in meditation. These are people who have become habituated to the self-observation of their train of thought, because they have been encouraged to do so, either as part of psychoanalysis or

an Eastern system of "spiritual growth." Yet this practice can be very destructive to our capacity to concentrate, because it encourages distractions while reducing our capacity to control them. We become more and more passive in dealing with the subconscious, until the associative mechanism detaches from our conscious focus, inducing a form of schizophrenia. The fact that these problems develop under the watchful eye of a psychoanalyst or teacher does not diminish the seriousness of the problems—it only indicts the incompetence and naiveté of the psychoanalyst or teacher.

There is no question that the exploration of our associations and memories is a vital part of self-discovery. Yet this activity must be kept within rational limits and seen as only one of many facets of self-improvement. To make the pursuit of stray thoughts the most important activity of a meditation is perhaps the greatest distraction of all. It takes us away from our real work—contacting the love and wisdom of the higher self. Common sense alone tells us that many stray thoughts are just that—entirely trivial impressions unworthy of any attention.

6. Too much interest in things which are not our business. Some people are too outwardly directed, allowing virtually any perception or sound that arises to command their attention. These people will go off to a restaurant and spend much of their time observing—or being irritated by—the other diners, taking in snatches of their conversations and absorbing the ambience of the restaurant, instead of enjoying the good food and companionship at their own table. Sometimes this outward-directedness is just a habit; sometimes it is a way of avoiding their own attitudes and memories. In either case, the tendency carries over into their meditations, producing difficulties in concentrating. They are too outward-directed to become absorbed in the meaning of inner events. The remedy, of course, is to break the habit and put more of a premium on

the inner tapestry of life. This is not easily done, *but it can be done,* if we want to. A good way of doing this is to take a little time to carefully plan what we will do in our meditation before we begin, then build up our enthusiasm for paying attention to these worthwhile projects.

7. A lack of ease in working with abstractions. Meditation is an activity which introduces us to worlds of subtle forces and abstractions. Some people are not very comfortable in working with abstract and symbolic thought; without the stabilizing focus of concrete data and images, they become uneasy. This creates a distraction which disrupts concentration. One way to remedy this problem is to use our creative imagination to visualize a comfortable mental retreat in which we can meditate. This might be a beautiful place in nature, a pleasant private study, a small private office or chapel, or any other kind of retreat which will convey the feelings of privacy and safety. This simple act stabilizes our inner state of consciousness by imposing imaginary boundaries on our memories and associations. It is then very easy to concentrate on the specific meditative techniques we intend to pursue.

There are a couple of other practices which can also help us become more comfortable in working with abstractions and symbols over a period of time—reading good fiction and occult literature and working with mantic devices such as the Tarot, the I Ching, and Sabian symbols. Both of these practices will help us go beyond the superficial phenomena of life and seek out their inner significance, causes, and implications. In these ways, we stimulate the same skills and abilities that we need in order to handle symbols and abstractions in meditation.

8. A guilty conscience. Everyone has thoughts and feelings they are not proud to acknowledge, but some people take the condition of a guilty conscience to an extreme, projecting it onto the higher self and assuming that the higher self is really just an omniscient nag that will condemn them for every mis-

take they have ever made. They therefore fear the higher self as some kind of wrathful god that will punish them.

The image of the wrathful god is primarily a product of Western religions, especially the more fundamental sects. It has done immeasurable damage to the well-being and self-expression of millions of people. There is no easy way to overcome the pervasiveness of this deadly poison in society, but individually we can work to make our relationship with God and the higher self more wholesome. This is done by appreciating the fact that an active conscience is a necessary part of any healthy and mature person. Ideally, it preserves the values and principles of the higher self. When we have violated these values and principles, the conscience lets us know, thereby helping us stay attuned to the best within us. The only time a problem arises is when we choose to feel excessively guilty about the mistakes we have made, *in lieu of correcting them!* Believing we deserve to be punished, we "give permission" to our conscience to become highly critical of our behavior.

This problem can be corrected by training our conscience to be a constructive influence on our life, not just a critic. Instead of struggling with our conscience, we draw up a truce in which we invite our conscience to work as our ally in self-improvement. We train ourself to respect our conscience, not fight it, and we teach the "critic within us" to help, not condemn. This may take a fair amount of work using the techniques for increasing self-esteem and mental housecleaning, but it will immeasurably improve our capacity to work effectively in meditation.

The other step to take in this regard is to make sure we are tuning into our higher self in our meditations, and not just the conscience. The conscience is an aspect of the personality—not a part of the higher self. If we embark on our meditation full of guilt, fear, and anxiety, this focus of attention will almost guarantee that we will align ourself only with the lowest levels

443

of our conscience, not the healthy part—and certainly not the higher self. If we *must* visit the cesspools of our subconscious, we should at least try to avoid doing it during meditation. Meditation should be reserved for the exploration of the noblest levels of our thought and feeling—the courage which will help us master anxiety, the goodwill which will help us become forgiving, the wisdom which will rout confusion, and the joy that will overcome guilt. It is a time for healing, not the gnashing of teeth in self-condemnation. We should therefore cultivate a reverence and aspiration for the higher self which will neutralize these interferences and distractions.

9. The feeling of worthlessness. A personality that feels rejected by spirit is likely to resist all efforts to grow, including meditation. The higher self does not reject the personality, of course, but many religious people have been led to believe that it does. Self-appointed experts have preached that the human personality is sinful, wretched, and worthless—and that the only way to redeem it is to annihilate it totally, by "getting the self out of the way" so that the life of spirit can enter. They view the personality as an impediment and insist on destroying it. Nothing could be further from the truth, but if a person believes these distorted views of life, they can seriously damage his self-perception.

The remedy to the distraction of self-rejection is to appreciate the personality as a temple of God, no matter how imperfect it may be. It may well need remodeling, but no good can be served by tearing it down! Instead, our goal should be to steadily improve it, making it always a more fitting temple for the expression of our indwelling wisdom and love.

This is the reason why the detachment drill which is used to enter the meditative state reviews the value and purpose of each aspect of the personality before shifting our attention away from it and focusing it on the higher self. The higher self needs the physical body to act in daily life, the emotions to set a tone of quality and love in living, and the mind to make sense of the many variables and principles of life. It respects the personality and seeks to use it as a vehicle for its strength, love, and wisdom. If we have a problem with self-rejection, we should make sure to dwell an extra moment on these stages of the detachment drill, communicating wholesome messages of approval to the subconscious.

10. The Dweller on the Threshold. The various distractions of resistance from the unconscious create problems not only for beginning meditators, but experienced ones as well. Indeed, these problems can occur at any time in the growth of the spiritual aspirant. Technically, they are not problems of meditation at all, but rather problems of human growth. But since they are often discovered in the meditative state, they deserve examination here.

As we grow and evolve, we may well strike deep substrata of old memories, habits, feelings, and convictions that strongly resist transformation. The deepest levels of this resistance are part of what is known esoterically as the Dweller on the Threshold. Many people melodramatize this Dweller on the Threshold, thinking it will sweep them away in "the dark night of the soul" or eternal conflict. It is much healthier to use our common sense, and see the Dweller for what it is—the sum of our strength, redeemed and unredeemed, at the unconscious levels of the personality. It contains a great measure of resistance to any effort to change the status quo, but is also one of the strongest elements of our individuality.

Nothing is gained by provoking direct confrontations with powerful areas of unconscious resistance. If we draw our sword and try to kill the Dweller, it will fight back. A far better alternative is to work quietly at increasing our dedication to and reverence for the light of the soul and its spiritual will, coupling this with an enlightened self-expression. The steady effort to be the right person and do the right thing in life is the most efficient way to neutralize the resistance of the Dweller on the Threshold—and ultimately transform it. Selfishness, for example, is never corrected by trying to become *selfless*. That is just a denial of selfhood. Rather, it is corrected by harnessing our self-expression to the impersonal life of the higher self. In this way, we fulfill the design of selfhood and raise the individuality embodied in the Dweller on the Threshold to its noblest level. This is a classic example of the enlightened way to "confront" the Dweller on the Threshold.

Common sense tells us the best way to lessen the strength of any kind of resistance is to build up the strength of its counterpart in spirit. If, for example, we are troubled by a persistent habit of hostility and resentment, we should spend time at least once a week building up the strength of our tolerance and goodwill. We should learn to express gratitude for the help we have received and the growth we have made, and then integrate these qualities of goodwill and gratitude into the mainstream of our attitudes and associations.

It is not to the advantage of the average meditator to confront and provoke the full force of the Dweller on the Threshold. There is a time when this can be safely done, but only after there is a full and constant rapport with the higher self. The person who provokes the Dweller prematurely will discover the prudence of these warnings.

In the final analysis, the central point of any effort to improve our concentration in meditation is to realize the higher self is interested in helping us make our meditations succeed. It cares for the personality and will respond to our honest aspiration and efforts. As we attempt to pursue the themes and ideals the higher self cherishes, our effort to concentrate will be magnetically reinforced by the life and love of the higher self. As always, it is the *partnership* between the higher self and the personality which makes meditation successful—never the solitary efforts of either the personality or the soul.

REBOUND PHENOMENA

It sometimes occurs that old resentments, guilty feelings, and frustrations will recur quite unexpectedly during a meditation or shortly thereafter. Often, this is the result of a rebound phenomenon at work; the personality is reacting negatively to the light of the higher self. It is as though the higher self has scolded the personality, and the personality is responding by pouting. If this response occurred "out in the open," where we could see it, we could see that it is just a reflexive response, and manage it quite easily. But it usually occurs at subconscious and unconscious levels, below the threshold of our conscious awareness. As a result, we only become aware of the *symptoms* of the problem—irritability, a sense of guilt, an overwhelming sense of inadequacy, anxiety, or resentment—and do not perceive the *cause*. It is therefore extremely easy to be swept away by the symptoms, and end up refighting old battles, stirring up old resentments, mentally ranting about old injustices, and rehashing old mistakes.

As with any problem, the rebound phenomenon can occur in either mild or severe doses. It can sneak in during the actual meditation—or pop up as a delayed reaction. The proper way to remedy the problem depends on its severity and frequency. If it only occurs after unusually long or intense meditations, or when we meditate an unusual number of times during a single day, the best cure is simply to cut back on the amount of time we are meditating. In this instance, the symptoms are primarily a sign that we are overworking the personality! But if our meditations habitually stir up troubling and unsettling reactions, we will have to take more substantive action.

The one thing we do not want to do is directly attack the symptoms which have been stirred up: the feelings of resentment, fear, guilt, or sadness. This is a matter of common sense. If a child is crying and we want to quiet him down, we do not spank or scold him harshly. Such punishment only makes the child cry more intensely. The best remedy is to cheer up the child. The same principle applies to remedying the rebound phenomenon in meditation. The child within us is crying. We therefore turn to the parent within us and act to generate a mature mood of goodwill, confidence, cheerfulness, courage, and forgiveness.

In other words, the key to resolving rebound phenomena lies in taking action on a long-term basis to reduce the possibility of the personality responding to the inflow of divine energies from the higher self in an immature, pouting way—either in or out of meditation. Two specific suggestions can be made in this regard:

1. We should improve our rapport with the higher self, building an ever stronger bond of affection, reverence, joy, and goodwill. Because so many people have been taught to view God as a harsh, scolding taskmaster—a tyrant that apparently does not believe we are capable of doing anything but sin—we have developed a strong cultural bias which subtly rebels against divine authority. This is a completely erroneous view, of course, but it has been reinforced by centuries of bad teaching and even worse theology. And the average person subconsciously transfers this picture of God to the higher self, *even if he intellectually knows better!* He feels he must approach the higher self with trepidation and contrition, which sets the stage for the rebound phenomenon in the personality. The best way to correct this problem, therefore, is to devote some meditative time, perhaps ten to twenty minutes each week, in adoring God and building dedication and reverence to the benevolence and wisdom of the higher self.

If the rebound phenomenon should become a severe problem, it could even be advisable to spend an entire week's worth of our meditations in rebuilding our devotion and reverence to the higher self. During such times, we are not looking especially for profound insights or messages from the higher self; our main intent is to train the personality to love and trust the higher self fully.

2. If we find ourself regularly refighting old battles or ruminating on old conflicts, we should recognize that the greatest problem confronting us is not the continuing memory of these difficulties but rather *our lack of self-discipline.* We are not exercising sufficient self-control. Before we can actually put these problems to rest, therefore, we will have to increase our self-discipline to a point where we are not overwhelmed by these rebounding memories. In severe cases, this may well require months of dedicated work to stay detached from the recurring memories, giving them as little attention as possible, but working instead to become more compassionate, tolerant, forgiving, or cheerful—whatever quality will neutralize the negative feelings we tend to be sabotaged by. Once we have disciplined ourself to give greater priority to the nobility and healing power of the higher self than to these memories, we will then be able to confront and resolve the struggle or resentment itself, using the technique for healing the emotions described in chapter ten.

Because the rebound phenomenon occurs primarily in the emotions, it is important to mobilize the power of our will and convictions to manage it. Many people prolong the problem because they fail to do this, working instead only within an emotional context. The emotions are an important part of our consciousness, but emotional problems are most easily solved if we can approach them from the perspective of our wisdom and will, rather than our feelings. If all we do is float around in nice sentiments, feeling good about overcoming our conflicts, nothing much will change. But if we charge up our strongest intentions and convictions to stay detached and confront these difficulties with self-control and dignity, we will tap the strength which will enable us to succeed.

DISTRESS FROM TOO MUCH MEDITATION

If we exercise the physical body too much, it becomes fatigued and achy. In very much the same way, if we exercise our subtle bodies too much, in strenuous or overly-long meditations, they may become strained, congested, or depleted. And because the physical body responds very quickly to the condition of our subtle bodies, it, too, can experience discomfort from too much meditation. Naturally, the amount and intensity of meditation which constitute an excess will vary from person to person. As always, common sense rules. Our capacity to meditate increases with practice. It would be foolish for a beginner to try to meditate forty-five minutes or an hour. But for the advanced meditator, these lengths may be no problem at all. The other significant factor is our current state of mind. If we are tired, upset, or irritated before we begin our meditation, our tolerance for lengthy or intense meditations may be greatly reduced.

It is useful to be able to recognize the symptoms which arise, both mentally and physically, from mild, medium, and major amounts of excess in meditation. These can be listed as follows:

The mental symptoms of mild excess: mental fatigue, difficulty in concentrating and remembering things, and irritability, lasting for brief periods.

The physical symptoms of mild excess: mild headaches, fatigue, a vague sense of fullness or a dull ache in the head or chest, a tendency to cough more than usual, and perhaps mild nausea.

The mental symptoms of medium strain: vague disorientation for up to an hour after meditating, an annoying forgetfulness and difficulty in concentrating which might last several hours, and a detached or "spaced out" feeling.

The physical symptoms of medium strain: moderate headaches, sinus congestion, a persistent cough, lung congestions or wheezing, moderate gastrointestinal disturbances, or the aggravation of preexisting illnesses.

The mental symptoms of major strain: very spaced out—the focus of attention drifts in and out between the physical plane and a deeply altered state of consciousness bordering on a trance. Sometimes, a rather goofy, pseudo-mystical state will persist for quite some time, making it impossible to work effectively at any significant task. The meditator becomes very irritable, especially in public; the slightest distraction, even the presence of another person, can become a source of severe irritation. There may even be hallucinations and delusions.

The physical symptoms of major strain: damage to the etheric web, the structure of the etheric body. This web can be torn by intensive meditations, usually involving the practice of concentrating on the movement of energy through the chakras. Once the web is torn, the damage is very difficult to repair, and there may be permanent conditions of uncontrolled muscle spasms or rippling of the muscles in the extremities and the back, irregular heart rhythm, disturbed motility of the digestive system, shaking and burning sensations in the pelvis and lower spine, and rushes of excitement. Sometimes so much energy will "leak" out of the hole which has been torn in the web that a condition of persistent low vitality and uncontrollable sapping of vitality from others ensues. The chronic low vitality leaves the physical body vulnerable to a variety of common physical ailments, especially infections and rapid advancement of degenerative illnesses.

It would be very rare that any of the severe forms of psychological or physical distress would ever arise out of the practice of the techniques of Active Meditation, unless the techniques were distorted or used fanatically. Common sense alone is enough to protect the meditator from significant distress; if we start to feel spaced out or nauseated, we should break off our practice of meditation until our consciousness has once more become stabilized.

As obvious as this basic principle is, there are nonetheless meditative systems which pointedly ignore it—insisting, for example, that the student meditate exactly twenty minutes in each session, regardless of the discomfort which might be experienced. Other systems set no limit on the amount of time which can be spent in meditation. It is not uncommon to hear tales of students of these systems meditating four or five—or even ten—hours straight, without a break! Almost always, they damage their physical and subtle bodies to some degree when they do.

Such systems are usually devoid of common sense and respect for the individuality of the person practicing the techniques. They are developed by authoritative teachers who insist on conformity to rigid, traditional practices. Quite often, these teachers have very little genuine knowledge about human nature, psychological processes, or even spiritual systems. If a student comes to them with a complaint about distress while meditating, these teachers will actually insist that the cure is more of the same!

When major psychological or physical problems develop during or after a meditation, then all meditative work should cease immediately, and not be resumed until the distress disappears and consciousness is stabilized. Even a number of non-meditative but passive activities—such as prayer, contemplation, and significant amounts of reading or television watching—should be drastically curtailed in favor of vigorous activity in the physical which forces the attention to be fixed on the outer world. The idea behind these recommendations is to restore balance to consciousness by utilizing the natural stabilizing influence of the physical plane.

"Vigorous physical activity" means exactly that. The idea is *not* to become earthy—by taking recreational drugs, eating meat, or pursuing hedonistic pleasures. These things are sometimes advocated as "cures" for the serious problems of meditative distress, but they are no real help. The genuine cure is to become active and productive in the physical plane.

If the use of a meditative technique or system produces a *major* psychological or physical distress, it ought to be permanently abandoned in favor of something more constructive. Once again, this is just common sense. Yet, it is amazing how seldom this simple dictum is followed. There are several people who, in their formative years, experienced extreme distress from improper meditative techniques, both physically and psychologically. But having recovered, they have become gurus who teach the same improper techniques to others. Surely this is the height of ignorance!

Naturally, far less drastic measures are required to correct the imbalances of mild or medium distress. In most cases, not meditating for a day or two will be sufficient to relieve the difficulty. Once balance is restored, the meditator should then be more careful not to exceed his practical limits of endurance and intensity. Almost every serious meditator will have problems of this nature until he learns these limits. In this regard, it is a little like sunburn—we do not know how much is too much until it is too late. But once we have learned the hard way, we never have to expose ourself to an excessive degree again.

If the problem is a mild amount of congestion in the subtle bodies, the unpleasantness can usually be reduced by shifting attention away from the affected area. It is generally not necessary, in these cases, to break off the meditation. If, for example, we are meditating quite intently on a divine archetype, using it to better understand a specific problem, we might accidentally stimulate the mental body to an excessive degree. This could produce stuffed sinuses (congestion in the forehead chakra) or a headache (congestion in the center at the top of the head). In such an event, shifting for awhile to devotional and adorational exercises, which will center us in the heart, may well relieve the achy sensation. As a rule, intensely focused mental meditations and those which involve concentrating intently on the will tend to produce more problems than devotional meditations, as the power contacted by thought and intention is many times greater than the power invoked by goodwill and devotion.

This is no reason to stick with purely devotional meditations, however. The ideal is to cultivate a balanced approach to spiritual growth, spending part of our time in meditation enriching the emotions, part of our time developing our mental powers of discrimination and discernment, part of our time exploring creative self-discovery, and part of our time building the spiritual will. If we balance our meditative activity in this way, there will seldom be any distress—and when there is, it will be quite mild.

The people who develop problems of congestion while meditating are usually those who are concentrating on a specific line of development at the time:

• Those who are rapidly developing the discriminating use of the mind are those who are most prone to congestion in the throat center and difficulty with coughing.

• Those who are working vigorously to integrate the higher self with the personality are the ones most apt to experience congestion in the forehead and sinuses.

• Those who are cultivating a more conscious use of the will are the ones who are likely to develop headaches and mild difficulties with memory and irritability.

In these cases, it is the *intensity* of the work they are doing which is causing distress, not the technique they are using or the goal they are pursuing. They need to decrease this intensity somewhat, but not eliminate their work altogether.

What we do *between* meditations can also be helpful in diminishing the discomfort of mild distress. If we notice congestion of our subtle energies occurring, for example, something as simple as taking a walk can help start them circulating again. Headaches, stuffed sinuses, and hoarseness can usually be remedied by shifting our attention away from these problems and involving ourself in engrossing and productive activities and responsibilities.

Usually, the best cure is just to get busy and do something constructive with the energies which have built up!

KUNDALINI BURNOUT

Unquestionably the greatest danger of distress to the meditator is the uncontrolled release of kundalini energy. This is not a significant problem in the Western tradition of Active Meditation, which places the emphasis on the energies of consciousness, not the energies of form. But it is a real and present danger in many of the meditative systems which have been imported from the East.

Kundalini energies are the subtle forces of matter—the "fire" of matter, to put it symbolically. They are the most highly refined and subtle energies of etheric, emotional, and mental substance. In the human system, the kundalini energies are concentrated in the chakras or force centers along the spine from its base to the top of the head. As these energies rise in their natural channels, overlying the area of the physical spine, they transmute the subtle matter of the etheric, astral, and mental bodies so it becomes progressively more pure. The action of the kundalini also helps prepare the subtle matter of these bodies so it will be more responsive to integration with the energies of spirit.

Kundalini is designed to rise naturally, as contact with the higher self is established and the purification of the subtle bodies progresses. The problems associated with kundalini all arise from one source: trying to stimulate the arousal of the kundalini energies prematurely.

Strangely enough, however, this premature arousal of the kundalini fire is *the avowed goal* of many Eastern meditative systems: kundalini yoga, laya yoga, and a number of systems which put heavy emphasis on breathing exercises. The stated intention of these systems is to purify and raise the quality of consciousness, but in practice little or no direct effort is actually given to improving the quality of thought or feeling in the meditator. Almost the whole of the meditator's attention is directed at acceleration of the movement of kundalini throughout the subtle bodies. It becomes a mechanistic attempt to bypass the integration of spirit and matter and forcibly cause the fires of matter to activate.

When these exercises succeed, the result can sometimes be a rather abrupt and vigorous change in the structure of the subtle bodies. The actual impact of arousing kundalini in these ways will vary from individual to individual. But when the etheric body is involved in these drastic changes, the kundalini can produce strong burning sensations along the spine and in the major chakras, shaking movements in the extremities, significant alteration of physical functions, especially those governed by the autonomic nervous system, and various degrees of confusion or delirium.

Yet none of these problems need ever arise in meditation! There may well be various physical sensations accompanying the *natural* arousal of kundalini, when this stage of development arrives, but they will never be uncomfortable—and certainly not harmful. The key, as always, is to use our common sense. The kundalini has been designed by the higher self to serve a specific role in the integration of spirit and matter. This role is understood by the higher self far better than the personality. If the higher self is our true source of wisdom, which it is, then surely the better part of common sense is to let the higher self choose the time and the manner in which the kundalini energies will be awakened. We need not fear that the higher self will be asleep and miss the opportunity. Instead, we should concentrate on making sure that the personality is attuned to the wisdom, love, and strength of spirit, and able to express these qualities maturely in daily life. If we can do this, then we will be well prepared to handle the challenge of kundalini when it arises.

The problem with the techniques of the East which seek to arouse the kundalini consciously is that they all end up encouraging the meditator to focus his attention on the material form of consciousness—kundalini—instead of the quality of consciousness. They have the cart before the horse; the transformation of consciousness is meant to awaken these changes in our subtle bodies—not the other way around. When full attention is given to improving the quality of our attitudes and thoughts, the awakening of the kundalini is spontaneous, well-modulated, and for the most part, uneventful.

If the techniques of Active Meditation are being used as the core of our meditative enterprise, it is highly unlikely that any adverse disturbances will ever arise in connection with the arousal of kundalini. If, however, an individual is using a different system of meditation and begins to experience the symptoms of kundalini burnout, it should be viewed as a major concern of both the meditator and his teacher, if he has one. The first step is to stop all meditative work and keep the attention off the body and the symptoms. If the symptoms are severe, it is important to cultivate an environment and lifestyle which is very stable and calm, until conditions improve—at least for several days. In other words, physical, psychological, and spiritual rest are essential.

Once a reasonable improvement is registered, it is essential to avoid repeating the kind of meditative practices which caused the problems to develop in the first place.

TOO MANY VISIONS

The average person is so grounded in the concrete use of the mind and the materialism of daily life that it is very hard at first to deal with abstractions and the invisible qualities of the higher self. For such a person, the use of the creative imagination, as described in chapter six and elsewhere, can be a vital and important skill during the beginning stages of meditation. It can help him translate abstract realities into an *image* he can visualize and manipulate. Nevertheless, visualization is really nothing more than a kindergarten practice in Active Meditation. After we have been meditating for a year or so, our dependency on images and visualizations ought to begin decreasing. We still use them from time to time, as appropriate, but ought to begin to learn to interact with wisdom, love, grace, and courage at their level, not ours.

In some people, however, the use of images does not decrease. They become more and more dependent upon visions and visualizations, not less. This can be a very serious problem, but strangely enough, it is almost never recognized as a problem. Some meditators, in fact, assume that a flood of images in a meditation is a sure sign that enlightenment is right around the corner! There are several other factors as well which contribute to this danger:

• Most people find images quite fascinating, and so they continue to watch them and hope for more.

• There are several spiritual and psychological traditions which encourage the invocation and observation of images in the mind.

• Even though there are none, shortcuts to enlightenment are always appealing to basically lazy people. The idea that we can learn about ourself and maybe even become enlightened while playing with images is guaranteed to attract a large following.

It is instructive to understand exactly what happens when we become too obsessed with images and visions in meditation. Instead of building contact with the higher self, we are encouraging the subconscious to churn out all kinds of dreamlike images and memories—most of them irrelevant. At this point, genuine meditative work ceases, because we have become absorbed in the subconscious. We have forgotten the higher self. The process becomes more like self-hypnosis—we are hypnotized by the images we are observing so intently.

For a year or two, nothing much will happen to alarm us. If the habit is not changed, however, it will grow in intensity, and one of two conditions is likely to arise eventually:

• Our awareness mechanism becomes connected to the department of the astral plane which stores the accumulated thoughts, dreams, and fantasies of the entire human race. This is an infinite reservoir of images which can best be described as "thought garbage." It contains the remnants of thoughts and images once entertained by humans but now discarded. Their appearance can be quite deceptive and fresh, however, as though they sprang to life only yesterday, in order to bring us a brilliant new revelation. They show no signs of wear—no bite marks or old stains of spaghetti sauce—to tip us off. If we *penetrate* these ideas, we quickly find that they are only shells, devoid of meaning and significance. But people who observe images and lust for mental visualizations seldom have learned to penetrate ideas. Their concept of "thinking" is to observe the outer appearance of images, not their inner meaning. So they are fully deceived and duped by this thought garbage, quite content to passively watch it hour after hour, while the rest of their life deteriorates. Eventually, they are unable to think about any subject or theme without the intrusion of these irrelevant images and feelings. Slowly, without realizing it, these people become victims and then slaves of the thought garbage which has accumulated in the lower psychic planes.

• If our interest in mental images has been only to observe them, we become so detached from daily life that we end up *disconnected* from our associative mechanism. We lose the ability to use the associative mechanism for normal purposes—such as remembering important items, analyzing the significance of events and ideas, and focusing on the right emotion at the appropriate time. If uncorrected, this disconnection gradually leads to a variety of schizophrenia in which our body of thoughts separates from the rest of the personality. As might be suspected, this is an intensely regressive step—and a problem which is very difficult to correct.

Of course, even this devastating blow to the evolution of consciousness has its champions—those people who are terrified of thoughts and condemn the mind as "the slayer of the real." When we disconnect the mind from the rest of the personality, a lot of the problems which characterize the unenlightened mind go with it. To the unintelligent observer, it may seem that a mighty breakthrough has been achieved. The rapture of abstract feelings becomes more possible, more frequent, and more seductive. But believing this to be a step forward is like claiming that having amputated our legs, we are now much lighter—and we do not have athlete's foot anymore, either!

To put the phenomenon of too many visions into its complete perspective, two other observations must also be made:

1. During the twilight phase between wakefulness and sleep, or between full alertness and a meditative state, it is possible to tune into special streams of images which circulate around the planet like jet-streams of thought shells. If this occurs, it will tend to be a spontaneous event which will last as long as we continue to concentrate on the streaming images. The distinguishing characteristic about this stream is that the images are moving at a pace which almost defies our ability to count them and they are all of a similar type—in other words,

all faces, all landscapes, or all buildings. Their appearance at these times is totally meaningless. No matter how fascinating, they are a pure distraction.

2. The problem of too many visions is far more likely to arise in people who use recreational drugs—especially marijuana and hallucinogens like LSD—than in anyone else. This is because of the toxic and damaging effect of these drugs. Unfortunately, this type of person is apt to believe that the appearance of these images and visions is proof that they are undergoing a profound mystical experience. The truth, of course, is just the opposite. Even people who have been off these drugs for some time will continue to tune in primarily to images in their meditations, and very little else. The impact of these drugs is to bind the attention of their users to the lower psychic levels of consciousness, while damaging the etheric body.

The cure for an excessive number of images and visions is to remember that the major purpose of effective meditation is to enrich consciousness. The focus of attention must therefore be kept on improving the quality of consciousness—the quality of our thoughts, feelings, and intentions. When images appear, we should seek to grasp their significance, if any, and understand what we can do with them. We should never just passively let the image itself fascinate us. In other words, we must penetrate beyond the appearance of the image and deal primarily with its meaning, its implications, and its power.

If the problem of too many visions is severe, they can be displaced by creating a neutral but stable mental image—for example, imagining that we continue to see our physical surroundings even after we close our eyelids. Or, we can try meditating in a relaxed state with our eyes open, if the physical surroundings are not too distracting.

Perhaps the best suggestion is to make sure we have a definite focus for every meditation, so that whenever stray images turn up, they can be easily ignored.

HYPERSYMBOLISM

Working with symbols is an important skill of Active Meditation. As in dealing with images, however, it is possible to overdose on symbolism to such a degree that we are not really meditating any longer. The primary problems which arise in working with symbols are:

1. We pay too much attention to the form of the symbol—the image—and ignore its meaning and power. The value of symbolism is that it helps us become aware of the inner dimensions of events, appearances, and images. The symbol represents a certain inner quality or force which can be used to enrich our attitudes, creative self-expression, or understanding. But the symbol is not a magical genie that will perform all of these things simply because we have rubbed the lamp of guided imagery. We must learn to look past the outer image and appreciate the real life of the symbol—what it means to us and how we can use it to change our life.

2. We become a collector of symbols. People who work intensively with dreams frequently develop this problem. They become fascinated by the symbols which arise in their meditations or dreams, and compile volumes of notes on the symbols they have received, but they never do much to integrate these symbols into the structure of their consciousness. One of the great characteristics of symbols is that they are a primary language of the subconscious. To a large extent, the associative mechanism of the subconscious operates symbolically. This is the reason why dreams are such a fertile source of symbols—and meditations, too. But if we summon symbols and then do nothing with them, it is the equivalent of stocking our pantry with food and then never preparing or eating it. One day, we may discover that our pantry—the subconscious—has been raided by rats who are gorging themselves on the food we did not use. The rats, of course, would be our own bad habits,

worries, and fears—and maybe even a few of our friends and colleagues who secretly delight in their ability to manipulate us.

The solution to this problem, of course, lies in learning to use symbols maturely and competently—not a common skill in meditative circles. This means learning not just to collect symbols, but more importantly learning to communicate with the subconscious symbolically—and conversely, learning to listen to the higher self symbolically.

3. We tune into the group mind associated with a symbol. Many symbols represent powerful archetypal forces. Most of these forces have been well-known for a long time, especially in religious and mystical traditions. As a result, the symbols are also well-known, and have been the subject of much commentary, both by intelligent and ignorant people, for centuries and centuries. Instead of using the symbols to become aware of the archetypal forces they represent, many meditators take the much easier route and tune into the standard interpretations of these symbols which have been popular over the centuries. It could be a Christian tuning into the popular Christian interpretations of the cross, the fish, or the star; it could be a psychic tuning into the gypsy fortune teller associations of the Tarot; or it could be a student of astrology tuning into the simplistic interpretations usually given for the various planets and signs of the zodiac. It is much easier to tune into these predigested interpretations of universal symbols than their actual archetypal power and force. It also gives us the sense that we are very, very good at interpreting symbols. But it is, of course, only an illusion.

4. We go on a color binge. Colors are a special form of symbolism, representing the quality and force of a certain type of energy. Some meditators will get so carried away with color that they will spend hours and hours visualizing it, wrapping themselves in color, breathing it in, or seeing their whole body

saturated with it. As is so often the case with symbolism, this use of color is more a digression from the real work of contacting the higher self than anything else. It becomes a game played by spiritual children, not a meaningful exercise in the lives of spiritual adults.

GLAMOURS AND ILLUSIONS

Like all human activities, the act of meditating has a tendency to build up certain glamours and illusions. We create expectations about what will happen while we meditate—and often these expectations have little to do with the actual experience which will follow. As a result, we get slightly lost on our journey to the higher levels of consciousness. We wander around in a self-created maze of wishes, self-deception, and pseudo-profound images for awhile, until we realize what we have been doing, and break through the fog of our illusion.

There are a number of "standard" illusions, glamours, and other distractions which seem to ensnare many meditators for awhile, until they see their self-deception. They are:

1. The glamour of contacting a "master teacher" who has taken us under his wing and will now provide us with careful tutelage and specific instruction in the ways of enlightenment. There is often the hint that we have been chosen for a "great mission" which will require a long and difficult period of preparation and probation. The fact that the instruction we receive usually seems obscure if not obtuse only serves to heighten the sense of mystery and reinforce our belief that we still have much to learn.

The meditator who "buys into" this illusion can go around in the circles of his own subconscious for years and years, if he is dull enough to do so. What makes this illusion at least somewhat credible is that there are teachers who can be contacted psychically and there are great missions that advanced individuals undertake. But for the average person, the most important mission is to discover and explore the higher self. It is this higher self which is supposed to be our real "master teacher," and to pursue a fantasy about being chosen for a great mission is only likely to delay the true beginning of genuine spiritual instruction. If our dedication to the spiritual life is strong enough, we will not accept such illusions.

It is also important to realize that we are under no obligation to trust every voice and whisper which arises in our meditations—and, in fact, we would be very foolish to do so. It would quickly lead either to schizophrenia or to utter chaos in our life.

Of course, there are always times when it is difficult to discern the merit or truth of the impressions we receive in meditation—especially if they involve something we very much want to believe. But whenever we are in doubt, all we have to do is rededicate ourself to the truth and our own highest good. As we hold our aspirations and thoughts in the light of this dedication, we will find that the strength of nonsense and mere fantasy is weakened, and we are able to see the truth more clearly.

As always, the key is common sense. And yet, common sense is the one faculty that the victims of "the great murky master from Jupiter" or the "teacher of the New Age Christ" or the "president of the Federation of Thirty Galaxies" never seem to possess. They never seem to wonder why such "great beings" are coming to them with such outlandish and often absurd missions.

The cure for this self-deception is to ponder on an ancient mantra: "Ignorance is its own punishment."

2. The glamour that a nice, warm feeling of bliss is the highest state of enlightenment. Many people sincerely believe that the ultimate meditative experience is total suspension in a nice, warm state of bliss. They want nothing to do with tech-

niques or growth or even the higher self; they just want to be able to rest in a pleasant emotional sensation. If they do include the higher self in their meditations, it is so that the higher self can cater to their need for praise and adulation. The genuine higher self would never actually do so, of course, so they create the illusion of a higher self out of their higher emotions to play the role. The subconscious is always quite willing to play this kind of game.

Positive emotional states *are* a vital part of the meditative process, but they do not constitute the crowning glory of meditation. Feeling good about spirit is *not* enlightenment; it is not even samadhi. It is just a pleasant emotional experience. The value of positive emotional states in meditation is to help boost our aspiration and devotion to the higher self, heal our negative emotions and associations, and enrich our attitudes and self-expression with the higher qualities of abstract emotion.

It should be noted that these are all *active* uses of the emotions. The practice of passively resting in a bland but pleasing emotional state is merely a surrender to the emotions, not a constructive use of them. It usually leads to a parasitic state of consciousness—not enlightenment.

3. The glamour that psychic contact with a spirit guide is the highest form of meditation. Many people are quite enthralled with the phenomena of mediumship—especially the possibility of contacting spirit guides who will help them solve their difficulties. They may be attracted to learning certain meditative techniques which will help them contact spirit guides and perhaps even develop some mediumistic attributes. It is certainly possible, and often useful, to contact various entities of the subtle realms in a meditative state. But if contact with these entities becomes the central core of our meditative experience, it can usurp an even more important kind of contact—contact with the higher self.

4. The glamour that meditating on the center of the uni-

verse is the highest form of meditation. Some people assume that as their meditations become more and more cosmic, they are becoming more and more advanced. So they spend the vast majority of their time meditating on the intergalactic Christ force, the origin of the universe, the destiny of the Planetary Logos, or some obscure point about life during the Krita-Yuga. Yet the higher self does not actually share their intense curiosity on these subjects. In fact, by spending too much time on esoteric nonsense in meditations, they run the risk of estranging themselves from the higher self. They need to ponder on the fact that excessive concern about the latest doings on Sirius is probably just a glamorized escape from the realities and responsibilites of their personal life.

5. The distraction of subtle physical sensations. From time to time in meditation, some people experience odd sensations in the physical body—buzzing noises, warmth in a particular part of the body, tingling sensations in the head, throat, chest, or back, or the feeling of spinning or being stretched out. Most of these minor phenomena are simply physical associations the subconscious connects with the inflow of new energy or slight alterations in our subtle bodies. We are not really spinning in our chair like a whirling dervish—we just have the temporary illusion of it. Yet many people take these sensations as signs their meditations are becoming "really deep and powerful." It is simple to prove they are not; if we ignore them and concentrate instead on the productive work of meditation, they will quickly disappear. The only danger that can come from these sensations is the temptation to devote too much attention to them. Since energy follows attention, we can easily magnify these sensations to the point where they are uncomfortable, forcing us to end our meditation. If this were to happen too frequently, we would run the risk of becoming locked into an earthbound state—more aware of what is transpiring in the body than what is happening in spirit.

6. The illusion that a trance state is a high level of meditative experience. Many people firmly believe that the goal of meditating is to fall into a near coma and lose contact with our body, our physical surroundings, and everything else. An intense focus of interest on inner themes often does cause our awareness of the physical plane and body to recede, but this lack of awareness of the physical level of expression is incidental. It should never be enshrined as a goal of meditation, because when it is, many people end up tuning out *everything*—not only the physical body but also the inner focus of interest! This is definitely not desirable—we are meant to stay active and alert during meditation, not drop into a coma where we totally "black out."

As obvious as this is, many practitioners of Eastern systems of meditation consider it perfectly acceptable to lose consciousness during a meditation—as though it represents the ultimate detachment from the "dreaded" physical plane. They entertain the pleasant self-deception that somehow their meditative work is continuing on at higher but unconscious levels.

There may well be times when any meditator briefly loses consciousness during a meditation. It is not an alarming condition, in most cases, but it is certainly nothing to covet or brag about. It is generally a sign that we need to cultivate a stronger measure of concentration and self-discipline. When a person *tries* to blank out during a meditation, however, he is likely to get out of the meditative experience exactly what he puts into it—nothing. It leads to advanced dopiness—not enlightenment. Over a long period of time, the personality will become more and more passive, and the mind will become dulled. Even if the unconscious does benefit, which is debatable, it is certain that the conscious personality does not. No integration between the higher self and our self-expression is occurring.

7. The glamour of out-of-body experiences. It sometimes happens that the consciousness of the meditator detaches

entirely from the physical body and is able to travel at will throughout the astral plane. When the meditator then returns to his physical body, he is able to remember the experiences he has had out of his body. Most meditators never experience this phenomenon, as it is quite rare. But an intense glamour has been built up among spiritual aspirants about the "value" of out-of-body experiences, causing a great deal of confusion and misunderstanding.

There are two types of people who spontaneously experience the out-of-body phenomenon. The first would be people with natural mediumistic talents, developed in earlier lives. The second would be people who have damaged their subtle bodies through the use of psychedelic drugs.

The seductiveness of the out-of-body experience is that the person who is able to detach in this way usually becomes convinced that it is a sign of profoundly effective meditation. It is not. In fact, most people, including mediums, who regularly travel out of the body start ignoring all other meditative practices in favor of astral travel. They abandon the daily needs of mental housecleaning, healing the emotions, training the mind, and learning more about the higher self, as though they are now above all these "common needs." As a result, the quality of their consciousness badly deteriorates.

It must be understood that most people who are able to travel out of the body journey only through the astral or lower psychic plane. They may be standing on a different landscape and able to converse freely with different entities, but they are still basically trapped in a mundane focus on life. Were they to travel through the mental plane and seek to make contact with the higher levels of consciousness, there would be value in their journeys. But the vast majority do not. Sightseeing is still sightseeing, even when it masquerades as an out-of-the-body experience. It can be interesting, but it is not a substitute for meditation.

Those who have difficulty in halting involuntary out-of-body experiences should try:

1. Spending an extra amount of time in bringing the spiritual qualities to earth, through the attractive force of their devotion, interest, and dedication to the life of spirit, instead of continuing to operate on the assumption that they must rise to them. The physical body is not a barrier to spirit—only an obsession with the physical form is a barrier. Spirit is meant to come to earth, and meditation should be designed to help spirit do just that.

2. Meditating with their eyes open.

3. Using the creative imagination to visualize their subtle bodies of thought and feeling enveloping the physical body, while contemplating their ideal attitude toward meditation.

4. Reviewing their attitudes about life to see if they have a tendency to want to escape from conditions of dullness or distress. It is usually the thrill seekers and drug users who have a problem with out-of-body experiences—not people with a serious dedication to the higher life.

DRYING UP

A common problem with many meditators is that their meditations begin to dry up after awhile—they become sterile and unproductive. They are going through the paces, but nothing much is happening. Of course, it is natural for anyone to have an "off day" every now and then, whether in meditation or any other activity. The occasional "off day" is not a cause for concern. But if our meditations in general become tepid, boring, and unproductive, then something definitely is wrong.

It is highly unlikely that this problem will ever arise in the use of the techniques of Active Meditation, which are designed to enrich consciousness, not dry it up. If it should, it is probably an indication that we are concentrating too much on a single technique, and need to put a little variety back into our meditative endeavors. It may also be a sign that we have been looking too much for "gee whiz" phenomena instead of genuine contact with the life of the higher self.

In other approaches to meditation, however, drying up can be a major problem. There are a number of reasons why:

1. The technique itself is boring. Many systems of meditation limit their students to a very simple practice, such as mumbling a mantra or concentrating on the breath. The *intelligent* response to such practices is to become bored and recognize them as unproductive! The sooner they are abandoned and the meditator moves on to more enriching practices, the better.

2. The technique encourages the meditator to render himself utterly passive and wait for spirit to guide him. The higher self, however, is not looking for a tree stump to sit on, but rather an intelligent partner to act through. If we become too passive, the higher self is far more likely just to ignore us than to try to reactivate us. Indeed, too much passiveness and surrender in meditation can actually disconnect us from the higher self. At that point, our meditations will become progressively more and more sterile and unproductive. The solution, of course, is to become more active and incorporate spiritual self-expression into our meditative experiences. We must try to understand how the higher self would ideally manifest through our personality and behavior, and then make it our top priority, *in and out of meditation*, to help the higher self do exactly that!

3. We are focusing too intently on one line of development to the exclusion of all others. The adoration of God, for example, is an important part of meditation, but if our entire meditative practice consists of adoring God, day in and day

out, we are likely to get rather tired of it. Even God is likely to get tired of it. So we would want to expand the scope of our meditative exercises, and include techniques which will help us understand God's nature and respond to God's will, as well as adore Him.

4. We have substituted an intellectual line of thought for meditative contact. The act of meditation occurs as we contact the higher self and direct its qualities of love, wisdom, and strength into our character and self-expression. But some people fall into a bad habit of merely thinking intellectually about this process, rather than actually doing it. They end up thinking about meditating, instead of meditating. As a result, their work becomes sterile and unproductive, because they are not tapping the actual power and love of the higher self, even though they devoutly believe themselves to be highly esoteric.

5. We have failed to balance our inner effort with an equally strong outer effort. In other words, we are not taking adequate steps to ground our new realizations and insights in our active self-expression. We have therefore become congested, as described in chapter fourteen, and this congestion blocks off the inflow of new insights and qualities. As a result, our meditations dry up. The solution in this case, of course, is to make a stronger effort to translate the qualities of the higher self into an active self-expression.

BECOMING EARTHBOUND

The state of being tied to earth is not limited exclusively to those people who are intensely materialistic in their attitudes and priorities. It can be found even in people who have made it their professed goal to become spiritual and who make it a daily practice to meditate. In fact, certain systems of meditation are almost guaranteed to make the meditator earthbound, if he or she pursues them for two or three years or more.

These are systems which put a great deal of emphasis on practices involving the physical body—breathing exercises, physical postures, and diet—instead of the development of consciousness. They are commonly found in hatha yoga, kundalini yoga, and zen. While all of these systems do have initial benefits in terms of calming agitated nerves and producing greater vitality in the physical body, the more they are used the more the attention of the meditator becomes absorbed in the physical body. Over a long period of time, this can become quite harmful.

The problems which arise, however, usually develop so gradually that they are not obvious to the meditator himself— only to others. The consciousness of the meditator becomes progressively denser, producing such changes as a loss of imagination, a slowing of the associative mechanism, a loss of memory, and a dulling of alertness, awareness, and creativity. At the subtle levels, there is an actual hardening of the etheric and astral auras—almost a crystallization. Consciousness is literally becoming more materialistic!

This is a high price for anyone to pay—especially someone who believes he is spiritualizing matter. In fact, he is doing just the reverse—he is losing his capacity to contact the higher self. The treatment for this problem is to *permanently* cease all practices which lead to earthbound conditions and to work at reintegrating our thoughts and feelings with the higher self. This cannot be done only in meditation; in fact, the bulk of the work must be done nonmeditatively, by immersing ourself in pursuits which will lead to a refined appreciation of the symbolic and abstract subtleties of life—the enjoyment of the fine arts, classical music, good literature, and poetry. We must gradually reorient our consciousness to appreciate the refined virtues of life, retraining it to act nonmaterially.

Most of the work, therefore, will have to occur in consciousness. The problem cannot be corrected by physical changes such as altering our diet or exercising. We must always remember that it is not possible to eat our way to God—or stretch or jog our way to God, either. There is, however, one physical treatment which is useful—frequent exposure to sunlight. Being out in the sun will expose our subtle bodies to the healing radiations of the sun and help break up the hardening of the auras.

The best solution, of course, is not to practice techniques which might make us earthbound.

PROBLEMS ARISING FROM GROUP MEDITATIONS

In addition to the problems which can arise in individual meditations, there is an entirely different set of difficulties which can arise from meditating in a group format. It is important for anyone who meditates in groups—either for his own self-improvement or the purpose of helping others—to learn to recognize and correct these problems, for many of them can lead to individual problems if left unchecked. The most common problems are:

• The group mind inhibits effective meditation. In the individual, there are many distractions which can interfere with making contact with the higher self—the wishes and fantasies of the subconscious, preconceived notions of what the higher self will be like, overheated expectations, prejudices, and resistances of the personality. When a group of people gather for the purpose of meditating together, these potential distractions will be magnified many times over. An individual who has largely succeeded in neutralizing his own inner distractions may suddenly find that he must now contend with the distractions of those around him! This can make it much more difficult than normal to make contact with the higher self.

474

This condition should in no way discourage us from participating in group meditations, as there can be great value in working in this way. But it does suggest that we should be careful about the groups we participate in, and it reemphasizes the value of each member of the group making contact with the higher self in his own way before the group meditative work begins. It also implies that we should get in the habit of comparing our individual meditations with our group meditations. If our group meditations are more enriched than our individual meditations, and the contact with the higher self seems to be of a more refined quality, then our association with that group is worthwhile. But if we tend to be more troubled by distractions, temptations, and weird ideas while we are meditating with a group, and we do not have these problems by ourself, then we ought to reevaluate our participation.

• Sapping. Some people love to meditate in groups because it gives them the opportunity to plug into other members of the group and sap their energy. But sapping is never part of the road to enlightenment. It is just a psychic form of theft which leaves the others in the group with a variety of unpleasant symptoms—irritability, anxiety, fatigue, headache, mild nausea, and a generally dopey state of awareness. As a rule, however, if a group is composed of intelligent and sincere spiritual aspirants, there will be little problem with sapping. Their collective aspiration and intent will keep the group climate wholesome.

If sapping is a persistent problem in any group situation, there are two ways to solve the problem. Either the group can suggest to the person who is doing the sapping that he not return in the future—if the offender is known—or the people who are victimized can drop out.

• Silly techniques. Sometimes the members of a group are good and sincere people, but the direction given by the leader of the group is not very knowledgeable. The group ends up using techniques which are more silly than useful. One such technique which is very popular among meditative groups at present is for everyone in the group to join hands and stay in physical contact throughout the meditation. There are even very precise ways the hands are to be interlocked! Once the circle is formed, the leader then instructs the members of the group to circulate the energy they have contacted around the circle.

This is a ludicrous technique. It instantly puts every member of the group in contact with the group mind, and makes it almost impossible to contact the higher self. Moreover, it guarantees that the only energy transfer which will occur will be from personality to personality within the group. It is a real boon to the psychic sapper, but everyone else in the group will end up with something he did not expect—*the psychic and psychological equivalent of taking a bath in someone else's dirty bathwater!*

• The limitations of the group. Many groups serve a useful role in helping people learn and develop meditative skills, but are unable to carry the meditator beyond a certain point. Perhaps the leader is limited in his or her understanding, or the group as a whole is limited by preconceived notions and beliefs. Once an individual member in that group has reached the outer limits the group has to offer, therefore, it is time to leave. If he tries to stay, he will find the accumulated force of the group mind and the psychological pressure to conform to the group experience to be deadening influences on his own meditations, by himself or with the group.

• Brainwashing. In some groups, the impact of the group mind on the individual is a bit more pernicious than just imposing limitations. Specific suggestions regarding conduct and attitude may have been fed into the group mind by the leader, in order to control the thinking and feeling of the individual members. This is a classic instance of brainwashing—at psychic levels. The individual member is made to conform by coercion, not by individual choice. If the member continues to insist on his or her individuality anyway, the group mind will retaliate, stirring up immense guilt, fear, and threatening images in the member's meditations. Once again, the best solution to this problem is to leave the group and focus attention on meditative themes which are different from the usual themes of that particular group.

• Irresponsible leadership. Some groups have no purpose except to enhance the ego and bank balance of the leader. The leader is usually quite charismatic and charming, but has little to offer in terms of constructive help to the other members of the group. Quite often, the leader exploits the group not only physically, but psychically as well, sapping their energies and manipulating their thoughts. No meditation, either individually or in a group, should ever be dominated by someone other than our own higher self. If it is, then once again this is a sign that it is time to leave the group.

In no way should these comments be interpreted to mean that as soon as something happens in a group not to our liking we ought to leave. This would just be escapism, and we would soon find we were unable to participate in any group activity. But some of the problems which arise in groups can be a genuine threat to our individuality, and there is often no alternative but to drop out. As always, the ruling factor should be our own common sense. If we are by and large getting more benefits out of the group experience than problems, then obviously our continued participation in the group is worthwhile. In a group dedicated to self-improvement, the benefits would be a sense of well-being, greater alertness, mental poise, a higher level of contact with spirit, and better health. In a group which is dedicated to helping others and humanity, the benefit would be more sublime—the opportunity to focus our self-expression into a worthwhile channel.

THE ONE PROBLEM

Ultimately, there is only one problem of meditation, and it is a problem all meditators must confront—the essential difference between the personality and the higher self and the difficulties which arise in harmonizing and integrating these two dimensions of selfhood so they begin to work together, as partners.

The many practices which have been outlined in this chapter are problems only because they aggravate this essential difference instead of diminishing it. Undoubtedly the intent in using most of these practices is sincere, but sincerity does not count for much if it only serves to make the problem worse. The techniques of Active Meditation are all designed with one primary purpose in mind—to help facilitate the integration of the higher self and the personality. It is for this reason that the major problems outlined in the preceding pages will not arise in the use of these techniques. They *solve* the one fundamental problem of meditation, rather than compound it.

Herman's Benediction

The buzz of the typewriters had died down. We had turned our minds to other tasks—editing, polishing, and preparing the manuscript for typesetting. But there was something portentous in the air. We scratched our heads.

Herman reappeared.

"Good job, boys!" the angel exclaimed. "I like the way you've handled it. It makes meditation simple."

"Simple?" Carl replied, frowning a bit. "Why do you say that? We tried to make this a complete statement on the fundamentals of meditation for Westerners. I don't think it's simple at all. In fact, we worked hard to make it as profound as possible."

"I keep forgetting that many of the words in your language have several meanings, and even shades of meanings," Herman replied, almost apologetically—as apologetic as an angel dares appear. "I didn't mean to suggest that the book is simplistic or lacking in depth. In fact, I was paying you a compliment. It makes meditation simple, so that everyone can understand it. Your ideas and descriptions are simple, even though the practice of meditation—and the wisdom and love you contact by meditating—isn't. It is complex, beautiful, enriching, infinite, expanding—something that cannot be captured entirely in mere words. And because of that, the best way to describe meditation is simply."

"Ah, I see what you are saying," Bob interjected. "In our effort to be precise, sensible, and logical, we have removed some of the mystery that has been hanging over meditation for century after century. Yet perhaps we haven't removed the mystery at all. The mystery is still there, a veil to be parted by each individual as he or she learns the skills of Active Meditation and seeks out the higher self. All we have done, I suspect, is remove the mystery which never was the real mystery—the fog, the smoke, and the obfuscations which have been created by people who did not really understand meditation."

Herman looked intently at the two of us. "I like the way you put that. The real mystery of meditation is not in your words or ideas—it's not even in *my* words or ideas. It is in the spiritual and invisible essence of life. That is the profound mystery which makes even my head ache at times in wonderment about its vastness, its splendor, its purpose. We should never lose our awe for that, whether we are angel or human. The 'ultimates' and the 'absolutes' and the 'laws' which you or I take so much delight in proclaiming have a way of seeming insubstantial and conditional once we discover something even more profound beyond them. This something more profound never negates the ultimates and absolutes and laws—it just makes them simple. It goes beyond them, and embraces a larger dimension. That is the mystery and the challenge of meditation. It's real, and it calls out to me—as it calls out to you. It is the mystery and challenge which we always need to keep in mind, no matter how much we understand the simple truth."

And having pronounced the benediction, Herman faded away.

It was quite awhile before either one of us spoke. Finally, Carl said, "I guess we need to write another chapter."

20

The Western Tradition

MOMENTUM FOR THE FUTURE

Human consciousness does not remain the same, century after century. It evolves, and as it evolves, civilization, society, the sciences, and human culture change, too. They become more powerful, more enlightened.

The spiritual customs and practices of humanity are meant to evolve as well. In the West, we are in a formative stage. The growth which has occurred in civilization in the last five hundred years has been rapid and most encouraging. There are excellent signs that we are leaving the Dark Age of ignorance behind. Our science is flourishing. The arts have made spectacular contributions. But above all, more and more individuals are training their minds and nurturing their God-given intelligence. There is an enormous momentum for future development—if we can tap it and harness it wisely.

But if we are going to tap this momentum for the future, we must add a rich esoteric tradition to the exoteric accomplishments we have already made. This cannot be done just by shopping among the existing esoteric traditions of the world, and taking the one which most appeals to us. We must develop our own tradition for spiritual growth and enlightenment—a tradition which is suited for our culture, our time, and our needs. Most of all, we must develop a tradition which will lead us into the future, not trap us in reliving the past.

To be meaningful, however, a tradition cannot be developed on the wishes and whims of those with the loudest voices. It must be based on intelligent discernment of the archetypal patterns which oversee and inspire the evolution of consciousness in our culture. We must strive to serve the same goals that the spiritual forces in the West are striving to serve.

These goals—the goals of the Western tradition—can be briefly stated as the following:

1. *To make the God within our primary source of enlight-*

enment, growth, and creativity. The God within, of course, is the higher self, the soul, the spirit. The label makes little difference. What is important is recognizing that the central source of life and all enlightened activity dwells within us, and can become our partner in living, if we are willing to be its partner in living. There is no higher priority in the Western tradition than recognizing the higher self, the God within, as the *gateway* to all growth, enlightenment, and creative expression. Finding this gateway should be the initial focus of all meditative work, and cultivating a stronger access to it should always remain our continuing theme. The failure of earlier spiritual traditions to emphasize the need to find and cultivate this gateway of the individual soul does not justify repeating the failure! Intelligent humanity is now capable of making this connection—and benefiting from it.

2. *To link the personality with the higher self, thereby producing a spiritualized individuality capable of responding to the forces and qualities of spirit.* It is not acceptable any longer to abandon the personality and simply love God. We must recognize our responsibility to train and prepare the personality so it is capable of acting as a representative of God, not just a worshipper of Him. This means we must live as a personality dominated by spirit, liberated from the fads and illusions of mass consciousness. We must also see it as our duty to achieve and maintain an illumined mind and purified emotions.

3. *To ground the life of spirit through the enlightened activities of the personality on the physical plane.* It is no longer practical for spiritual aspirants to "escape to heaven." It is time, instead, to learn to bring heaven to earth—to integrate the divine qualities of wisdom, love, and power into our daily self-expression. Even our meditations are to become active and practical—and meditation is to be seen as a tool for facilitating the integration of the higher and the lower, not an end in itself.

486

4. *To learn and use the skills of devotion, understanding, and obedience to link the personality with all three of the major aspects of divine life—love, wisdom, and will.* In the past, most spiritual traditions have stressed training the personality to be responsive to one of the major aspects of divine life, ignoring the others. Some taught devotion to divine love but ignored understanding and obedience. Others taught understanding of divine wisdom, but ignored the need for love and will. In the Western tradition, all three approaches to the life of God must be balanced.

5. *To purify and illumine all aspects of the personality so they become agents of spiritual force.* When the emphasis of a spiritual tradition shifts from passively adoring God to actively participating in the life and work of God, greater emphasis must be put on purifying and preparing the subtle vehicles of the personality to carry and transmit spiritual force without major distortion. The purpose of this purification is not just to make us "feel good," but rather to increase our effectiveness in translating the life of God into a constructive self-expression.

6. *To cultivate the spiritual intuition, by linking an illumined mind with the wisdom of the soul.* One sign that a spiritual tradition has lost its momentum is the appearance of rigid dogma which dictates how people should think, feel, and act toward God. One of the basic tenets and goals of the Western tradition is that each individual must learn to discern truth and wisdom for himself, by directly contacting the divine archetypes and ideals of life, through the higher self. This is done by cultivating the spiritual intuition and an illumined mind. The spiritual intuition bears no resemblance at all to the psychic abilities of the personality. It is the sword of truth that cuts us free from materialistic blindness, self-deception, illusions—and dogma.

7. *To nurture a constant awareness of the underlying goodwill and unity in the divine presence.* This constant

awareness is something more than just a belief or a hope; it is an ongoing realization of the fact that we all have our spiritual roots in the one life of God—the One in Whom we live and move and have our being. The ability to commune with the presence of God, through our dealings with all others, is a key factor in establishing the kingdom of heaven on earth.

8. *To recognize that it is our duty and privilege to serve the purpose of the soul.* Life is not a game which is played in competition with one another. We have been designed to fulfill a certain purpose, and it is both our duty and our privilege to work to fulfill it. This purpose is to integrate divine life into our conscious thoughts, attitudes, and activities, thereby becoming an agent of divine force and a participant in the work of humanity.

9. *To become consciously aware of the reality of the Hierarchy and its plan for the evolution of humanity and civilization—and to assist in implementing it.* The Hierarchy is the group of enlightened beings which guides and inspires the development of human civilization and consciousness. It incorporates that portion of the divine plan which specifically pertains to humanity and civilization. As part of our effort to cooperate intelligently with the plan of God, therefore, it is important to learn to participate in the work of the Hierarchy.

10. *To become consciously aware of the spiritual groups the higher self is part of—and to learn how we can contribute to the work of these groups.* This is the active mode of brotherhood. True brotherhood is a reality to the higher self, the fabric of its relationship with specific spiritual groups. We can best serve the ideal of brotherhood on the personality level by learning to contact the spiritual light of the groups the higher self belongs to and transmitting it into the world around us, through the work we do in meditation and in daily life.

The work of reaching these ten goals *is* the momentum of the Western tradition.

WHAT THE FUTURE HOLDS

The benefits of the Western tradition are available to any individual who adopts the practices of Active Meditation and uses them to pursue a greater contact with the higher self and the other goals of spiritual growth. They do not come instantly, nor if we fail to make the effort. But if we are willing to work toward these goals constructively and with dedication, we will gradually attain them.

The same is true for society as a whole. As large numbers of individuals embrace these traditions and work with them, our science, religion, education, arts, and civilization will be enriched. Mass consciousness will be purified, at least to a degree. Over a long period of time, remarkable changes may well occur. But it must be understood from the outset that there are no miracle cures for society. It requires hundreds of years to change the patterns of thought and feeling in society. Nevertheless, once the work of a new tradition is set in motion, the process of change will pick up momentum, as moıe and more individuals join the ranks of the enlightened servants of the Hierarchy and its plan for humanity.

Here are some of the benefits we can look forward to, if the Western tradition is embraced by the intelligent and dedicated people of the world:

• There will be far more cooperation and sharing among communities and nations. Conflicts, when they arise, will be resolved more commonly in the realm of ideas than on the battlefields of prejudice and nationalistic pride—or physical confrontations.

• The progressive elements of religion will lead a reformation to replace the worship of a remote and petty god with the worship of the living God of love, Who is a benevolent influence in our daily life and work.

• Governments will be inspired to attend more to the duty

of encouraging the growth of civilization and spiritual themes than to meeting the material wants of the irresponsible members of society. Order and justice will be seen as qualities which must be fostered in a climate of self-sufficiency, self-reliance, and individual responsibility—not in a climate of enforced restriction. The value of the individual and his responsibility will become dominant themes.

- Science will discover that its true work is not to discover the laws of the physical universe, but to reveal the principles which govern all of the planes of form—and to participate in implementing the "technology of divine ideas."

- Psychology will learn to distinguish between consciousness and sensation, and see the central reality of the soul in understanding human behavior and activity. It will become more interested in promoting the health of human consciousness through activating the life of the soul.

- Education will begin to see the higher correspondences of the learning process, and come to appreciate that we all dwell in an invisible realm of pure thought which can be tapped by any intelligent person who trains himself or herself to become aware of this subtle presence.

- The arts will be seen more fully as an opportunity to communicate directly with the symbolic and intuitive dimensions of human consciousness—not just as a personal dumping ground for the idiosyncrasies and hang-ups of the artist, writer, or musician.

There is, of course, no guarantee that any of this will come to pass. Yet it can be stated truthfully that the momentum of the archetypal forces which govern the emerging Western tradition is moving us in these directions. How far we go depends on what we do, individually and collectively. Each of us must play our part. No one has the right to indulge in the smug assumption that society must reform itself first, before we take up our own duty.

OUR ROLE

The Western tradition and the practice of Active Meditation are both based on the fundamental precept that human individuality is the key to human advancement and productivity. Society can only grow as the individual members of society recognize their duties and responsibilities to becoming productive citizens of life. A spiritual tradition can only grow as individuals become responsive to its goals and work to participate in it.

The techniques of Active Meditation are designed to help us better understand the secret of our individuality and cooperate with the emerging directions of the Western tradition. In practicing them, we should always keep in mind the basic principles upon which they are founded:

• Our higher self is the center of all our meditative work—not a guru, or even the allness of God. Teachers should be seen only as midwives to the birth of enlightened consciousness. And the allness of God should be seen as the environment in which the higher self lives and acts.

• Our link to spirit lies in the most pure and noble aspects of the personality's emotions, thoughts, and will. Mantras, symbols, colors, prayers, and visualizations do not link us with the higher self. They can facilitate the meditative process, but only our devotion and aspiration, trust and understanding, and dedication and intention can *link* us with spirit.

• The interaction between personality and spirit is meant to be creative and dynamic. The love, wisdom, and power of the higher self can only enter into our character and self-expression as we work to integrate these qualities with our attitudes, habits, and activities.

• The ideal relationship between personality and spirit is a creative partnership. The higher self provides inspiration, wisdom, and the full resources of divine love; the personality provides the form of outer activity and expression—which includes its talents, experience, and interest. Together, they are able to contribute to the spiritualization of the worlds of form. But if they do not serve as partners, neither the higher self nor the personality is able to perform this work.

• The focus of attention in meditation should always be on the *quality* of consciousness—not the *form* through which consciousness is being expressed, whether that is a chakra, a mantra, a color, a posture, a guru, or anything else. Our goal is to enlighten our understanding, enrich our emotions with compassion and goodwill, and mobilize our intention with dignity and skill.

• All progress is dependent upon our ability to ground our spiritual development in our self-expression. It is not enough just to grow in awareness and to refine our character; we must become a helpful, constructive force in society and civilization.

In striving to fulfill these principles of Active Meditation, it is important to remember a few key points:

1. The popularity of a practice is not an indication of its usefulness. In fact, it may be a sign that it appeals to the basic laziness or materialism in mass consciousness.

2. Long-standing religious or spiritual traditions are not necessarily the best for present day enlightenment. A new tradition is emerging, which is meant to take us into the future, not the past.

3. Feeling good is not an intelligent criterion for evaluating the richness of our meditation.

4. Enlightenment has nothing to do with the ability to see light in a meditation. It is the process of dominating our thoughts, feelings, and actions with the light of the higher self—its qualities and forces.

The genuine signs that our meditative work is developing according to plan are the changes which occur within us. They are similar to the changes which will occur in society, as the Western tradition emerges, but with an individual focus.

We become more tolerant, patient, and able to remain faithful to the ideals and principles we cherish.

We better understand the meaning and relevance of our work, our relationships, our talents, and the events of life.

We are better prepared to recognize and meet our responsibilities and opportunities.

We become more joyful in the way in which we approach life—especially the difficulties of life.

We become more self-sufficient, self-disciplined, and self-directed in our thinking, planning, and behavior.

We become more productive and useful to the world.

We become more aware of our inner talents and beauty—and are able to see and respect similar qualities in others.

We are more able to recognize the underlying qualities of goodwill and unity which permeate all of life.

To some, of course, this particular listing of the results of effective meditation will be one final proof that the Western tradition is inferior to the traditions of the East—it does not give proper due to God consciousness. But in the West, these results *are* the signs that we not only know God and adore God, but are busy working to participate in the divine plan of God for humanity—which is the real God consciousness.

THE FINAL WORD

We have tried to make this book a comprehensive guide to the principles and practices of Active Meditation. Yet in no way do we consider it the final word on meditation. The "final word" of what to do—and not to do—in the practice of Active Meditation should come from one source and none other:

Our own higher self.

The needs of each of us are unique and individual. The techniques suggested in this book are meant to provide a structure upon which to build a strong bond with the higher self—but it is something each of us must build for ourself. As we try, we will find that the higher self is quite able—and willing—to assist us. From the very beginning, this will always be our most reliable source of guidance.

Nevertheless, not all voices we hear in our meditations will be the guidance of the higher self. Our own misconceptions, desires, and prejudices are likely to speak quite loudly at times. So will the traditions, prejudices, and desires of mass consciousness. We must learn to discriminate between these false voices and the true voice of the higher self.

When all else fails, and we are confused about the meaning of what is happening or the value of a specific idea, there are always three things we can rely on:

1. Our common sense.
2. Our own experiences.
3. The invocation of Truth and a renewed dedication to honoring the life of the higher self. It is not just understanding which clears up confusion and doubt, but even more importantly, the power of Truth and our constant loyalty to it.

AN ENVOI

We have written this book out of our own experiences in using meditation as well as teaching it. We have tried to include the kind of practical suggestions we wish had been available years ago when we first began to meditate. It is offered to you, the reader, in the hope that these ideas will help make your own experiments in meditating more successful—and more active.

Recommended Reading

The following are some of the many books which will enrich the practice of Active Meditation:

NONFICTION

The Art of Living, by Robert Leichtman, M.D. & Carl Japikse

The Life of Spirit, by Robert Leichtman, M.D. & Carl Japikse

Leadbeater Returns, by Robert Leichtman, M.D.

Yogananda Returns, by Robert Leichtman, M.D.

The Inner Life, by C.W. Leadbeater

Man, Visible and Invisible, by C.W. Leadbeater

The Chakras, by C.W. Leadbeater

The Brotherhood of Angels and Men, by Geoffrey Hodson

The Light of the Soul, by Alice A. Bailey

Letters on Occult Meditation, by Alice A. Bailey

Divine Healing of Mind and Body, by M. MacDonald-Bayne

The Finding of the Third Eye, by Vera Stanley Alder

Psychosynthesis, by Roberto Assagioli

FICTION

Winged Pharaoh, by Joan Grant

The Earthsea Trilogy, by Ursula LeGuin

The Saga of the Well World, by Jack L. Chalker

Stranger in a Strange Land, by Robert Heinlein

Childhood's End, by Arthur C. Clarke

The Secrets of Dr. Taverner, by Dion Fortune

The Time Trilogy, by Madeleine L'Engle

Siddhartha, by Hermann Hesse

The Mind Parasites, by Colin Wilson

Great Lion of God, by Taylor Caldwell

GLOSSARY

ARCHETYPE: A pattern of creation. Archetypes are found at the abstract levels of the mental plane and are used by the higher self as it creates the personality, its destiny, and its behavior. They are also the source of creative inspiration.

ASHRAM: A place for learning the lessons of spiritual unfoldment. Esoterically, the word is used to refer to a group dedicated to common forms of spiritual service.

ASPIRANT: One who actively seeks to be more attuned to the higher self and better able to express its light, love, and strength in his or her daily circumstances.

ASSOCIATIVE MECHANISM: A principle of the mind, operating largely at subconscious and unconscious levels, which enables us to relate the contents of relevant memories, feelings, and speculations to our conscious focus of attention. A healthy associative mechanism is of great importance in maintaining the skills and capacities of memory and the ability to understand what we read and observe.

ASTRAL MATTER: The substance of the astral plane.

ASTRAL PLANE: The plane of the emotions and desires. The astral plane is an inner world made of matter that is more subtle than physical substance, yet interpenetrates all physical substance. It is teeming with life of its own. The phenomena of the astral plane differ from physical phenomena in that they occur fourth dimensionally.

AURA: The light which surrounds all life forms. An aura emanates from the surface and interior of the etheric, astral, and mental bodies. Clairvoyant observation of the aura can give an indication of the quality of health or consciousness of the individual or life form.

BROTHERHOOD: The bond in consciousness that links all human beings together. Brotherhood is not an utopian fantasy, but an actual *fact*—a living presence of common purpose, shared experience, and loving potential. It is the divine ideal for all community and governmental activity, and ought therefore to be studied and honored by all leaders, all citizens. For further insight into the presence of brotherhood, see part one of "The Noblest Masterpiece," an essay in *The Art of Living* series by Robert R. Leichtman, M.D. and Carl Japikse.

CHAKRA: A Sanskrit word meaning "wheel," a poetic allusion to the general shape of major and minor focal points of energy within the threefold human aura. In the West, chakras are often called "force centers." There are seven major chakras and scores of lesser ones in each of the subtle bodies. The science of how energies circulate throughout these chakras—and their impact on human expression—is a complex one. The physical correlates of the seven principal chakras are the pineal gland, the pituitary body, the thyroid gland, the heart, the solar plexus, the gonads, and the adrenals and the kidneys.

CONSCIOUSNESS: The capacity to know and be aware. It must be distinguished from *sensation*, which is the perception of objects, feelings, events, or ideas through the five physical senses or their emotional and mental counterparts. *Consciousness* is the ability of a unit of intelligence to reason on, reflect about, and draw conclusions regarding the nature of any other unit of intelligence or manifestation—and also itself. Esoterically, consciousness is the mechanism used by the higher self to perceive life and interact with it, whereas sensation is the mechanism used by the personality.

DESTINY: The combined plans and commitments made by the higher self of an individual or a group for its future. A destiny would include plans for creative fulfillment, achieving enlightenment, and the events of life. It is not imposed from without—it is formulated by the higher self itself.

DIMENSION: A measurement of size, space, movement, or consciousness. There can be dimensions of thought and feeling as well as physical dimensions.

DWELLER ON THE THRESHOLD: Those elements of the personality, usually unconscious, which an individual must face at "the threshold" of new expansions of consciousness or self-discovery. The challenge to the aspirant in facing the Dweller on the Threshold is to know which elements to preserve, which to redeem, and which to discard.

EARTHBOUND: The state in which consciousness is trapped in the materialistic forces of earth.

ENLIGHTENED: Focused in the light of the higher self. An enlightened mind is able to contact directly the higher self and use its light to perceive, comprehend, and apply archetypal wisdom. An enlightened personality is governed and directed by the higher self.

ESOTERIC: An adjective which refers to knowledge of the inner worlds and inner life.

ETHERIC MATTER: The substance of the etheric plane.

ETHERIC PLANE: The most subtle realm of the physical plane. It is composed of the finest grades of physical matter, exceeding even the "fineness" of gases. In physics, the term "plasma" would be used for this grade of matter.

EVIL: Anything which retards the evolution of human consciousness. Contrary to public opinion, evil is not measured by our likes and dislikes. Unpleasant experiences may help us evolve, and would therefore not be evil. By contrast, the indulgence of one person by another may be pleasant—but quite harmful. A more thorough description of evil can be found in the essay "Defeating Evil and Sin" in *The Life of Spirit* essay series by Robert R. Leichtman, M.D. and Carl Japikse.

EVOLUTION: The growth of any life form to its destined perfection. It is the response of consciousness to the divine impulse to grow.

FIFTH DIMENSION: A realm of existence in which there can be five different planes of movement from a single point, each of those planes being separated by ninety degrees or its abstract equivalent. All physical solids are part of this larger, fifth-dimensional context. The impact of the fifth dimension on third-dimensional solids can be seen as changes in shape of a whole species or class of those objects. In other words, if the growth registered in a single tree is fourth-dimensional in nature, the evolutionary growth of the species to which that tree belongs is fifth-dimensional. Archetypal ideas, from which whole species and classes of objects are produced, are part of the fifth dimension. The higher self also exists in the fifth dimension, as does heaven. Therefore, the true focus for Active Meditation is the fifth dimension. It is not, however, a common environment for the average human being.

FOURTH DIMENSION: A realm of existence in which there can be four different planes of movement from a single point, each of these planes being separated by ninety degrees. All physical solids are part of this larger, fourth-dimensional realm. The movement of a fourth-dimensional solid through the physical plane would be recognized as a change in the apparent three-dimensional shape of that object, such as in the growth of a tree. We act in fourth-dimensional ways every day—by associating relevant memories to current experience, by speculating about our future, and by perceiving underlying motives and attitudes of other people. Loosely speaking, the astral plane could be considered the fourth dimension.

GLAMOUR: Before the word acquired its modern, popular meaning, it meant "an enchantment" or "magic spell." In esoteric writings, the word still preserves this basic meaning, and is used in a technical sense to refer to the illusions and distortions of reality generated by the emotions, either of an individual or of mass consciousness. Fears and worries, for example, would be negative glamours, because they cast a spell on the thinking apparatus of the person who is afraid or worried, deluding him. Strong wishes and fantasies would also be glamours, although more pleasant by nature. Dispelling glamour is one of the great challenges the spiritual aspirant must face—and one of the most difficult.

GOD: The Creator of all that exists, visible and invisible; the life principle and creative intelligence underlying all life forms and phenomena. In spiritual practices, it is common to think of God in two ways—as God Transcendent, referring to the universal presence of *all* divine forces, and as God Immanent, referring to the indwelling divine elements in a particular life form.

GROUP MIND: The combined ideas, attitudes, illusions, and thoughts of any group of humans relative to the purpose or common interest which brings them together as a group. Every individual in a group contributes to the group mind, and the group mind influences every member's own ideas, attitudes, illusions, and thoughts. This influence is subtle and often difficult to discern, but nonetheless can be quite powerful.

GURU: A Hindu term for "teacher."

HEAVEN: The state of consciousness of the higher self. Heaven is not a place for those who have died; it is a center of consciousness for incarnate and discarnate humans alike—a state of mind. Heaven is the home of the archetypal patterns and spiritual ideals of life.

HYPNOSIS: A psychological technique for communicating more directly (and sometimes more forcefully) with the subconscious of an individual. It is an artificial technique which does not make contact with the higher self.

I CHING: The Chinese Book of Changes, a complex system of philosophy which can be used to interpret the movement of archetypal forces in life. It is also used popularly as a method of divination. The I Ching is based on sixty-four hexagrams which are selected by the random fall of coins or sticks.

Its purpose is to indicate the significance of events and forces, rather than predict the future.

ILLUSION: A distorted or limited perception of reality. The term "glamour" is usually used to refer to the distortions and limitations of the astral plane, whereas the term "illusion" is used to describe the distortions and limitations of the mental plane. As the mind learns to dispel illusion, it becomes a better vehicle for the wisdom of the higher self.

INNER PLANES: A term used to refer to any one of several inner worlds of levels of existence, all of which interpenetrate the dense physical plane. Each physical human being exists on these inner planes as well as on the physical level, by dint of having bodies composed of matter drawn from them.

KUNDALINI: A Sanskrit term for the subtle energies of matter which flow up the spine in the etheric, astral, and mental bodies, connecting various force centers or chakras. As the quality of consciousness changes, corresponding changes occur in the quality and intensity of these energy flows.

LIGHT: Esoterically, there are many octaves of light, of which visible light is the densest. In its higher octaves, light is consciousness itself.

MANTIC DEVICE: A set of symbols, either deliberately or fortuitously assembled, that can be used for the divination of destiny, duty, and purpose. A mantic device can be a highly-organized system such as numerology, astrology, palmistry, the Tarot, or the I Ching; or it can be a more spontaneous arrangement of symbols, such as the fall of coins or body language. The more inspired and organized the system, the wider its application.

MANTRA: A word or phrase that is silently repeated for the purpose of calming our thoughts and feelings, or some other effect. As we concentrate on this mental sound, it produces a harmonious response in our subtle bodies. Mantras come in many lengths and languages and are designed to help in entering the meditative state. Using a mantra as a substitute for the entire meditative process is an abuse of its purpose.

MASS CONSCIOUSNESS: Literally, the mind and emotions of the human race as a single whole. To some degree, the thinking and feeling of every human being contributes to mass consciousness and—to a much larger degree—is powerfully influenced and conditioned by mass consciousness.

MASTER: A term used by esoteric students to refer to an individual who has reached complete enlightenment and perfection as a human.

MATERIALISM: The belief or attitude that the physical plane is the only plane of existence, or at least the most powerful and important. Materialism denies the central importance of spirit, the existence of universal intelligence, and the invisible realms of life. It is the basis of black magic and leads the person who believes in it to become "earthbound"—a state in which all values, decisions, and acts are formulated in selfish and temporal terms.

MATTER: The substance of life. There is mental and astral matter as well as physical matter.

MEDIUMSHIP: The phenomenon of a nonphysical intelligence, usually a discarnate human, assuming some degree of control of a physical body in order to communicate something useful and meaningful. Mediumship is usually used for the transmission of information and inspired guidance, but can also be used to transmit varieties of healing energies.

MENTAL MATTER: The substance of the mental plane.

MENTAL PLANE: The dimension of intellectual thought. One of the inner planes of existence, it also interpenetrates the dense physical plane. It teems with active life of its own, in addition to providing the substances for the mental bodies of all humanity.

METAPHYSICS: The philosophical and intellectual inquiry into the spiritual nature of all things.

MYSTIC: One who loves, reveres, and *finds* God and His entire Creation.

OCCULT: The hidden secrets of nature. The study of the occult deals not just with the esoteric aspects of man's being, but also the entire universe. It includes the study of the function, operation, purpose, origin, and destiny of nature and man. The word literally means "that which is hidden."

PLANE: An octave in consciousness. All planes of consciousness interpenetrate the same space; they differ from one another in the quality of their substance. The three planes in which the human personality exists are the physical, astral, and mental planes.

PSYCHIC: A person who is able to perceive events and information without the use of the physical senses. The word is also used to refer to any event associated with the phenomena of parapsychology.

SABIAN SYMBOLS: A series of 360 symbols derived by Marc Edmund Jones and a psychic in 1925. The symbols represent the key meaning of specific degrees of the zodiac and are used by some astrologers in interpreting horoscopes. The term "Sabian" comes from the name of the group Jones led, the Sabian Assembly.

SAMADHI: An exalted state of consciousness, reached during meditation or contemplation, in which the consciousness of the meditator becomes absorbed in God and contacts divine wisdom, love, and unity. There are a number of degrees of samadhi.

SANSKRIT: An ancient language, now dead, in which many of the Hindu scriptures are written.

SELF: A psychological term used to describe the center of the totality of the unconscious and conscious aspects of the human being. The self acts to unite and integrate the diverse elements of the individual.

SENSATION: The reaction we register in our mind, emotions, or physical body in response to stimuli. Memories and ideas are mental sensations. Feelings and sentiments are emotional sensations. Sensations should never be confused with *consciousness*, which is our ability to be aware of the meaning, purpose, design, and creative uses of the forces, elements, and entities of our spiritual, mental, emotional, and physical environments. Detaching from mental and emotional sensations and identifying with consciousness is one of the major problems the spiritual aspirant faces.

SIN: The act of engaging in evil or condoning it in others or society.

SOUL: The individualized principle of consciousness and creativity within the human being. It is the soul that evolves and acts; it is the soul that creates the potential of the personality, vivifies it, and guides it through certain life experiences designed to increase competence in living. The soul is a pure expression of love, wisdom, and courage; its destiny is not damaged by changes or tumults in the life of the personality.

SPIRIT: The highest immortal, divine essence within the human being.

SUBCONSCIOUS: The part of the personality that is not being consciously used at any given moment. The subconscious is always active and greatly influences our conscious moods, thoughts, acts, and attitudes. It is psychically in tune with other portions of the inner planes—even if we are not consciously psychic at all.

SYMBOL: An image, thought, feeling, or event which contains a deeper significance than what is obvious from the outer form. It points to inner dimensions of reality, force, and meaning. To discern these inner dimensions, however, the symbol must be interpreted. The study of symbolism is useful only if it leads to a discovery of the reality the symbol veils.

TAROT: A set of 78 cards, each card featuring a symbolic portrayal of an esoteric quality of force. The esoteric purpose of the Tarot is to provide an allegorical key to the structure of life. By studying and using the Tarot, one can gain knowledge of the hidden aspects of life. It is interconnected with aspects of the Kabalah, astrology, and alchemy.

TELEPATHIC: Pertaining to direct mind-to-mind communication, with or without associated physical contact and communication. Most often, telepathic communication occurs on the astral plane.

TRANSCENDENCE: The state of having risen above the mundane levels of consciousness and self-expression. Many people falsely assume that the mere retreat into a state of psychological quietness is enough to achieve transcendence, but that is only a withdrawal from sensation. Transcendence involves the movement of our level of awareness and perception toward spiritual consciousness; it may or may not involve significant withdrawal from outer sensation.

UNCONSCIOUS: The part of the mind not ordinarily accessible to the conscious mind. It is filled in part with repressed memories, desires, fears, and feelings. But there are other parts to the unconscious as well: the seeds of noble qualities, creative impulses, and memories of earlier lives.

WILL: The force of our impulse to act and its expression. The spiritual will is the power and focused direction of our spiritual life and force.

YOGA: A Hindu system of personal or spiritual development. There are many kinds of yoga—the yoga of the physical body (hatha yoga), the yoga of action (karma yoga), the yoga of devotion (bhakti yoga), the yoga of wisdom (jnana yoga), and the yoga of the mind (raja yoga) are some of the better known. The word "yoga" means "union."

ZEN: A form of mysticism practiced in Japan. Although the principles of zen are gaining some popularity in the United States, its passive nature tends to interfere with the development of the mind, rather than encourage it.

INDEX

ABOUT THE AUTHORS

In the late 1960's, Dr. Robert R. Leichtman's interest in intuition and spiritual growth caused him to close his medical practice and devote his energies to lecturing, teaching, and writing. Out of his experiences and personal insights, he developed the basis of "Active Meditation," a comprehensive course in personal growth and meditative techniques which he has now been teaching for seventeen years. In addition, he has devoted much of his time to refining his intuitive skills. His pioneer work as a psychic consultant to medical doctors, psychiatrists, and psychologists has earned him recognition as one of the premier psychics in America today. Dr. Leichtman currently resides in Baltimore, where part of his time is spent participating in the healing services of the New Life Clinic.

A graduate of Dartmouth College, Carl Japikse began his work career as a newspaper reporter and freelance writer. He has worked for several newspapers, including *The Wall Street Journal.* In the early 1970's, he left the field of journalism to pursue his current interests: teaching "Active Meditation" and other courses in personal growth, writing, lecturing, and consulting psychically with businesses and individuals. He is also the developer of The Enlightened Management Seminar, an educational program for executives and managers, and various courses in spiritual growth.

Dr. Leichtman and Mr. Japikse are the authors of *Forces of the Zodiac: Companions of the Soul, The Art of Living,* and *The Life of Spirit,* all published by Ariel Press. In addition, Dr. Leichtman is the author of *From Heaven to Earth,* a series of 24 interviews with the spirits of famous individuals, and Mr. Japikse is the author of *The Hour Glass: Sixty Fables For This Moment in Time,* a collection of esoteric fables and parables.

They are the founders and principal officers of Light, a charitable organizations serving humanity worldwide.

THE WORK OF LIGHT

Active Meditation: The Western Tradition is issued by Ariel Press, the publishing house of Light, a nonprofit, charitable foundation.

The purpose of Light is to stimulate the growth of the mind and the creativity of people throughout the world. It was founded by Dr. Robert R. Leichtman and Carl Japikse, two authorities on human consciousness, personal growth, and the creative process. The work of Light is to enrich the human capacity to use the mind and spirit wisely and productively.

The activities of Light include the publications of Ariel Press, the Books of Light book club, and the presentation of lectures and forums such as the Enlightened Management Seminar and the Enlightened Classroom.

Contributing members of the work of Light receive a newsletter, "The Work of Light" and automatically become members of Books of Light.

The cost of a contributing membership is $35 a year for an individual, $50 a year for a family. There are also three other levels of contributing membership: the *fellow*, who contributes $100 a year; the *benefactor*, who contributes $250 a year; and the *angel*, who contributes $1,000 a year. Those who donate $2,000 a year for three years become members of our Founders Club. A brochure describing the work of Light will be sent on request. Information on making larger gifts to Light is also available.

To become a contributing member of Light, send a check and letter of application to Light, 289 S. Main Street, #205, Alpharetta, GA 30201. Or call us toll free at 1-800-336-7769 and sign up by MasterCard, VISA, Discover, Diners, or American Express.

All contributions to the work of Light are tax deductible and greatly appreciated.